A MAGIC STILL DWELLS

A Magic Still Dwells

Comparative Religion in the Postmodern Age

EDITED BY
KIMBERLEY C. PATTON
AND BENJAMIN C. RAY

UNIVERSITY OF CALIFORNIA PRESS
BERKELEY LOS ANGELES LONDON

University of California Press
Berkeley and Los Angeles, California

University of California Press, Ltd.
London, England

Library of Congress Cataloging-in-Publication Data

A magic still dwells : comparative religion in the
postmodern age /
edited by Kimberley C. Patton and Benjamin C. Ray.
p. cm.
Includes bibliographical references.
ISBN-13: 978-0-520-22105-5 (pbk. : alk. paper)
ISBN 0-520-22105-2 (pbk. : alk. paper)
1. Religions.   2. Postmodernism.   I. Patton, Kimberley C. (Kimberley Christine), 1958–
II. Ray, Benjamin C., 1940–
BL80.2.M278   2000
200'.71—dc21   99-31468
CIP

Printed in the United States of America
08 07 06
10 9 8 7 6 5 4 3

CONTENTS

Acknowledgments   vii

A Note to the Reader   ix

Introduction
Kimberley C. Patton and Benjamin C. Ray   I

Prologue: In Comparison a Magic Dwells
Jonathan Z. Smith   23

**Part One. Comparative Religion:
The State of the Field**

The Scholar as Mythographer:
Comparative Indo-European Myth and Postmodern Concerns
David Gordon White   47

Contested Identities:
The Study of Buddhism in the Postmodern World
Malcolm David Eckel   55

Post-modern and -colonial -structural Comparisons
Wendy Doniger   63

**Part Two. Case Studies:
Critical Issues in the History of Religions**

What's Beyond the Post?
Comparative Analysis as Critical Method
Barbara A. Holdrege   77

The Contextual Illusion:
Comparative Mysticism and Postmodernism
Jonathan R. Herman   92

Discourse about Difference:
Understanding African Ritual Language
Benjamin Caleb Ray   101

American Religion Is Naturally Comparative
Winnifred Fallers Sullivan   117

Dialogue and Method:
Reconstructing the Study of Religion
Diana L. Eck   131

Part Three. A Revised Comparison: New Justifications for Comparative Study

Juggling Torches:
Why We Still Need Comparative Religion
Kimberley C. Patton   153

Methodology, Comparisons, and Truth
Huston Smith   172

Elements of a New Comparativism
William E. Paden   182

The Magic in Miniature:
Etymological Links in Comparative Religions
Laurie L. Patton   193

The Net of Indra:
Comparison and the Contribution of Perception
Lawrence E. Sullivan   206

Epilogue: The "End" of Comparison:
Redescription and Rectification
Jonathan Z. Smith   237

Contributors   243

ACKNOWLEDGMENTS

The editors wish to thank each of the contributors for the scholarly dedication and vision that brought about the creation of this volume. We would also like to express our gratitude to our editor at the University of California Press, Douglas Abrams Arava, for his steadfast support of this project from its inception, and to his assistant, Reed Malcolm, for his dedicated effort. Our copy editor, Nick Murray, dealt with our protean manuscript with sensitivity, intellectual appreciation, and a heroic attention to detail. Jan Spauschus Johnson, the production editor, midwifed the project graciously and in record time. Thank you.

Finally, we are indebted beyond measure to the intelligent, tireless, and careful work of Dr. Margaret Studier, Faculty Assistant at Harvard Divinity School, who assembled and prepared the manuscript for publication.

K.C.P. & B.C.R.

A NOTE TO THE READER

Acknowledgment is gratefully made to the University of Chicago Press for permission to reprint the essay by Jonathan Z. Smith, "In Comparison a Magic Dwells," chapter 2 of *Imagining Religion: From Babylon to Jonestown* (1982), pp. 19–35, as pp. 23–44 of this book.

Throughout, references to "In Comparison a Magic Dwells" cite page numbers in the original edition, followed by page numbers in this book in italics.

INTRODUCTION

tells where going - gives main points (handwritten annotation)

KIMBERLEY C. PATTON AND BENJAMIN C. RAY

Whither comparative religion in the postmodern age? The essays in this volume seek to break through the seemingly intractable division between postmodern scholars who reject the comparative endeavor and those who affirm it. In various ways, this volume seeks to demonstrate that a broader vision of religion, involving different scales of comparison for different purposes, is both justifiable and necessary.

Drawing from as wide a range of fields of expertise and vantage points as possible, *A Magic Still Dwells* brings together historians of religions who are outstanding in their respective areas of scholarship. Their essays take up a common set of questions that are reflected in their papers. They take seriously the postmodern critique, explain its impact on their own work, uphold or reject various premises, and in several cases demonstrate new comparative approaches.[1] Despite the rich range of difference in their grounds for and use of comparative method, they are united in the claim for the continuing necessity—and relevance—of the comparative study of religion.

Postmodernism represents a variegated critique of the Enlightenment humanism that undergirds modernism with its totalizing, rationalist gaze. The substantial and often well-founded charges brought against the comparative method are many: intellectual imperialism, universalism, theological foundationalism, and anti-contextualism. In particular, the work of Mircea Eliade, the late doyen of the history of religions, is held to be unredeemable, based as it is on the vision of a universal,

1

transcendent "sacred" refracted in the ritual and mythic behavior of a cross-cultural human archetype called *Homo religiosus.*

The standpoint of the comparativist was once privileged as a vantage-point of objective description, classification, and comparison of "other peoples" and their beliefs. The focus of deconstructive scrutiny "reveals" it instead, at worst, as a subjective mélange of culturally biased perceptions that cannot but distort or, at best, as an act of imaginative, associative "play." The application of postmodern thought to analytical reflection on religious narrative or worldview is problematic at best. Postmodernism denounces order and ordering principles in favor of "otherness, difference, and excess," and further wishes to "destruct the status quo in favor of the fluxus quo";[2] the religious worldview is nothing if not global, universal, systemic, unequivocal, and symmetrical in its claims, "totalizing" in its metaphysics or anti-metaphysics. If we are to take the philosophical claims of postmodernism seriously, the possibility of describing religious systems with integrity or comparing them to one another is thus permanently compromised.

Once confined to poststructuralist, neo-Marxist thought and literary studies, the impact on the field of religion—as on all other fields in the humanities and social science—of a postmodern critique such as Jacques Derrida's deconstructionism has been profound. Words appear no longer to be connected to the world but to be merely unrooted signifiers, shifting counters in the many language games we play. There is also the political charge implied by the work of a Lyotard or that of an Adorno: to compare is to abstract, and abstraction is construed as a political act aimed at domination and annihilation; cross-cultural comparison becomes intrinsically imperialistic, obliterating the cultural matrix from which it "lifts" the compared object.

Thus to compare religious traditions, particularly unhistorically related ones, or elements and phenomena within those traditions, is to attempt to control and ultimately to destroy them. Following this logic, scholarly integrity is only to be found in the self-reflexive study of the "other" that locates itself in the uniquely local and the particular. Whereas Enlightenment-nourished modernism confidently affirmed that "nothing human is foreign to me" and went about making the human intelligible, some postmodernists reverse the adage and affirm with equal confidence, "everything human is foreign to me," and go about denying the intelligibility of the "other" and promoting cultural criticism and intellectual relativism. "There is no way definitely, surgically, to separate the factual from the allegorical in cultural accounts," says anthropologist James Clifford; ethnography is only "a fantasy reality of a reality fantasy," says his colleague Stephen Tyler.[3]

Responding to these recent developments, the field of the study of religion has undergone a profound change. With a few outstanding exceptions, comparative studies have virtually disappeared in graduate programs in favor of increasingly narrow "area studies" research into specific religious texts and communities. This represents a trend identified by Jonathan Z. Smith in 1995:

> In a wholly understandable over-reaction against the well-meaning, endlessly tolerant amateurs who often comprised religion programs prior to the 1960s, a new set of standards was forged: competence in a particular religious tradition measured largely by the acquisition of philological expertise accompanied by an emergent ethic of particularity which suggested that any attempt at generalization violated the personhood of those studied. Lip service might be paid to more general issues, but only in the most introductory courses, never to be studied again.[4]

Perhaps the most cogent and eloquent challenge to the very possibility of responsible comparison came from Smith himself in his seminal 1982 essay, "In Comparison a Magic Dwells." We reproduce his essay as the prologue to this collection because so many of our contributors acknowledge their indebtedness to it, especially its deconstructive attack upon previous comparative studies in anthropology and the history of religions. Smith's essay argues that comparison in the human sciences has been problematic and unscientific and lacking in any specific rules. It contains a kind of "magic," he asserts, like Frazer's idea of homeopathic magic, "for, as practiced by scholarship, *comparison has been chiefly an affair of the recollection of similarity.* . . . The procedure is homeopathic. . . . The issue of difference has been all but forgotten."[5] For Smith, the unfortunate "magic" of previous comparative studies lies in their resemblance to Frazer's notion of primitive magic, the association of ideas by superficial similarity, thus confusing subjective relationships with objective ones. Smith finds wanting several types of comparison in the history of religions for their confused, impressionistic, and unscientific character.

Acknowledging the importance of this essay, we borrow Smith's linkage between magic and comparison for the title of the present volume, *A Magic Still Dwells.* Recognizing that Smith used the term "magic" derogatorily, we do so, not as an act of defiance nor even one of irony, but rather to highlight a reenvisioned potential for comparative study. We reclaim the term "magic" to endorse and to extend his claim that

comparison is an indeterminate scholarly procedure that is best undertaken as an intellectually creative enterprise, not as a science but as an
art—an imaginative and critical act of mediation and redescription in
the service of knowledge. In keeping with this view, these essays offer
an illuminating discussion of the scholarly "manipulation of difference,"
to use Smith's words, a playing across the "gap" of differences, for the
purpose of gaining intellectual insight.

The present volume is divided into three parts. The essays in Part 1,
"Comparative Religion: The State of the Field," offer an overview of
the current status of the comparative enterprise, with particular reference to the methodological challenges posed by postmodernism.

Inaugurating the volume, David White argues that postmodernism's
lessons have been absorbed, and that the "self-indulgent pursuit . . . of
talking about ourselves talking about other people is one whose time
has passed." "We would do better," White continues, "to do what we
do, which is to attempt to make sense of other people's religions," despite the ultimately provisional, non-final nature of the effort. Responding to Jacques Derrida's criticism of Western metaphysics as a kind of
"Indo-European mythology," White defends the modern field of
Indo-European studies as consistently responsive to cultural difference,
religious specificity, and historical change. White ends by invoking Jonathan Smith's idea of the comparative enterprise as an imaginative act
of mediation and redescription, concluding that Smith has "artfully
shown us how we may take issue with our modernist forebears without
embracing the rhetoric of certain of our postmodernist contemporaries."

In "Contested Identities: The Study of Buddhism in the Postmodern
World," David Eckel eloquently remarks upon the "implosion," like
many of the "rational" housing projects of the 1970s, of the "grand
old" projects of classification that typified modern phenomenologies of
religion. He meditates on Jonathan Smith's dismissal of comparative
similarities as a kind of Frazerian-style "magic," but, resonating with
David White's observations, rescues out of Smith's *Imagining Religion*
a new kind of comparison—a style of "imaginative and ironical juxtaposition" (e.g., the Jonestown mass suicide, a cargo cult in the New
Hebrides, the Dionysia of Euripides' *Bacchae*) as a way of stripping
away illusions of "uniqueness" for each religious situation. Buddhist
studies, Eckel shows, provides a superb exemplar of the debates within
a particular field of religious studies, with recent attacks on notions of
Buddhism as a monolith, a kind of totalizing narrative philosophy rather
than a religion, that is unique in its utterly experiential orientation. Yet

just as Eckel redeems "comparison," he also argues for a lexical rehabilitation of the much-maligned idea of "essence" in the pragmatic sense
of what is "necessary" to any Buddhist community's self-understanding
and therefore to the work of the scholars who study it.

Noted mythographer Wendy Doniger's essay vigorously reframes the
recurrent issues of sameness and difference. She proposes that we salvage
a broad comparativist agenda in the study of religion and myth, even
when it means bringing into a single conversation "the genuinely different approaches that several cultures have made to similar (if not the
same) human problems." Acknowledging the reductionism of extreme
universalism, she counters by outlining the ironic pitfalls of extreme
nominalism: one can "essentialize" the contextualized "group" as one
homogeneous mass, whose various individual members may view the
same story quite differently. Doniger urges that, in order to sidestep
these twin intractable dangers, we focus our vision on individual insight,
or, as she puts it, "anchor our cross-cultural paradigms in an investigation of the unique insights of particular tellings of our cross-cultural
themes, to focus on the individual and the human on both ends of the
spectrum—one story, and then the human race—thus not so much ignoring the problematic cultural generalizations in the middle as leaping
over them altogether." Thus she avoids a "quasi-Jungian universalism"
and posits a kind of "pointillism," formed by the views of individual
authors whose insights transcend their particular moment and "speak
to us across space and time." Doniger searches for these points "not
merely in the bastions of the Western canon, but in the neglected byways
of oral traditions and rejected heresies." Thus we arrive at "a wider
construction of cross-cultural inspiration."

Part 2, "Case Studies: Critical Issues in the History of Religions,"
offers in-depth case studies by different scholars working in various
traditions within the history of religions. Each scholar demonstrates how
her or his work has interacted with postmodernism, and how she or he
has used a comparative approach as a valuable analytical tool in the
development of specific cultural as well as cross-cultural categories.

Barbara Holdrege, known for her ambitious study, *Veda and Torah:
Transcending the Textuality of Scripture*,[6] asks with her colleague
Charles Long, "What's beyond the 'post' of the various intellectual
movements that characterize themselves using this prefix?" Her emphatic answer is that there is a place "beyond the post" for the comparative study of religion, agreeing with Jonathan Smith that, in her
words, comparison is itself a "constitutive aspect of human thought and

an inextricable component of our scholarly methods." In her essay, Holdrege attempts to "redress" the comparative method by highlighting the problems that emerge from the work of the phenomenologists and their inadequate attention to differences, the diachronic dimension, and context. Using her own work as an example, Holdrege outlines a method of comparison that gives "proper attention to differences as well as to similarities and to diachronic transformations as well as to structural continuities."

Building on the problematic of the illusion of "uniqueness" examined by Smith and underscored by Eckel, Holdrege argues that comparative analysis can claim a rightful place within the postmodern enterprise as "an important corrective to the strategies of domination through which we privilege certain categories and models over others in our academic discourse. . . . [It] can serve as a heuristic tool not only to establish taxonomies but also to critique and dismantle their tyrannies."

Jonathan Herman, a scholar of Chinese religious traditions, plunges into possible new directions for the comparative study of mysticism. In his essay, "The Contextual Illusion: Comparative Mysticism and Postmodernism," Herman chronicles a particular comparative project, namely, the unlikely juxtaposition of Martin Buber's *I and Thou* and the ancient Taoist classic *Chuang Tzu*. Herman's discussion of the ways in which *Chuang Tzu* influenced Buber's work, and conversely, the latter's dialogical principle, provides a valid lens through which one may creatively reapproach the original Chinese text. Herman suggests that the resonances between Chuang Tzu's model of mystical fulfillment and that of Buber—which Maurice Friedman called "a mysticism of the concrete and the particular"—are so strong as to provide a single typology of mystical experience.

Herman also notes that "the fact that comparativists are frequently accused before the fact of dilettantism, perennialism, or relativism . . . demonstrates that there is a widespread presupposition that phenomena belonging to observably different contexts are self-evidently unrelated to one another." Championing a comparative method that starts not with *a priori* assumptions about the nature of a category like mysticism, but instead grows organically out of a careful respect for particular contexts, Herman is willing to let such an investigation produce profound similarities as well as the differences so beloved of—and expected by—postmodern scholars.

Benjamin Ray takes up one of the popular claims of postmodern anthropology, cultural particularism, and examines its problems, and recommends a solution. In *Writing Culture: The Poetics and Politics of Ethnography* (1986), several anthropologists offer the postmodern argument of cultural particularism—the view that different societies are culturally unique and hence fundamentally unknowable by outsiders and incomparable. Ray argues that in rejecting older-style ethnographic realism, postmodern anthropologists have mistakenly advocated their own brand of philosophical antirealism and cultural solipsism. They have taken the moral and political failings of older-style colonial anthropology as evidence of epistemological incompatibility between cultures, arguing that each constitutes a conceptually unique domain of thought and reality. Thus they believe they can only "represent" other cultures and never engage in issues of meaning and truth. While the difficulties and responsibilities of describing and interpreting other cultures will always remain, Ray offers the work of Edith Turner and Paul Stoller as examples of ways in which anthropologists and historians of religion can open up the realities of other religious worlds, while still engaging questions of meaning and truth. Ray concludes that comparative religion should have both an intellectual and a moral purpose. Its aim should be to advance the conversation of humankind, while building religious bridges and political relationships.

Like other contributors, legal scholar and religious historian Winnifred Sullivan takes as her starting point Jonathan Z. Smith's insistence in *Map Is Not Territory* that "[t]he process of comparison is a fundamental characteristic of human intelligence."[7] She argues in "American Religion Is Naturally Comparative" that "the goal is to historicize morphology." Unlike other contributors, Sullivan is trained primarily in Christianity and American religion. Whereas once "American Religion" was studied as the history of the Protestant Church in America, it is now "about everyone": Native Americans, Spanish conquistadors, Franciscan missionaries, French trappers, and Jesuit priests. Implicitly acknowledging the postmodern charge that certain "metanarratives," most notably ones of European origin, are by nature hegemonic, Sullivan shows how the "starting point" of the story makes all the difference: a Navajo or Iroquois rather than a Puritan framework gives the scholar a view of "early" American religion that comprises symbol and myth, one that sanctifies space, time, birth, or violence, rather than one that is only about "baptism, conversion, and the work of the spirit." She remarks upon an issue related to the very problem that postmodernism has identified in the "history of religions school": the fact that "American religion has been studied by historians while other religions have been studied as reified ahistorical systems." She lobbies for the inclusion of the religious traditions of America in the comparative study of religion, based, of course, on the richly variegated nature, the multicultural diaspora of American religious history. As Sullivan puts it, "American religion might be almost regarded . . . as a controlled experiment in comparative religion."

Emerging as the primary cartographer of the kaleidoscopic contemporary American religious landscape, Diana Eck writes out of her own scholarly history as a "boundary-crosser, even a trespasser," one who has repeatedly moved in her scholarly and religious life between the religious traditions of India to the field of Christian theology to the field of American religious history. Observing a "new geo-religious reality" in the United States and across the globe, wherein "there are mosques in the Bible Belt in Houston, just as there are churches in Muslim Pakistan," Eck notes the tremendous changes in the religious map of the world that have been brought about by migration, cultural assimilation, and most importantly vast new opportunities for dialogue and religious exchange (Jews practicing Buddhist meditation; Christians reading the *Gita;* interfaith monastic exchanges; and so forth).

These new realities simultaneously bring with them urgent imperatives in the comparative study of religion. Eck calls into question whether the "hybrid" or converging forms such as American Buddhism should be so easily dismissed by scholars who cling to purist notions of classical traditions; perhaps instead the new paradigms are more historically typical than atypical. Just as postmodern thought represents reality as a non-fixed, unreifiable, and uncategorizable stream of events, so Eck urges us as scholars to consider the world's religious traditions, not as fixed systems, "boxes" of texts and commentaries transmitted between generations, but rather as rivers, converging, recombining, perpetually in motion. She charts both the hardening and softening of boundaries in the "worldwide backlash of colonialism." Recalling her own work in *Banaras: City of Light,*[8] in which she acknowledges using interpretive methods and a voice that "no Hindu" would have used, she argues that she has nevertheless articulated "an understanding of Hindu religious life that Hindus themselves would recognize."

Herein, then, lies the paradox. As scholars, we do not have to be the "other" to speak to or even for the "other," but we must ourselves first change. Ultimately, Eck calls for "dialogue as method" in the comparative study of religion. This approach draws both from postmodernism and from its critics, requiring mutuality and critical awareness, and especially interaction with the "other," as she puts it, "in a way careful and sustained enough to be able to see, and even to articulate, the other's point of view—both the others who are before us and the others whose multiple voices speak within us. Gradually we become bilingual or multilingual . . ."

The third and final major section of the volume, "A Revised Comparison: New Justifications for Comparative Study," comprises synthetic essays. Resonating with and in some cases building on the previous essays, they argue for the possibility of a re-visioned comparative method. This "new comparative religion" grows out of cultural specificity and may or may not begin with the assumption of a shared ontology across the world's religious traditions. It is receptive to using cross-cultural categories as an imaginative tool to enable us to begin to know each tradition more profoundly, and paradoxically, more on its own terms. In "Juggling Torches: Why We Still Need Comparative Religion," Kimberley C. Patton challenges some of the underlying premises of postmodern thought as it is applied to the study of religion, and defends the comparative enterprise. She notes how a comparative approach was instrumental in her own research as she attempted to solve a "ritual paradox" in ancient Greek iconography. Patton rejects the postmodern concept that comparison by its nature abstracts and annihilates. In investigating its suspicion of organizing schemata, she points to its own reactive heritage in the aftermath of World War II, provoked as that conflict was by "grand plans" and "final solutions." Turning to issues of ontology, she questions postmodernist constructions of religion as invariably and primarily a matter of "local" or "political" concerns, with metaphysical or theological issues serving only as a pretext. "If we maintain a relentlessly closed mind toward the claims of religious traditions that what they describe is real or true," she asks, "how on earth can our descriptions of how they work, however 'thick,' be authentic?" Finally, using Robert Kiely's recent discussion of Hildegard of Bingen as a focus, she problematizes the postmodern obsession with "marginalization" when it is applied to the religious text. Patton argues against the "surrender of the whole comparative enterprise just because it is hard to do it right."

Like many postmodernists, but for utterly different reasons, Huston Smith deplores the intellectual legacy of the Enlightenment. Particularly damaging, he argues, has been the secular developmentalist model of history that "wipes out religion's key concepts, revelation and transcendence, with a stroke." Even if we agree with Enlightenment atheism,

how can we pretend to "give our students the impression that our Enlightenment-vectored courses show them what religion objectively is?"
Smith identifies what he calls two "half-truths" on the part of the detractors of comparative religion that have become false "truths." First
of all, "it is indeed the case that thinking is embedded in cultural-
linguistic contexts and is affected by them, but to argue that those contexts are so insulated from one another that it is impossible to understand what goes on in them except from the inside is going too far."
Secondly, Smith is in agreement with Kimberley Patton about the significance of Jean-François Lyotard's rejection of "the nostalgia for the
whole and the one" on the grounds that, continuing to quote Lyotard,
"the nineteenth and twentieth centuries have given us as much terror as
we can take." While conceding that "wholes can be misused and have
been, and differences do have their place," Smith reveals the absurdity
of the postmodern notion that "wholes are bad because they produce
terror" and that "differences, by contrast, are good and should be activated." The revolt against wholes, Smith concludes, namely, "metaphysics, metanarratives, and pejoratively, totalism—has severely impacted the idea of Truth," caricatured in Foucault and elsewhere as little
more than a power play. Smith rejects the charge that "belief in absolute
Truth lands one in dogmatism" and, redeeming the millions of adherents
of the religions we study over and against their learned detractors, defends "the spiritual wholeness that can come from the sense of certainty."

William Paden's essay emphasizes the inevitability of comparativism,
renouncing the notion that knowledge in our field (or any field) can
advance without transcontextual concepts; "[L]ike it or not," he writes,
"we attend to the world not in terms of objects but in terms of categories.
Wherever there is a theory, wherever there is a concept, there is a comparative program." Anticipating Jonathan Smith's notion in his "Epilogue" of the rectification of categories, Paden argues that we can always
improve categories. Building on Nelson Goodman's notion of "world-
making," Paden argues for the universality of the "forms" of world-
making activities, including classifications, which render them comparable despite the uniqueness of culturally specific "contents." He
thoroughly outlines how a "reconstructed sense of comparativism"
might look through the discussion of five factors or functions: its bilateral function as a window onto both similarities and differences; its
heuristic nature as a resource for further investigation and discovery; its
expanded idea of patterns; its stress on controlled, aspectual focus rather

than *in toto*, wholesale analysis of traditions; and finally its careful (and respectful) distinction between meanings seen by the comparativist and the believers themselves.

In her piece, "The Magic in Miniature," Laurie Patton seeks to expose some of the assumptions that both comparative and postmodern (particularly deconstructionist) approaches unexpectedly share. In particular, she examines the uses of etymology in the work of Mircea Eliade, W. C. Smith, Jacques Derrida, and Mark Taylor. In all four works, etymology—the history of the use of particular words—remains a means by which these authors make their intellectual moves. Patton argues that this common intellectual engagement reveals an underlying, shared belief in the magical power of what a single word can "do" throughout time. After demonstrating these (for some, uncomfortable) continuities between comparative and postmodern approaches, she proposes that this common "faith" in the magical power of individual words in intellectual argument might be seen as parallel to faith in the magical power of the miniature in ritual, as recently discussed by Susan Stewart and Jonathan Smith.

A conversation with Lawrence Sullivan focuses on the implications for the field of recent neurophysiological research indicating that the intellectual act of comparison itself seems to be a kind of primeval ocular-cortical function. Sullivan suggests in this conversation that through the twin epistemological principles of pattern formation and the continual factoring of elements, human experience itself is inherently comparative. Hence, to exclude the study of religion from comparative method based on misguided, purist premises of cultural self-containment is to shut down methods that have been logically and uncontestedly available to disciplines as diverse as physiology and linguistics. Sullivan particularly emphasizes the contribution of perception itself: "It may be a mistake to think of inner consciousness and our world as entirely separate. . . . Notions of comparison can be drawn from aspects of the material universe such as the brain, where there is a promising possible convergence of the study of material structure, formation through time, and reflexive understanding of these processes of structure and development. Given what the comparative study of religious history can bring regarding human intention, imagination, and orientation, it can look forward to joining the effort."

And what, finally, of Jonathan Smith, so crucial a player in these discussions? A respondent to the 1996 AAR Panel (see note 1 on p. 18), he reflects in the epilogue presented here on the significance of his early essay, "In Comparison a Magic Dwells." Smith softens his previously unequivocal assessment (and rejection) of the possibility of a valid comparative approach. Whereas in 1982 he wrote, "In no literature on comparison that I am familiar with has there been any presentation of rules for the production of comparisons; what few rules have been proposed pertain to their post facto evaluation," in 1999 he offers the groundwork for such a set of rules. Drawing from the few successful cases in comparative anatomy, in linguistics, folklore, and archaeology, Smith observes three such preconditions by which "genealogical comparisons" might be accomplished in the study of religion: (1) the relationship to strong theoretical interests; (2) the wealth of the data available and the level of "micro-distinctions" between those data; (3) the consequent ability of the comparison to provide "rules of difference" (as well, presumably, as those of similarities). He then highlights four "moments" in a successful comparative enterprise: description, comparison, redescription, and rectification. At the same time, Smith insists that "the end of comparison cannot be the act of comparison itself," but rather, "the aim . . . is the redescription of the exempla (each in light of the other) and a rectification of the academic categories in relation to which they have been imagined."

It is important to recognize that the authors of these essays, unlike most of their theological predecessors in the comparative study of religion, were trained as area studies specialists. They take for granted the linguistic and historical skills and the varied cultural experiences of the area studies scholar. Their work is shaped by immersion in primary texts, by interdisciplinary conversation with area studies specialists, and by collaboration with members of other religious communities. In reference to the comparative study of myths, Wendy Doniger describes the area studies perspective this way: "The way to study them is to *study* them, learning the languages in which they were composed, finding all the other myths in the constellation of which they are a part, setting them in the context of the culture in which they were spawned—in short, trying to find out what they mean to the people who have created and sustained them, not what they mean to us."[9] This remains the area specialist's goal, even if it is imperfectly achieved. David Eckel emphasizes that the scholars of Buddhism have been trying to achieve this goal in recent years: "Buddhist scholars have been going through their own therapeutic struggle to shake off the remnants of the modernist dream— the totalizing narratives and the unified visions—to achieve a more accurate understanding of the diversity and contradictions of their chosen object, the object that some, at least, still call by the name 'Buddhism.' "

Like Eckel, the comparativists in this volume are connoisseurs of difference; indeed, they are connoisseurs of the postmodern condition itself in which modernist thinking is also strong. Concerning this scholarly environment, Eckel expresses a certain optimism: "In the complexity, eclecticism, and irony of this situation I find much cause for hope." If the postmodern condition is marked by the process of decentering of the Eurocentric visions that were imposed upon the "other," this is the environment in which our contributors have pursued their work. All have traveled "out there" and conducted their work in collaboration with "others," and all have brought the "out there" into themselves and into their scholarship and reexamined their assumptions. Indeed, they recognize that in the late twentieth century, the "other" is no longer "out there" but also among us—we are all "other to one another," as Diana Eck has put it. We teach in increasingly diverse classrooms, and engage in dialogue with a range of "others," both jet-setting scholars and local believers.

As North American scholars trained after World War II, when area studies scholarship developed rapidly in the United States, our authors have long since abandoned the great modernist building in which they were schooled, to use David Eckel's apt metaphor, with its totalizing and essentializing architecture. Now, like postcolonial citizens with multiple passports, historians of religions dwell alternately in the polyglot villages of area studies programs and in established religion departments in the secular university. Many of us share Eckel's experience of finding that our old books containing the grand systems of comparative religion have gathered dust upon the shelves. Referring to one of the more important of these books, David White remarks that "a cursory re-reading of the 1959 *The History of Religions* leads . . . to the conclusion that the days of the history of religions metanarratives chronicled in that work are well behind us. Our thinking has changed, just as our world has changed since that time."

Much of the postmodern critique, then, has long resonated within the discipline of the history of religions and led to a revisioned comparativism, but without undermining its old Enlightenment purpose of enlarging our understanding and commitment to a wider embrace of humanity. "I am unwilling to close the comparativist shop," Doniger asserts, "just because it is being picketed by people whose views I happen, by and large, to share." Laurie Patton argues that in rejecting the static, generic comparisons of the past, postmodernism also urges moral engagement with the world, like the previous generation of comparative religionists. Having listened to the cultural particularists, Jonathan Herman proposes that "the best hope for rigorous comparative study is to work within the prevailing—and I believe, well-placed—concern for context, but to do so with the renewed methodological self-consciousness and a receptivity to the types of resonances that may indicate connections buried beneath the surface." Thus our contributors show their indebtedness to the postmodern critique while retaining the older humanist goals.

While today's historians of religions are not necessarily secular humanists, the contributors to this volume are all humanists in the general sense of their commitment to understanding the moral and spiritual condition of humanity in all its variety. They are also committed to the pragmatic, contested, and negotiated nature of the comparative enterprise. Unlike their predecessors, they do not see themselves as taking a God's-eye point of view—making totalizing claims and "finding" universal sacred realities. Nor do they believe that positivistic forms of postmodernism are the only alternative. "It is possible," argues White, "for comparative studies . . . to steer a middle course—between the universalism of our modernist forebears and the nihilism of certain of our postmodern contemporaries—through the opening afforded by the cognitive activity of reading and interpretation."

No one in this volume is willing to follow the postmodernist strategy of today's reductionisms—the turning of religion's perceived truths into merely exploitive systems of power, the fantasies of the weak, or the sociobiological strategies of the human species. Nor do our authors practice theological apologetics. Nevertheless, as Kimberley Patton points out, the similarities that comparativists perceive between different religious traditions are often realities for the believers themselves: "If human religious thought did not function in equivalencies, much missionary thought would have fallen on deaf ears, rather than, in many cases, relying so heavily on the translation of new concepts or divine figures into indigenous ones."

To those who would deny the possibility of any universal understanding across cultures or the possibility of shared concepts of virtue, as Alisdair MacIntyre does in *Whose Justice? Whose Rationality?*[10] Huston Smith responds by referring to the simple fact that Maasai warriors with whom he had absolutely nothing in common and with whom he could not communicate saved his life in East Africa. MacIntyre's naïve assumption that there might exist entirely self-contained cultures in today's polyglot, multicultural, postcolonial world is, of course, a philosopher's fantasy. MacIntyre intends this concept to support the culturalist's claims about the hyper-particularized character of human existence. Such a view, Doniger points out, "seems to deny any shared base to members of the same culture, much less to humanity as a whole." As globally oriented historians of religion, we can affirm with Doniger that there is no periphery to humanity, but only, of course, if we use the term "humanity" as with its inclusive Enlightenment meaning.

Nevertheless, as Jonathan Z. Smith rightly maintains in a more recent work, *Drudgery Divine*, "[T]here is nothing 'natural' about the enterprise of comparison."[11] This means that the comparativist must be acutely self-conscious of her task, not ignoring differences, despite the "oneness" of humanity. "A newer comparative frame," writes William Paden, "will neither ignore resemblances nor simplistically collapse them into superficial sameness; and it will neither ignore differences nor magnify them." The newer comparativism, he continues, "unavoidably involves the factor of reflexivity: self-awareness of the role of the comparativist as enculturated, classifying, and purposive subject, a cleaner sense of the process and practice of selectivity, and an exploratory rather then hegemonic sense of the pursuit of knowledge." For Diana Eck, scholarly reflexivity involves a self-consciousness about the scholar's situatedness and voice: "[W]henever I write or speak, I must be clear about which argument I am currently participating in. . . . We are, as my colleague Michael Sandel has put it, 'multiply situated selves.' We speak and write in multiple contexts—religious, academic, civic, familial. Recognizing this is what being aware of 'voice' means. As teachers and writers, we must work to discern clearly the distinctive voices we ourselves speak, and when we shift lanes, we are obliged to use a turn signal."

Just where do our comparativists stand on the question of religious truth claims and the existence of religious universals? None assumes the scholar must automatically endorse or deny them. Certainly, as Huston Smith and Benjamin Ray emphasize, the pursuit of meaning and understanding requires judgments about truths that are commonly perceived. But no one wishes to turn today's universities into theological seminaries of perennial religion. The scholar's first aim is intelligibility, and she must make up her mind about the reality claims and moral principles she can accept, and whether she has discovered shared religious truths.

All of our contributors recognize that it is only by identifying our common as well as separate cultural and religious beliefs that we gain greater understanding of ourselves and others. All implicitly accept Huston Smith's recognition that as members of secular universities they are engaged in "Enlightenment-vectored" teaching and research that is value-centered and morally engaged. This involves investigating religious meanings for their full moral and spiritual significance in peoples' lives and their role in shaping cultural systems.

For the historian of religion whose work concerns the ancient world, of course there can be no "historical" or dialogical interaction with the peoples and traditions of the past. There can, however, be moral, analytical, and even spiritual engagement with them—and in turn they can and will affect the historian. As Kimberley Patton writes, "[I]n the study of religion we are not playing a game that is purely intellectual, one that will leave us unaffected as we go about our business." Emboldened by J. Z. Smith's vision of the scholarly challenge involved in comparative study, she emphasizes both its risks and its rewards: "I know it now to be a bit more like the juggling of torches; either we will mishandle them and they will burn and wither us, or else our faces will begin to glow." The very concepts and terms of the scholar's analysis, whether it be of the past or the present, are enmeshed in contemporary social, religious, and academic arguments which the engaged scholar must confront if she is to examine their value. Winnifred Sullivan emphasizes, for example, that "a comparative perspective would give needed perspective" to the study of American religion which "occurs in the context of a highly politicized and polemical local debate concerning the interpretation of the First Amendment . . . and the appropriate location of religion in contemporary American life."

Finally, as this latter statement implies, our contributors' principled aim of increasing understanding is implicitly linked to wider intellectual, moral, and ideological norms, indeed, to the metanarratives of Western political liberalism: respecting cultural differences, recognizing the rights of others, listening to multiple voices, discovering shared truths, achieving mutual understanding, and developing what Martha Nussbaum calls "normative skepticism."[12] In postmodernist language, these goals belong to the West's totalizing vision of free society, equal rights, and distributive justice, to which our comparativists are committed. For them, universal moral principles may change, but they cannot be abandoned for the sake of solipsistic relativism. The goals of mutual understanding and self-critical scholarship are, as these essays demonstrate, the foundation of any situated scholar's work.

Our authors do not, then, adopt the modernist pose of "value-free" scholarship. Laurie Patton observes that "comparison reinforces ethical relations between scholars and the objects of their study" and asserts that "the comparative move and the ethical move can be one and the same." For Benjamin Ray, moral engagement ought to be one of the goals of comparative study—the tearing down of hideous stereotypes of the "other" and the encounter with moral and political issues that affect the communities we study.

The contributors would agree that postmodernism in its extreme form goes too far in rejecting all metanarratives and all essentializing and totalizing claims. As the critical theorist Terry Eagleton has pointed out, postmodern scholars committed to equal rights and distributive justice can reject the totalizing concepts of anti-racism and political emancipation, which comparative scholarship exposes, only on pain of contradiction.[13] The global story of imperialism and colonialism is, in fact, one of the metanarratives which the postmodernist critic takes as a basic premise. Finally, Eagleton reminds us that "it was by virtue of our shared human nature that we had ethical and political claims upon one another, not for any more parochial, paternalist, or sheerly cultural reason."[14] The authors of these essays reassert the old humanistic view that it is only by coming to understand our shared cultural and religious beliefs and practices that we gain greater understanding of ourselves and others.

In sum, our contributors argue that scholars can risk positing a comparative framework not to reach closure in service of a particular theory, nor to achieve moral judgment or to gain intellectual control over the "other," but to empower mutual dialogue and the quest for understanding. Although no author presents a simple formula or definitive method—an inadvisable strategy—each offers the vision of a renewed comparative enterprise. It is a vision that attends as strongly to difference as to similarity, while recognizing that both depend upon the scholar's choices and assumptions. This renewed and self-conscious comparativism is eclectic and circumscribed, dialogical in style and heuristic in nature; and it is self-confidently situated within interdisciplinary area studies programs and religion departments of the secular academy. Its ultimate purpose is not to create more generic patterns of the sacred in support of grand theories but to enlarge our understanding of religion in all its variety and, in the process, to gain renewed insight into our-selves and others.

While comparative religion must come to terms with its past, the contributors to this volume argue that it can be contextualized and re-fashioned so as to yield significant insight into particular aspects of re-ligious ideas and practices, while still recognizing that comparison is the scholar's own *inventio*—the "magic" of creative insight and mutual un-derstanding.

In titling this volume—which seeks to rehabilitate the comparative approach—*A Magic Still Dwells*, we note that the term "magic" has undergone its own rehabilitation. Particularly in studies of Mediterra-nean antiquity through the Hellenistic and Byzantine periods, and in Indo-European thought,[15] the term "magic" emerges as a concept de-scribing religious practices and sciences that involve internally consistent, tightly logical relationships between a wide variety of phys-ical elements and metaphysical principles of power. As Bruce Lincoln writes, " 'Magic' . . . is not idle superstition . . . it is a system of non-Aristotelian, homologic causality, whereby items are considered capable of acting on one another."[16]

The argument that in the case of comparative religion the items com-pared really don't "act" on one other except in the scholar's mind can hardly be defended, as Diana Eck shows: on-the-ground interaction be-tween traditions has never been more prevalent than today. But even in scholarly discourse, it is time to recognize that our discipline is more than a scholarly language-game with no relationship to its purported field of inquiry. Like magic, comparative religion can be an efficacious act of conjuring, of delineating and evoking homologous relationships while simultaneously holding in view, and thus in fruitful tension, un-disputed differentials. In the act of comparison, the two original com-ponents juxtaposed in scholarly discourse have the potential to produce a third thing, a magical thing, that is different from its parents. Not only is it "different," but it can illumine truths about both of them in ways that would have been impossible through the exclusive contemplation of either of them alone.

Notes

1. This volume grows out of two panels presented under the title "The Comparative Study of Religion: Contemporary Challenges and Re-

sponses" at the Annual Meetings of the American Academy of Religion in 1995 and 1996.

2. David Tracy, On Naming the Present: Reflections on God, Hermeneutics, and the Church (Maryknoll, NY: Orbis Books, 1994), p. 16.

3. James Clifford, "Introduction: Partial Truths," in Writing Culture, ed. James Clifford and George Marcus (Berkeley: University of California Press, 1986), p. 119; Stephen A. Tyler, "Post-Modern Ethnography: From Document of the Occult to Occult Document," ibid., p. 139.

4. Jonathan Z. Smith, "Afterword: Religious Studies: Whither (wither) and Why?" Method and Theory in the Study of Religion 7-4 (1995): 407-414.

5. Jonathan Z. Smith, Imagining Religion: From Babylon to Jonestown (Chicago: University of Chicago Press, 1982), p. 21; 25-26.

6. Barbara A. Holdrege, Veda and Torah: Transcending the Textuality of Scripture (Albany: State University of New York Press, 1996).

7. Jonathan Z. Smith, Map Is Not Territory (Leiden: E. J. Brill, 1978), p. 240.

8. Diana Eck, Banaras, City of Light (Princeton: Princeton University Press, 1982).

9. Wendy Doniger O'Flaherty, Other Peoples' Myths (New York: Macmillan, 1988), p. 16.

10. Alisdair MacIntyre, Whose Justice? Whose Rationality? (Notre Dame, IN: University of Notre Dame Press, 1988).

11. Jonathan Z. Smith, Drudgery Divine: On the Comparison of Early Christianities and the Religions of Late Antiquity (Chicago: University of Chicago Press, 1990), p. 51.

12. Martha C. Nussbaum, Cultivating Humanity: A Classical Defense of the Reform in Liberal Education (Cambridge, MA: Harvard University Press, 1997), pp. 136 ff.

13. Cf. Terry Eagleton, The Illusions of Postmodernism (Oxford: Blackwell Publishers, 1996).

14. Ibid., p. 113.

15. See, among many others, the works of Christopher Faraone, Dirk Obbink, Hans Dieter Betz, Fritz Graf, John Gager, Albert Henrichs, Sarah Iles Johnson, Alan Segal, Henry McGuire, Roy Kotansky, Rebecca Lesses, Bruce Lincoln, Susan Stewart, and Jonathan Z. Smith himself.

16. Bruce Lincoln, Myth, Cosmos, and Society (Cambridge, MA: Harvard University Press, 1986), p. 110.

PROLOGUE

IN COMPARISON A MAGIC DWELLS

JONATHAN Z. SMITH

If I read a myth, select certain elements from it, and arrange
them in a pattern, that "structure" is bound to be in the material unless I have misread the text or demonstrably misren-
dered it. The fact of its being there does not, however, indicate that my arrangement is anything more than my personal
whim. . . . A myth is therefore bound to have a number of
possible "structures" that are both in the material and in the
eye of the beholder. The problem is to decide between them
and to determine the significance of any of them.

David Maybury-Lewis

We stand at a quite self-conscious moment in the history of the study
of Judaism. There are a variety of ways of articulating this self-
consciousness, perhaps the most relevant formulation being our awareness that our scholarly inquiries find their setting (indeed, their legitimacy) within the academy. This provides not only the context for our
endeavors, but their raison d'être. This is to say, no matter how intrinsically interesting and worthwhile the study of the complex histories and
varieties of the several Judaisms may be, they gain academic significance
primarily by their capacity to illuminate the work of other scholars of
other religious traditions, and by the concomitant desire of students of
Judaism to be illuminated by the labors of these other scholars. Judaism,
for the academy, serves as exempli gratia. In the words of Jacob Neusner:

I believe that section meetings in the history of Judaism [at the American Academy of Religion] should be so planned as to interest scholars in diverse areas of religious studies. If these [section] meetings do not win the attention and participation of a fair cross section of scholars in the field as a whole, then they will not materially contribute to the study of religion in this country. There is no reason for the study of Judaism to be treated as a set of special cases and of matters so technical that only initiates can follow discussions—or would even want to.

This, I would submit, is a new voice and a new confidence. It is that of the study of Judaism come of age!

To accomplish such an agendum, it is axiomatic that careful attention must be given to matters of description and comparison—even more, that description be framed in light of comparative interests in such a way as to further comparison.

I

For a student of religion such as myself to accept willingly the designation "historian of religion" is to submit to a lifelong sentence of ambiguity. I cannot think of two more difficult terms than "history" and "religion." Their conjunction, as may be witnessed by every programmatic statement from this putative discipline that I am familiar with, serves only to further the confusion. It is necessary to stress this at the outset. If Judaism may assert no special privilege, neither can the historian of religion. The reflections embodied in this essay make no claim to be the result of clear vision from the "head of Pisgah." It is not the case that there is a model "out there" that needs only to be applied to the study of Judaism. There is no consensual format into which the scholar of Judaism needs only to feed his data. To the contrary, I intend this essay to be an exercise in collaboration. We need to think together about the issues presented to us by the assignment to be attentive to description and comparison. For me, this implies some attempt to map out the options in order to clarify what is at issue. The issues might as well be discussed in terms of Judaism.

I take my point of departure from the observation that each scholar of religion, in his way, is concerned with phenomena that are historical in the simple, grammatical sense of the term, that is to say, with events and expressions from the past, reconceived vividly. The scholar of religion is, therefore, concerned with dimensions of memory and remembrance—whether they be the collective labor of society or the work of the individual historian's craft.

The earliest full theory of memory (setting aside the Platonic notion of *anamnesis*) is in Aristotle's *De memoria et reminiscentia* 451b, which describes memory as an experience of "something either similar or contrary to what we seek or else from that which is contiguous to it." Within discourse on memory, this triad remains more or less intact through a succession of writers as distinct in character but as similar in excellence as Augustine (*Confessions* 10.19) and Samuel Taylor Coleridge (*Biographia Literaria*, chaps. 5–7). In the complex literature on mnemotechnics, it led to the elaborate Late Antique through Renaissance handbooks on visualization and *topoi*,[1] while, shorn of its specific context in memory, it was developed into the notion of the Laws of Association which so preoccupied the philosophical generations of Locke, Berkeley, Hume, Hartley, and Mill, receiving its definitive history in the famous appendix, "Note D**," in William Hamilton's edition of the *Works* of Thomas Reid.

As many will recognize, the formulation of the Laws of Association has played a seminal role in the development of theory in the study of religion. E. B. Tylor, in his first comparative work, *Researches into the Early History of Mankind* (first edition, 1865), postulated that a "principle of association" supplied the underlying logic for magical praxis: "any association of ideas in a man's mind, the vaguest similarity of form or position, even a mere coincidence in time, is sufficient to enable the magician to work from association in his own mind, to association in the material world."[2] J. G. Frazer, building explicitly on Tylor, developed a typology of magic:

> If my analysis of the magician's logic is correct, its two great principles turn out to be merely two different misapplications of the association of ideas. Homoeopathic magic is founded on the association of ideas by similarity; contagious magic is founded on the association of ideas by contiguity.

And Frazer repeats Tylor's charge that magic is a confusion of a subjective relationship with an objective one. Where this confusion is not present, the Laws of Association "yield science; illegitimately applied they yield magic."[3]

It requires but a small leap to relate these considerations of the Laws of Association in memory and magic to the enterprise of comparison in the human sciences.[4] For, as practiced by scholarship, *comparison has been chiefly an affair of the recollection of similarity. The chief explanation for the significance of comparison has been contiguity*. The procedure is homeopathic. The theory is built on contagion. The issue of difference has been all but forgotten.

Regardless of the individual scholar's theoretical framework, regardless of the necessary fiction of the scientific mode of presentation, most comparison has not been the result of discovery. Borrowing Edmundo O'Gorman's historiographic distinction between discovery as the finding of something one has set out to look for and invention as the subsequent realization of novelty one has not intended to find, we must label comparison an invention.[5] In no literature on comparison that I am familiar with has there been any presentation of rules for the production of comparisons; what few rules have been proposed pertain to their post facto evaluation.

Perhaps this is the case because, for the most part, the scholar has not set out to make comparisons. Indeed, he has been most frequently attracted to a particular datum by a sense of its uniqueness. But often, at some point along the way, as if unbidden, as a sort of déjà vu, the scholar remembers that he has seen "it" or "something like it" before; he experiences what Coleridge described in an early essay in *The Friend* as the result of "the hooks-and-eyes of the memory."[6] This experience, this unintended consequence of research, must then be accorded significance and provided with an explanation. In the vast majority of instances in the history of comparison, this subjective experience is projected as an objective connection through some theory of influence, diffusion, borrowing, or the like. It is a process of working from a psychological association to an historical one; it is to assert that similarity and contiguity have causal effect. But this, to revert to the language of Victorian anthropology, is not science but magic. To quote from a masterful study of this issue from a representative of one of the more lively and unembarrassed of the comparative disciplines, comparative literature:

> When we say that *A* has influenced *B*, we mean that after ... analysis we can discern a number of significant similarities between the works of *A* and *B*. ... So far we have established no influence; we have only documented what I call affinity. For influence presupposes some manner of causality.[7]

We are left with a dilemma that can be stated in stark form: *Is comparison an enterprise of magic or science?* Thus far, comparison appears to be more a matter of memory than a project for inquiry; it is more impressionistic than methodical. It depends on what Henri Bergson, in his study of memory, termed an intermediate knowledge, [derived] from a confused sense of the *striking quality* or resemblance: this sense [is] equally remote from generality fully conceived and from individuality clearly perceived.[8]

This may be tested against a review of the major modes of comparison.

In an essay written some years ago (and rather sarcastically entitled, to translate the tag from Horace, "When you add a little to a little, the result will be a great heap"), I tried to map out a paradigm for comparison, based on a survey of some 2500 years of the literature of anthropological comparison.[9] Four basic modes or styles of comparison were isolated: the ethnographic, the encyclopaedic, the morphological, and the evolutionary.

The *ethnographic* is based essentially on travelers' impressions. Something "other" has been encountered and perceived as surprising either in its similarity or dissimilarity to what is familiar "back home." Features are compared which strike the eye of the traveler; comparison functions primarily as a means for overcoming strangeness. As such, ethnographic comparisons are frequently idiosyncratic, depending on intuition, a chance association, or the knowledge one happens to have. There is nothing systematic in such comparisons, they lack any basis, and so, in the end, they strike us as uninteresting, petty, and unrevealing. In Lévi-Strauss's critique of Malinowski, such comparison loses "the means of distinguishing between the general truths to which it aspires and the trivialities with which it must be satisfied."[10]

The *encyclopaedic* tradition was not limited by the external circumstances of travel or contact. Rather than presenting items from a single culture that had been encountered by the author, as the ethnographic mode characteristically did, the encyclopaedic style offered a topical arrangement of cross-cultural material culled, most usually, from reading. The data are seldom either explicitly compared or explained. They simply cohabit within some category, inviting comparison by their coexistence, but providing no clues as to how this comparison might be undertaken. The encyclopaedic mode consists of contextless lists held together by mere surface associations in which the overwhelming sense is that of the exotic. Malinowski's description remains apt when he wrote of "the piecemeal items of information, of customs, beliefs and rules of conduct floating in the air" joined together in "lengthy litanies of threaded statement which make us anthropologists feel silly and the savage look ridiculous."[11]

The *morphological* approach is more complex with regard to the theoretical assumptions that are entailed (largely derived from Romantic *Naturphilosophie*). For the purposes of this essay, we can largely abstain from a consideration of these matters. Fundamentally, morphology allows the arrangement of individual items in a hierarchical series of increased organization and complexity. It is a logical, formal progression which ignores categories of space (habitat) and time. It has as its necessary presupposition an *a priori* notion of economy in which there are relatively few "original elements" from which complex systems are generated: the "all-in-all" and the "all-in-every-part." Both internal and external forces operate on these "original elements" to produce variety and differentiation in a manner which allows the morphologist to compare individuals in a morphological series using rubrics such as "representative/aberrant," "progressive/degraded," "synthetic/isolated," "persistent/prophetic," and to compare the individual with the generative "original element" (the archetype), either through direct comparison or as "recapitulation" or "repetition." The discovery of the archetype, as represented in the literature, has a visionary quality; it appears to be the result of a sudden, intuitive leap to simplicity. Characteristic of morphological presentations will be a dated account of the vision—Goethe gazing at a palmetto while strolling in an Italian botanical garden on 17 April 1787; Lorenz Oken accidentally stumbling over a deer's skull while walking in the Harz Forest in the spring of 1806. Nevertheless, in both the biological and the human sciences, morphology has produced major comparisons that have stood the test of time.

The *evolutionary* approach, which factors in the dynamics of change and persistence over time in response to adaptation to a given environment, has produced useful theory and comparisons in the biological sciences. I know of nothing in principle that would prevent fruitful application to the human sciences as well.[12] However, what is usually known as the evolutionary approach within the human sciences, related inextricably to what the late nineteenth century termed "The Comparative Method," is not fruitful, nor does it represent a responsible use of evolutionary theory. Evolution, as represented by the nineteenth- and early-twentieth-century practitioners of anthropology and comparative religions, was an illegitimate combination of the morphological, ahistorical approach to comparison and the new temporal framework of the evolutionists. This impossible and contradictory combination allowed the comparativist to draw his data without regard to time or place and, then, locate them in a series from the simplest to the more complex, adding the assumption that the former was chronologically as well as logically prior. While such approaches to cultural materials are still practiced, albeit on a more modest scale, such attempts came quickly under the sort of criticisms leveled by F. Boas:

> Historical inquiry must be considered the critical test that science must require before admitting facts as evidence. By means of it, the comparability of the collected material must be tested and uniformity of processes must be demanded as proof of comparability . . . comparisons [must] be restricted to those phenomena which have been proven to be the effects of the same cause.[13]

I suspect that the majority of my readers would agree with this statement as well as with its concomitant stricture that comparison be limited to cultural artifacts contiguous in space and time—the method of "limited" or "controlled" comparison.[14] Unfortunately, these statements and strictures have also been used as the smug excuse for jettisoning the comparative enterprise and for purging scholarship of all but the most limited comparisons. As the Stranger from Elea reminds us, "A cautious man should above all be on his guard against resemblances; they are a very slippery sort of thing" (*Sophist* 231a).

We stand before a considerable embarrassment. Of the four chief modes of comparison in the human sciences, two, the ethnographic and the encyclopaedic, are in principle inadequate as comparative activities, although both have other important and legitimate functions. The evolutionary would be capable in principle of being formulated in a satisfactory manner, but I know of no instances of its thorough application to cultural phenomena. What is often understood to be the evolutionary method of comparison embodies a deep contradiction which necessitates its abandonment. This leaves only the morphological, carried over with marked success from the biological to the cultural by O. Spengler, and which has a massive exemplar in religious studies in the work of M. Eliade, whose endeavor is thoroughly morphological in both presuppositions and technical vocabulary, even though, in specific instances, its principles of comparison remain unnecessarily obscure. Yet, few students of religion would be attracted by this alternative. Because of the Romantic, Neoplatonic Idealism of its philosophical presuppositions, because for methodologically rigorous and internally defensible reasons, it is designed to exclude the historical. The only option appears to be no option at all.

In the past two decades, three other proposals have been made: the statistical (especially as embodied in the Human Relations Area Files [HRAF] model), the structural, and "systematic description and comparison."

The statistical methods proposed are, without doubt, essential for evaluating comparisons in any mode, but they provide little, in themselves, by way of rules for the generation of comparisons. The only programmatic proposition, the HRAF project, is essentially a refinement of the encyclopaedic mode and is subject, with appropriate qualifications, to the strictures recited above.[15] However, the various discussions generated by this approach have yielded, as an urgent item on any comparativist's agenda, the question of the isolation of a unit for comparison with an invariant frame of reference. At present, the answers are too easily divided into those that resemble the ethnographic and those that resemble the encyclopaedic.

Structuralist comparison is more complex, and I shall be exceedingly brusque lest I distract from my theme. In terms of the descriptions presented above, I would classify structuralism as a subset of morphology, although with Marxist rather than Idealist presuppositions. The formal, comparative procedures of structural analysis appear to me to be identical with those in morphology. While I welcome the shift to Marx, who seems to me to be the necessary base for any responsible anthropological approach to culture, I do not find, as yet, that the structuralist program has come to clarity on the historical. To the degree that it is comparative, it falls prey to the strictures on morphology already presented; to the degree that it has been interestingly historical (e.g., M. Foucault), the comparative has been largely eschewed.

This leaves the proposal for systematic description and comparison which will be the subject of the third portion of this essay. To anticipate, although this is the least developed of the recent proposals, it is my suspicion that this may be but an elegant form of the ethnographic to the degree that the descriptive is emphasized, and the comparisons thus far proposed remain contiguous.

The new proposals have not allowed us to escape our dilemma. Each appears to be but a variant of one of the four modes of comparison. The embarrassment remains. The only mode to survive scrutiny, the morphological, is the one which is most offensive to us by its refusal to support a thoroughly historical method and a set of theoretical presuppositions which grant sufficient gravity to the historical encapsulation of culture. Therefore, I turn briefly to a consideration of a historical proposal from within the morphological mode.

II

Perhaps the most difficult literature from the past history of the human sciences for the modern reader to appreciate is the vast library that might be assembled on the hoary question of diffusion versus parallel or independent invention. It is a matter which has preoccupied comparativists from Herodotus to the present, and it is one of the few places where the validity of comparative evidence has been explicitly and continuously debated. From the perspective of our endeavor, this debate becomes of interest to the degree that it can be seen as a tension between a concession to the centrality of historical processes over against ahistorical constructs such as the "psychic unity of mankind."

It is to be regretted that much of this debate is so arid. Where there has been color and interest, it is usually the product of a long line of distinguished monomaniacs from G. Elliot Smith and W. J. Perry through Thor Heyerdahl. But there is one group among this number that I would want to argue deserves further attention, not so much for accomplishment as for endeavor. I refer to the Pan-Babylonian school, whose name is sufficient to drive usually calm scholars to a frenzy of vituperation. "Pan-babylonianism!—the word awakens the idea of an extreme generalization . . . of fantastic audacities."[16] From our perspective, their prime "audacity" was the daring attempt to historicize morphology from within.

To put the matter as succinctly as possible, what the Pan-Babylonian school introduced was the notion of a total system, to use their favorite word, a *Weltanschauung*. The importance of this cannot be overstated. Culture was removed from the biological to the realm of human artifact. It is man's intellectual and spiritual creation.[17] Concomitantly, the object of religion, for them the most total expression of "world view," is man's cultural and intellectual world, not the world of nature.[18] It is the inner relationships of the "elements," their system, their internal logic and coherence, that validates a "world view," not conformity to nature. Therefore, the "world view" may be articulated in a rigorously systematic manner. Hence the "audacity" of the founder of the school, Hugo Winckler:

> I claim to have established a formula which explains every conception of Babylonian theology. In mathematics, a formula is a general expression for the reciprocal connection of isolated facts, which, when it has been stated once for all, explains the phenomenon and settles the question. One may prove the truth of a formula by countless examples, illustrate it and show its

practical utility, but when once the root principle has been found, there is nothing further to discover.[19]

The school—and in what follows I will summarize the work of Alfred Jeremias as a typical and eloquent example—takes its departure from the fact that, while anthropology brings ever new evidence for the contemporary "Stone Age" man (the "savage"), the then newly recovered and deciphered literature of ancient Near Eastern civilizations reveals a cultured, urban, rational, and spiritual man. Jeremias argued that we find, "not hordes of barbarians, but an established government under priestly control" in which "the whole thought and conduct of the people were governed by a uniform intellectual conception . . . a scientific and, at the same time, a religious system." This "system" had, as its chief aim, "to discover and explain the first causes of visible things," these being discerned as a "microcosmic image of the celestial world."[20]

Jeremias concludes that the evolutionists are factually wrong, for there is no sign of nature worship and the like in the Near Eastern materials, no sign of slow development. Of more gravity, the evolutionary approach failed to account for the "inner unity of the cults"[21] or, when it did, turned to notions of independent or parallel development based on a presupposition, which lacks all basis in fact, of the "psycho-mental unity" of mankind.

Common to both these critiques, is the Pan-Babylonian notion of a complex, well-integrated, primordial system at the base of culture. The incremental hypothesis of evolution can be rejected because it cannot yield this whole, but rather only a series of parts; the thesis of independent or parallel development can be rejected because it cannot account for systematic similarity (i.e., it can point only to highly general resemblances or parallel single motifs, not to their similar formal combination). Hence the school's preoccupation with diffusion.

> The ancient Oriental conception of the universe entirely precludes the possibility of independent origin in different places by the exact repetition of certain distinctly marked features that only migration and diffusion can satisfactorily explain.[22]

In his argument, Jeremias breaks with a set of explanations which have hitherto characterized most comparative endeavors: single-trait comparisons which fail to show how they are integrated into similar systems; "mental unity" which yields general similarities but cannot account for agreement of details or structures; borrowing, which will not allow the "specific character" of a nation to be expressed. He does so by postulating a rich model of cultural tradition that has three levels: (1) that of "world view," which is characterized by "imposing uniformity"; (2) that of "culture complex," the particular *Weltbild* or *Gestalt* of a given people; and (3) the linguistic manifestation of the interaction of these two. It is the "world view" which is diffused, modified by a particular "culture complex" and linguistically particularized in a text with its own quite specific context.

To put this model in a more contemporary translation. The "world view" is expressed by the unconscious syntactics of intellectual thought when applied to first principles. The "culture complex" provides the semantics—in Jeremias's view, a lexicon self-consciously transmitted by elites. The particular text is pragmatics, an individual expression reflecting, both consciously and unconsciously, the conjunction of syntax and semantics within a personal and historical environment. Or, to translate into yet more recent terminology, the "world view" is the unconscious deep structure, the "culture complex" is *langue*, the text is *parole*.

While the details of the various interpretations and patterns generated by this approach are fascinating, especially as many of them have been taken over in wholesale fashion, without acknowledgment, in the works of subsequent historians of religion, I give only one concrete example of their most imitated pattern.

Given the basic law of correspondence between the celestial world and the terrestrial, Jeremias postulates two ideal types which he designates the "Babylonian" and the "Canaanite" (he insists that the names be written with sanitary pips). The "Babylonian" is "original," it is a "purely astronomical theory," a cosmological pattern, which maintains the general correspondence of microcosm/macrocosm and traces world history as a cycle leading from chaos to creation to redemption by a savior sent by the creative deity to overcome the forces of chaos. The "Canaanite" is a secondary, "corrupt" system. (Corruption is a technical term in morphology.) Here a seasonal, naturalistic interpretation has been given to the "Babylonian" cosmic cycle: the god of sun and spring who, after his victory over winter, built (or rebuilt) the world and took charge of its destiny. These two patterns, representing dual aspects of a "single, intellectual system," "spread throughout the world and, exerting a different intellectual influence over every civilization according to the peculiar character of each, developed many new forms." But each remains based on "die gleichen Grundlagen des Geisteslebens."[23]

Of course, the Pan-Babylonian school was wrong. At the factual level, its exponents placed too great a reliance on the high antiquity of Near

Eastern astrological texts, dating them almost two thousand years too early. On the theoretical level, they placed too great a reliance on diffusion. Yet, in many ways they were right. They saw clearly the need to ground comparison and patterns in a historical process, saw clearly the need to develop a complex model of tradition and the mechanisms for its transmission, saw clearly the need to balance generalities and particularities in a structure which integrated both, saw clearly the priority of comparative systematics over the continued cataloging of isolated comparative exempla, saw clearly the power of pattern (and hence, of comparison) as a device for interpretation. They bequeathed to us this rich heritage of possibilities—and they bequeathed to us the problems as well. The two chief options followed by students of religion since then have been either to continue its diffusionist program shorn of its systematic and theoretical depth (e.g., the Myth-Ritual school) or to cut loose the pattern and the systematics from history (e.g., Eliade). We have yet to develop the responsible alternative: the integration of a complex notion of pattern and system with an equally complex notion of history.

As will be detected, with my evocation of the ghost of the Pan-Babylonian school, I have been slowly moving closer to the matter of systematics and to the particularized portion of this essay, that of description and comparison in the history of Judaism. Not that the preceding has been remote. For example, I know of no idea so influential on biblical scholars, students of Judaism and of religion than the groundless distinction, first generated by the Pan-Babylonian school, between cyclical and linear time, the former associated by them with the Near East and myth, the latter, with Israel and history.[24]

III

It is most likely an accident, but it is also a fact, that three of the most distinguished, creative, native-born American historians of religion should have devoted substantial portions of their academic careers to undertaking systematic descriptions and comparisons of early Judaism: George F. Moore, Erwin R. Goodenough, and Jacob Neusner.

It is the task of the third part of this essay to review their work from the limited perspective of the considerations on comparison already advanced.

Considering its date of publication (1927) in the midst of the controversies over the *Religionsgeschichtliche Schule* and his own considerable comparative labors as the holder of one of the first endowed chairs in history of religions in this country, George Foot Moore's *Judaism in the First Centuries of the Christian Era: The Age of the Tannaim* is remarkably, in fact deliberately, free from explicit comparisons. Indeed, one of Moore's central theses (against Bousset and other members of the school)[25] is that Judaism is incomparable as a religious system. An examination of his work with an eye toward comparison reveals a consistent pattern. (1) "Normative Judaism" is autochthonous. Any comparisons which imply significant borrowing are to be denied.[26] (2) Therefore, the largest class of comparisons to normative Judaism are negative. They are used to assert the difference, the incomparability of the tradition.[27] (3) The second largest group of comparisons are internal, to other forms of Judaism: the biblical, the Alexandrian or hellenistic, the Samaritan. These comparisons are occasionally used to measure the distance from the normative, but are more usually employed to assert the overall unity of the system.[28] (4) Where non-Jewish parallels can be adduced, where borrowing may be proposed, is always in the area of "nonnormative" Judaism, in those materials "ignored" or rejected by the normative tradition. Hence, the greatest concentration of comparisons will be found in the seventh part of Moore's work, devoted to "the hereafter," which focused on apocalyptic and pseudepigraphic literature.[29] In other rare instances, when borrowing or imitation is postulated, Moore emphasizes that it occurs in "late" post-Tannaitic texts, materials presumably "leaking" out from under control.[30] (5) A final class of comparisons may be called pedagogic. These result from Moore's presumption that he is writing for a largely Christian audience. Thus, while he is usually at pains to deny Jewish precedents for Christian doctrine (especially those associated with elements in Roman Catholic dogma),[31] he is prepared to offer analogies to Protestant religious doctrines, presumably to help his reader understand.[32]

I can find only two interesting theoretical statements on comparison within the three volumes of *Judaism*. Both raise the question of the systematic, although in quite different ways. The first is the last paragraph of the work, the conclusion of the section on the nonnormative "hereafter":

> Borrowings in religion, however, at least in the field of ideas [in a note Moore writes, "the adoption of foreign rites and the adaptation of myths are another matter"] are usually in the nature of the appropriation of things in the possession of another which the borrower recognizes in all good faith as belonging to himself, ideas which, when once they become known to him, are

seen to be the necessary implications or compliments of his own . . . [for example] the Persian scheme must have been most strongly commended by the fact that it seemed to be the logical culmination of conceptions of retribution which were deeply rooted in Judaism itself.[33]

While I do not quarrel necessarily with the notion in this passage (it reminds me of the exciting work of scholars such as Robin Horton),[34] Moore nowhere clarifies the meaning of terms such as "necessary implication" or "logical culmination," which hint at a generative, systematic logic. Rather, one feels when reading this paragraph as if one is in the presence of that remarkable figure in Borges's narrative, "Pierre Menard, Author of Don Quixote," who labored for years to produce a manuscript which repeated, word-for-word, Cervantes's masterpiece.[35] Jews did not borrow, for what they "borrowed" turned out to be already their own.

The second passage is the closest Moore comes to the articulation of an indigenous system—alas, it concerns the Levitical Code and not Tannaitic materials:

> They were ancient customs, the origin and reason of which had long since been forgotten. Some of them are found among other Semites, or more widely; some were, so far as we know, peculiar to Israel; but *as a whole, or, we may say as a system*, they were distinctive customs which the Jews had inherited from their ancestors with a religious sanction in the two categories of holy and polluted. Other peoples had their own [systems] . . . and *these systems also were distinctive*.[36]

But the thought remains undeveloped. We are left with only the atomism: each religion has one or more systems; they are each distinctive; they are each incomparable.

Neither of these statements is developed further in Moore. They remain as hints of the possibility of describing systems with generative logics of their own.

What Moore did accomplish in *Judaism* in an explicit fashion requires no rehearsal. Despite his statement that he has "avoided imposing on the matter a systematic disposition which is foreign to it and to the Jewish thought of the times,"[37] Moore applied to the Tannaitic documents a traditional Christian dogmatic outline ("Revealed Religion," "Idea of God," and the like), arranging his materials in a synthetic sketch in which the discrete items, despite his historical introduction and his catalog of sources, are treated ahistorically without individuality. Moore's *Judaism*, although confined to a single tradition, is clearly in the encyclopaedic mode. What he produced, in a most elegant and thoughtful form, was, essentially, an expanded chapter on Judaism from his two-volume textbook, *History of Religions*.[38] The suppressed member of the comparison throughout Moore's work is Protestant Christianity; it is this comparison that provides the categories for description and the occasions for exegesis. But, as it is suppressed, we are left with a dogmatic formulation of incomparability and an equally dogmatic description. Moore's work is unfortunately typical of most Jewish and Christian handbooks on Judaism. It is the supreme achievement of this genre, but it provides no model for our inquiry.

The work of Erwin R. Goodenough richly deserves a monograph that has yet to be written. From our limited perspective, he presents himself as, perhaps, the most interesting single author. For, unlike Moore, from whom he self-consciously distances himself, comparisons abound, between Judaism and other Mediterranean cults, between "hellenistic" and "normative" Judaisms, between iconographic and literary materials. The comparisons are in the service of both a complex (and largely psychological) general theory of religion and of an equally complex historical reconstruction of Judaism. "I have not spent thirty years as a mere collector; I was trying to make a point."[39]

Fortunately for the reader's patience, it is not necessary to produce such a monograph at this time. From the various methodological statements Goodenough issued in the course of his long career, a consistent set of assumptions may be gleaned. He was successful in making his "point"![40] Baldly stated, Goodenough sought to establish several points: (1) Any given symbol (and it was crucial to Goodenough that one was dealing with an exceedingly economical group of symbols) had wide currency in the Mediterranean world; that is to say, it was part of a Mediterranean "lingua franca." The fact of currency could be established by the enumeration of examples drawn from the ancient Near East, Egypt, Greece, Rome, the Iranian empire, and the religious traditions of Judaism and Christianity. (2) The same symbol possessed a "common meaning," and this meaning was singular. He insisted that this meaning could be recovered by the (usually cultic) setting of the iconic symbol, as well as by its occurrence in texts (especially ritual materials). On occasion, a meaning may be explicitly given a symbol in literary materials (here, "theological" statements were given priority). Goodenough also held that symbols were effective primarily through "emotional impact," that they retained this capacity for the modern interpreter as well as for the ancient religionist, and thus could directly "give" their meaning to the modern student "attuned" to their "language." The contemporary scholar "must let the lingua franca speak to him . . . directly. . . . If this be subjectivism, let my critics make the most of it."[41] And so we should! (3) The symbols have been taken over in "living form" from the general milieu by Judaism. (4) They have retained the same "value" in Judaism when borrowed. (5) Although they retain this common "value," they have been subjected to a specifically Jewish "interpretation" (here, Philo and the rabbinic materials have priority). (6) In addition, there are a few specifically Jewish symbols, but these participate in the same general system of value and the same framework of meaning as those symbols which are part of the lingua franca. Around this skeleton, the vast exegetical and comparative labors of Goodenough on text and symbol are articulated.

I would hope that, in this summary, the reader would have anticipated my judgment. Shorn of his idiosyncratic psychologism (itself a powerful ahistorical presupposition), Goodenough's work is a variant of what has been previously described as the attempt to historicize morphology as exemplified by the Pan-Babylonian school. The system of "life" and "mysticism" at the level of the lingua franca functions as an analogue to "world view." Judaism and other national and religious systems which stamp their own peculiar understanding on this "common language" function as analogues to "culture complexes." The particular expressions, be they the writings of Philo or the murals at Dura Europos, function as analogues to the "linguistic" formulations.

I intend no criticism of Goodenough by labeling him a morphologist or by comparing him to the Pan-Babylonian school. He has opted for the most promising, but most unattractive, of the modes of comparison. In the same way that the structuralists have attempted to modernize the presuppositions of morphology by turning to Marx, Goodenough turned to his own understanding of Freud and Jung. This allowed him to affirm a generally ahistoric point of view, while asserting a modified diffusionism in specific instances (as when he described "syncretism" or the "Orphic reform"). However, he stands under the same strictures already articulated for both classical morphology and the Pan-Babylonian variant.

The last proposal to be passed under review is that by Jacob Neusner. While much that he has written is of direct relevance, he has summarized his program in an important essay, "Comparing Judaisms," which is also a review of E. P. Sanders's massive work, *Paul and Palestinian Judaism: A Comparison of Patterns of Religion*.[42]

Neusner takes as his start point Sanders's introduction, where, after criticizing the frequent comparativist tactic of reducing the various world religions to "essences" which are then compared and the alternative comparativist device of comparing single, isolated motifs between religions, Sanders ventures a proposal for what he terms the "holistic comparison of patterns of religion."[43] This is to be the comparison of

> an entire religion, parts and all, with an entire religion, parts and all; to use the analogy of a building, to compare two buildings, not leaving out of account their individual bricks. The problem is how to discover two wholes, both of which are considered and defined on their own merits and in their own terms, to be compared with one another. I believe that the concept of a "pattern of religion" makes this possible.[44]

Allowing, for the moment, the language of "entire" and "wholes" to stand unquestioned, and setting aside the difficulty, indeed the impossibility, of comparing two different objects, each "considered" and "defined in their own terms"—a statement which he cannot mean literally, but which he gives no indication as to how he would modify—Sanders compounds confusion by further defining the notion of pattern. It is not a total, historical entity (e.g., Judaism, Christianity, Islam), but "only a given more or less homogenous entity." How much "more," how much "less" is needed to posit homogeneity and, hence, a pattern is left unclear. It is a matter of seeing "how one moves from the logical starting point to the logical conclusion of the religion." But the notion of "logic" is nowhere clarified. Indeed, it seems thrown aside by Sanders's exclusion of what he terms "speculative matters" of methodology and by his strange insistence that the logic is one of "function."[45] Given these restrictions, I am baffled by what "entire religion, parts and all" could possibly mean for Sanders. I find no methodological hints on how such entities are to be discovered, let alone compared. His results give me no grounds for confidence.

It is at this point that Neusner joins the discussion. He affirms the enterprise of comparing "an entire religion, parts and all, with other such *entire* religions"[46] and goes on to state as a prerequisite for such "systematic comparison" (the term Neusner substitutes for Sanders's "holistic comparison") "systematic description." Who could disagree? We must describe what we are comparing before we compare. But much hinges on the meaning of the term "systematic." In Neusner's generous, initial proposal:

> Systematic description must begin with the system to be described. Comparative description follows. And to describe a system, we start with the prin-

cipal documents. . . . Our task then is to uncover the exegetical processes, the dynamics of the system, through which those documents serve to shape a conception, and to make sense of reality. We must then locate the critical tensions and inner problematic of the system thereby revealed: What is it about?[47]

Here the difficulties begin. Despite the bow to the notion of the social construction of reality, for Neusner, a system is a document, located at a quite specific point in space and time, a system is the generative logic (in Neusner's term, the "agendum") of a quite particular document, its "issues." The more one goes on with Neusner, the more it becomes clear that each important document may well be a system in itself. How, then, is each documentary system to be compared with each other? Let alone with "an entire religion, parts and all"? I can find no answer to these questions in Neusner. Rather I find an elegant ethnography of Mishnah, and, to some degree, of Tosefta and Sifra. As I have argued above, comparison in such an ethnographic mode is necessarily accidental.

It would appear that Neusner has proposed what might be taken for an effort in historicizing atomism, a proposal for comparing "Judaisms,"[48] an enterprise seen as problematic by Neusner. He appears to eschew wider comparison which he views as that which often "compares nothing and is an exercise in the juxtaposition of incomparables."[49] If this be an exaggeration, and there is much in Neusner's recent writings that suggests that it is, what in method and theory prevent it? We are left with the dilemma shrewdly stated by Wittgenstein:

> But isn't *the same* at least the same? We seem to have an infallible paradigm of identity in the identity of a thing with itself. . . . Then are two things the same when they are what one thing is? And how am I to apply what the one thing shows me to the case of two things?[50]

Wittgenstein's last question remains haunting. It reminds us that comparison is, at base, never identity. Comparison requires the postulation of difference as the grounds of its being interesting (rather than tautological) and a methodical manipulation of difference, a playing across the "gap" in the service of some useful end.

We must conclude this exercise in our own academic history in a most unsatisfactory manner. Each of the modes of comparison has been found problematic. Each new proposal has been found to be a variant of an older mode: Moore, of the encyclopaedic; Goodenough, of the morphological; Neusner, of the ethnographic. We know better how to evaluate comparisons, but we have gained little over our predecessors in either the method for making comparisons or the reasons for its practice. There is nothing easier than the making of patterns; from planaria to babies, it is done with little apparent difficulty. But the "how" and the "why" and, above all, the "so what" remain most refractory. These matters will not be resolved by new or increased data. In many respects, we already have too much. It is a problem to be solved by theories and reasons, of which we have had too little. So we are left with the question, "How am I to apply what the one thing shows me to the case of two things?" The possibility of the study of religion depends on its answer.

Notes

This essay originally appeared as chapter 2 of *Imagining Religion: From Babylon to Jonestown* (Chicago: University of Chicago Press, 1982), pp. 19–35. Copyright 1982 by the University of Chicago. All rights reserved.

1. On these handbooks, see H. Hadju, *Das mnemotechnische Schriften des Mittelalters* (Vienna, 1932); P. Rossi, *Clavis Universalis arti mnemoniche e logica combinatoria da Lullo a Leibniz* (Milan and Naples, 1960); F. Yates, *The Art of Memory* (Chicago, 1966). I should note that I was led to take the starting point in memory for this essay by rereading the classic study by M. Halbwach, *Les cadres sociaux de la mémoire* (Paris, 1952).

2. E. B. Tylor, *Researches into the Early History of Mankind*, 3d ed. (London, 1878), p. 130. See also Tylor, *Primitive Culture*, 2d ed. (New York, 1889), 1:115–16.

3. J. G. Frazer, *The Golden Bough*, 3d ed. (New York, 1935), 1:53, see also, 1:221–22.

4. Note that David Hume, in his discussion of the Laws of Association in the third chapter of *An Enquiry Concerning Human Understanding*, writes of the similarity between words in different languages "even where we cannot suspect the least connection or communication," and thus moves from association as a matter of individual psychology, to association as an anthropological issue (in the edition by C. W. Hendel [Indianapolis, 1955] the passage quoted occurs on p. 32).

5. E. O'Gorman, *La idea del descubrimiento de América* (Mexico City, 1951). Compare his own English-language version, *The Invention of America: An Inquiry into the Historical Nature of the New World and the Meaning of Its History* (Bloomington, 1961). I have oversimplified O'Gorman's important argument as to the nature of invention. He maintains that the "New World" was invented over time as explorers came to realize that it was a world that their traditional world view had not anticipated. See further, W. Washburn, "The Meaning of 'Discovery' in the Fifteenth and Sixteenth Centuries," *American Historical Review* 68 (1962): 1–21.

6. *The Works of Samuel Taylor Coleridge* (New York, 1854), 2:31.

7. Ihab H. Hassan, "The Problem of Influence in Literary History: Notes toward a Definition," *Journal of Aesthetics and Art Criticism* 14 (1955): 66–76. I quote p. 68. At the present, comparative law and comparative literature are the only two humanistic enterprises that function in such a way as to merit the title discipline. The question of "influence" has been much debated in comparative literature. In addition to Hassan, I have been much influenced by C. Guillén, "Literatura como sistema: Sobre fuentes, influencias y valores literarios," *Filologia romanze* 4 (1957): 1–29, in its clarification of the psychological nature of the postulation of influence—although I dissent from the conclusions he reaches.

8. H. Bergson, *Matter and Memory*, 5th ed. (Garden City, N.Y., 1959), p. 152.

9. J. Z. Smith, *Map Is Not Territory: Studies in the History of Religion* (Leiden, 1978), pp. 240–64.

10. C. Lévi-Strauss, *Structural Anthropology* (New York, 1963), 1:14.

11. B. Malinowski, *Crime and Custom in Savage Society* (Paterson, 1964), p. 126.

12. J. H. Steward, *Theory of Culture Change: The Methodology of Multilinear Evolution* (Urbana, 1955); S. Toulmin, *Human Understanding* (Princeton, 1972), 1:133–44 *et passim*.

13. F. Boas, "The Limitations of the Comparative Method of Anthropology," *Science* n.s. 4 (1896): 901–8. I quote pp. 907 and 903–4.

14. See F. Eggan, "Social Anthropology and the Method of Controlled Comparison," *American Anthropologist* 56 (1964): 743–63 for a useful overview.

15. HRAF comparison is embodied in G. P. Murdock's classic *Social Structure* (New York, 1949) and his proposal "World Ethnographic Sample," *American Anthropologist* 59 (1957): 664–87. For the methodology, see F. W. Moore, ed., *Readings in Cross-Cultural Methodology* (New Haven, 1961), and R. L. Merritt and S. Rokkan, eds., *Comparing Nations: The Use of Quantitative Data in Cross-National Research* (New Haven, 1966). The encyclopaedic nature of the enterprise will become apparent to even the most casual reader of these works. This is not surprising inasmuch as the first proposal for such a study was made by E. B. Tylor, "On a Method of Investigating the Development of Institutions," *Journal of the Royal Anthropological Institute* 18 (1889): 245–72 (see the important note by F. Galton on p. 272). Within the sociological literature chiefly concerned with intrasocietal comparison, see, among others, G. Sjöberg, "The Comparative Method in the Social Sciences," *Philosophy of Science* 22 (1955): 106–17, and R. M. Marsh, *Comparative Sociology: A Codification of Cross-Societal Analysis* (New York, 1967).

16. H. Pinard de la Boullaye, *L'Etude comparée des religions* (Paris, 1922), 1:385 and 387.

17. Hence, their sharp critique of the evolutionary school.

18. Hence, their sharp critique of the naturist school. See further, J. Z. Smith, "Myth and Histories," in H. P. Duerr, ed., *Mircea Eliade Festschrift* (Frankfurt, 1982).

19. H. Winckler, *Altorientalische Forschungen* (Leipzig, 1900), 3: 274.

20. A. Jeremias, *Das Alte Testament im Lichte des Alten Orients* (Leipzig, 1904). For the historian of religion, the most important edition of this work is not one of the three German editions (Leipzig, 1904, 1906, 1916), but rather the English translation by C. L. Beaumont, *Old Testament in Light of the Ancient East* (London, 1911), vols. 1–2, with new materials added by Jeremias. The bulk of vol. 1 constitutes a major essay by Jeremias on the *Weltbild*, which was not incorporated into the German version.

21. Jeremias, *Old Testament*, 1:4, n.2.

22. Ibid.

23. Jeremias, *Old Testament*, 1:4.

24. On the debt to the Pan-Babylonian school, see, among others, B. S. Childs, *Myth and Reality in the Old Testament* (London, 1960), p. 74.

25. See G. F. Moore, "Christian Writers on Judaism," *Harvard Theological Review* 14 (1921): 243–44, and Moore, *Judaism in the First Centuries of the Christian Era: The Age of the Tannaim* (Cambridge, Mass., 1927–30), vols. 1–3, esp. 1:129 and n.1.

26. Moore, *Judaism*, 1:16, 115, 135; 2:295; 3:vii–viii. It should be understood that the passages in Moore cited in notes 26–33 are intended as clear examples of the point in question and do not constitute exhaustive lists.

27. Moore, *Judaism*, 1:22 and n. 1, 110, 220, 281, 323, 386; 2:22, 395.

28. Moore, *Judaism*, 1:ix, 23–27, 44, 119; 2:154.

29. Moore, *Judaism*, 2:279–395, esp. pp. 289, 292–95, 394–95. Cf. 1:404.

30. Moore, *Judaism*, 1:551.

31. Moore, *Judaism*, 1:332, 417, 544–46. Whether this is Protestant bias or a caution to his own formulation of the "church" of Judaism, or "catholic (universal) Judaism" (1:111)—a formulation which is derived from S. Schechter—I cannot determine. I suspect the former.

32. Moore, *Judaism*, 1:460, 476, 515; 2:65, 88 n.1.

33. Moore, *Judaism*, 2:394–95.

34. R. Horton, "African Conversion," *Africa* 41 (1971): 85–108.

35. J. L. Borges, *Ficciones* (New York, 1962), esp. p. 49.

36. Moore, *Judaism*, 1:21–22 (emphasis mine). Note that the first sentence is a statement of the doctrine of "survivals," on which see 2:8.

37. Moore, *Judaism*, 1:viii.

38. G. F. Moore, *History of Religions* (New York, 1913–19), vols. 1–2. See the pungent remarks on this work in J. Baillie, *The Interpretation of Religion* (London, 1928), pp. 130–31.

39. E. R. Goodenough, *Jewish Symbols in the Greco-Roman Period* (New York, 1953–70), vols. 1–12. The quotation is taken from 12:vii.

40. In my attempt to construct a synthetic account of Goodenough's model, I have drawn on Goodenough's essays: "Symbolism in Hellenistic Jewish Art: The Problem of Method," *Journal of Biblical Literature* 56 (1937): 103–14; "The Evaluation of Symbols Recurrent in Time," *Eranos Jahrbuch* 20 (1951): 285–319; "Symbols as Historical Evidence," *Diogenes* 44 (1963): 19–32, as well as on the relevant sections in *Jewish Symbols*, 1:3–32; 4:3–70; 11:3–21, 64–67; 12:64–77.

41. I have combined two passages, one from "Evaluation of Symbols," p. 298, the other from *Jewish Symbols*, 8:220.

42. J. Neusner, "Comparing Judaisms," *History of Religions* 18 (1978): 177–91.

43. E. P. Sanders, "Patterns of Religion in Paul and Rabbinic Judaism: A Holistic Method of Comparison," *Harvard Theological Review* 66 (1973): 455–78.

44. E. P. Sanders, *Paul and Palestinian Judaism: A Comparison of Patterns of Religion* (Philadelphia, 1977), p. 16.

45. Sanders, *Paul*, pp. 16–18.

46. Neusner, "Comparing Judaisms," p. 178.

47. Ibid., p. 179.

48. On the problem of defining and classifying early Judaisms, see J. Z. Smith, *Imagining Religion: From Babylon to Jonestown* (Chicago: University of Chicago Press, 1982), chap. 1.

49. J. Neusner, *The Talmud as Anthropology* (New York, 1979), p. 28, n. 33.

50. L. Wittgenstein, *Philosophical Investigations*, 3d ed. (London, 1958), p. 84e (no. 215).

Part One

COMPARATIVE RELIGION:
THE STATE OF THE FIELD

THE SCHOLAR AS MYTHOGRAPHER

Comparative Indo-European Myth
and Postmodern Concerns

DAVID GORDON WHITE

In preparing this contribution, I had the occasion to refer, for the first time since graduate school, to the 1959 volume *The History of Religions: Essays in Methodology*, edited by Mircea Eliade and Joseph Kitagawa, that many have identified as a landmark in our field. Now, some forty years after its publication, that collective effort appears more as a period piece than a landmark, quite nearly as antiquated in its Enlightenment presuppositions or Romantic agendas as the earlier works of Frazer, Freud, and Max Müller. In a word, this is a modernist document, the mere reading of which should suffice to alert us to the fact that ours are postmodernist methodologies, and have been so for a good many years.

Loosely defined, postmodernism is a critique of modernist thought, the legacy of such modernist thinkers as Leibnitz and Descartes, but ultimately of all metaphysics going back to Plato. In his typically rhetorical fashion, Jacques Derrida has described metaphysics as

> the white mythology which reassembles and reflects the culture of the West: the white man takes his own mythology, Indo-European mythology, his own *logos*, that is, the *mythos* of his idiom, for the universal form of what he must still wish to call Reason. Which does not go uncontested.[1]

Now, some would argue that this is precisely the sort of insight that historians of religions, and particularly Mircea Eliade, had already had several decades prior to Derrida's deconstructionist endeavor, that is, that Western *logos* is always already grounded in Western *mythos*. But this would be a misrepresentation of both Derrida and Eliade. Derrida's argument is against White Man's *logos* rather than in favor of any *mythos* whatsoever: he is, after all, a deconstructionist. This makes his agenda quite different than that of Eliade, who, in his theory of "primitive ontology," attempted to valorize *mythos* as the narrative expression of authentic being for Religious Man, *Homo religiosus*.

While one might be tempted to read Eliade's as a proleptic "deconstructionist" strategy, wielded to undermine the hegemony of White Man's Reason, this is in fact not the case. Rather, it is more accurate to see Eliade's construction of Religious Man as the swan song of Romanticism, a last nostalgic Western imagining of archaic or primitive people that, while it opposed itself to the Enlightenment view of these as so many benighted heathens, was fully as Western and modernist in its appropriation of other people's myths as were the Enlightenment rationalists. Eliade used the Australian aborigines' dreamtime to attack Hegelian historicism, but he never truly sought to understand dreamtime on its own terms. Rather, he used dreamtime to demonstrate a theory of "meta-dreamtime," arguing that the West too had had its own mythic dreamtime before "profane," rationalist, historicist thought occulted it with its *logos*.

So, in the end, Eliade was constructing his own White Man's metanarrative, and the unmasking of such metanarratives is what much of postmodernism is about. This is at the heart of Jean-François Lyotard's critique of modernism, of "totalising metanarratives, great codes which in their abstraction deny the specificity of the local and traduce in it the interests of a global homogeneity, a universal history. Such metanarratives would include Marx's historicist narrative of emancipation, the narrative of psychoanalytic therapy and redemption proposed by Freud, the story of constant development and adaptation proposed by Darwin,"[2] as well as, we might add, the theories of myth and religion offered by the likes of Frazer, Eliade, and Lévi-Strauss (even if structuralism itself belongs to an early phase of postmodernism).

Now, if we follow Lyotard's argument to its conclusions, as some postmodernists have done, we find ourselves forced to grapple with the question of the legitimacy of conducting comparative studies of culture, societies, or religions, that is, of pursuing the discipline of the history of religions as it has been constituted over the past century. This argument runs as follows: modernist metanarratives, in order to accommodate widely diverging local histories and traditions, abstract the meaning of those traditions, by way of a "translation" into the terms of a master code, which leaves the specific tradition simply unrecognizable. Such metanarratives also become coercive and normative: they systematically control and distort the local under the sign of the universal. Such a drive to totality cannot respect the specificities of the genuinely heterogeneous traditions.[3]

If we accept this argument uncritically, then we are forced to conclude that we, as comparativists, must be the witting or unwitting propagators of the sorts of modernist metanarratives that produced Auschwitz. By "signing on," through an uncritical acceptance of the modernist categories that ground our discipline, to a form of reason that is hegemonic, coercive, and even demonic, we are participating in the carnage. However, as already stated, a cursory re-reading of the 1959 *The History of Religions* leads me to the conclusion that the days of the history of religions metanarratives chronicled in that work are well behind us. Our thinking has changed radically, just as our world has changed since that time.

And so it is that I would maintain that the postmodernist critique of modernist metanarratives is pretty much a dead horse as the millennium draws to a close.[4] If we are talking about contemporary Western scholarship—on art, architecture, law, literature, economics, politics, society, and yes, even religion—the postmodern message has been received and acted upon. Educating politicians, technocrats, the media, and land developers is another question altogether, but the fact is, these have never paid much heed to the Academy in any case. The demonization of modernism by the postmodernists is more a matter of rhetoric than of substance, just as is the demonization of the postmodernist Academy by neoconservatives. And while it may be the case that postmodernism has been, in the sociology or economics of knowledge, a short-term windfall for a number of subfields of the humanities, the self-indulgent pursuit (even if self-indulgence often takes the form of self-flagellation) of talking about ourselves talking about other people is one whose time has passed. We would do better to do what we do, which is to attempt to make sense of other people's religions, even if we do so in the certain knowledge that everything we say and write is provisional and condemned to revision if not ridicule by future generations, as well as by our own proximate and distant others.

In practical terms, this means that we need not feel ourselves compelled to front-load our own discussions with deconstructions of the theories of all who have preceded us on our path, nor need we worry out loud over what facets of our discussion are "essentialist," or attempt to render our scholarship "self-consciously performative . . . reflecting on itself in such a way that it reveals its own rhetorical nature."[5] All of these issues ought to be present in what we say and write, but as subtext rather than text. Postmodernism has been around long enough for us to take it more or less for granted. Watching ourselves talking about talking about what we do is not what we are about: we are about doing what we do, interpreting religions.

Behind the ever-expanding, always already expendable rhetoric of postmodernism, there nonetheless remains the substantive question of its implicit critique of comparativism, which needs to be addressed seriously. If, as Lyotard and others maintain, comparativism jettisons cultural specificity in favor of theoretical comprehensiveness, then we as historians of religion need to address the issue of how we compare the traditions we study. Here, we would do well to recall the insights of Antoine Meillet, who states in the introduction to his *Comparative Method in Historical Linguistics* that

> the linguistic sign is arbitrary: it has value only by virtue of a tradition. If unity is expressed in French by *un, une,* duality by *deux,* etc., this is not because the words *un, une—deux—*etc. have by themselves any connection whatsoever with unity, duality, etc., but solely because such is the usage taught by those who speak to those who are learning to speak. Only the totally arbitrary character of the sign makes the historical and comparative method possible. . . . [6] There are two different ways of practicing comparison: one can compare in order to draw from comparison universal laws or historical information. These two types of comparison . . . are entirely different.[7]

Here, Meillet's discussion identifies the great divide between the two types of comparative studies that we encounter in the humanities and social sciences. The first, whose goal is to uncover universal laws, has been followed by semioticians (De Saussure), general linguists (Jakobson), folklore specialists (Propp), structuralists (Lévi-Strauss), as well as phenomenologists or morphologists of religions (Eliade). Here, the analysis is synchronic, and based on the assumption that all the varied data that fall within the purview of these approaches are viewed as so many "accidental" events (*parole*) within a timeless, immutable system (*langue*). Similarity is the watchword of this approach, which is patently deductive, interpreting particulars on the basis of universal principles. The second, whose goal is to interpret historical data, is diachronic, inductive, and as such, most attentive to *différence*. Scholars who have followed Meillet most closely in this historical approach have included Benvéniste, the comparative Indo-European philologist, and a number of (mainly European) *historians* of religions; as for Meillet himself, he takes for his example of the historical approach none other than the "young French scholar Georges Dumézil,"[8] who salvaged the field of comparative Indo-European mythology from the reef upon which Max Müller had thrown it a half century before.

With this division in mind, let us now revisit Jacques Derrida's broadside against metaphysics, which he characterized as a White Man's mythology, the Indo-European mythology, parading under the guise of "the universal form of what he must still wish to call Reason." If we read this as a critique of a Western ideology-laden endeavor to correlate individual expressions of, say, religious experience, to universal laws (the Sacred, the Holy, structures of cognition), then Derrida's criticism is not unwarranted. If, however, we take what Derrida has referred to here as the Indo-European mythology seriously, then we must take issue with his rhetoric.

I say this for two reasons. The first concerns the highly ambiguous term "mythology," which, as Marcel Detienne has noted, is employed both as a synonym for "myth" (as in Greek mythology), and for the study of myths (or of mythology). The term "mytho-logy" itself indicates an effort of interpretation: just as anthropo-logy is the study of human beings, so mytho-logy is the study of myths. Detienne maintains that mytho-logy emerged with the emergence of writing, which opened up a space for synoptic exegesis, comparison, reflection, and interpretation of the immediate, orally transmitted data of myths. By extension, our modern-day Western studies of world mythology are so many interpretations of interpretations: this is a case of double mimesis.[9] Thus, whereas the Greek mytho-graphers catalogued variants of their own "authorized versions" of myths, certain present-day comparative mythologists catalogue Greek and Amerindian and Chinese myths as so many variants on universal mythemes. Derrida has not told us which sense of the term "mythology" he intends, which leaves me with the impression that his understanding of mythology in both senses of the term is a rather naïve and uncritical one.

If Derrida is, as one would suspect, taking Indo-European mythology in the sense of the oral and literary traditions of the Indo-European language area, then he may be accused of presuming a homogeneity of tradition that never existed. If he is using the term to denote the modern-day study of Indo-European mythology, then he is misrepresenting that discipline which is, I would maintain, more interested in difference and historical change than it is in immutable ideologies or cross-cultural mythemes.

Now, it is not my aim here to rehabilitate the scholarly reputation of Georges Dumézil, but rather to argue that the field of comparative mythology, Indo-European or otherwise, when grounded in a diachronic, inductive attention to difference, may be used to advantage in formulating a model for a "new comparativism," in which difference is not explained away, but rather mustered to thicken the description of similarity. An excellent example of this is Georges Duby's *The Three Orders*, a study of class ideology in medieval France, in which the orders of society were always three in number, but with the social group filling the three "slots" changing from century to century, if not from decade to decade, according to religious, social, political, and economic reconfigurations.[10] Another example would be millenarian accounts of a race of Dog-Men, whose transformations across European, Chinese, and Indian traditions tell us fully as much about the cultural specificities of those traditions as about the "core myth" itself as it was reconstructed in the mind of this scholar.[11] Here, a new comparative mythology, driven by attention to historical change and cultural difference, emerges as a sophisticated and self-conscious endeavor that corresponds neither to Derrida's "White Man's mythology" nor to the earlier universalist or diffusionary models that preceded it.

How is it that we as twentieth-century scholars may legitimately tap into the mythology of other peoples from other times? Here, let us recall the dual sense of the term "mythology." The myths that we as textualists study have, by the simple fact of having been committed to writing, been subjected to a primary exegesis by their mythographers: it is therefore mythology that we read, myth that has already been sifted through, with this "variant" thrown out and that "reading" retained as "authoritative," a process that already involves an effort of comparison and interpretation. In this perspective, the effort of the scholar is a continuation of that of the mythographer: in both cases, the cognitive activity of the reader intervenes between the text and its truth content, between the realms of language and being.[12]

It is at this point that the ruminations on comparativism by Jonathan Z. Smith commend themselves to our discussion. It is Smith who recalls for us, in one of his earliest articles on comparativism,[13] the acronym OTSOG for "on the shoulders of giants," a commonplace dating back to the thirteenth-century Thierry of Chartres for the relationship of medieval and modern thinkers to the ancient philosophers. Here I wish to propose a new acronym, which I believe applies to any history of religions discussion of comparativism: we are OTSO-JZS, because we are standing on the venerable shoulders of Jonathan Z. Smith (if you disagree, you're NOTSO-JZS), who has artfully shown us how we may take issue with our modernist forebears without embracing the rhetoric of certain of our postmodernist contemporaries.

Here, I wish to concentrate on Smith's discussion of the central role of difference in the comparative enterprise on the one hand and, on the other, the mediating role played by cognitive activity of the person making comparisons. Referring to "the rich vocabulary of similarity and difference," Smith notes that its terminology

> presume[s] *intellectual operations* on the part of the individual making the comparison, as well as the notion that we are comparing *relations and aspects and not things*. . . . Similarity and difference are not "given." They are the result of mental operations. . . . In the case of the study of religion, as in any disciplined enquiry, comparison, in its strongest form, *brings differences together within the space of the scholar's mind for the scholar's own intellectual reasons* [my emphasis]. It is the scholar who makes their cohabitation—their "sameness"—possible, not "natural" affinities or processes of history. . . . Comparison does not necessarily tell us how things "are." . . . [L]ike models and metaphors, comparison tells us how things might be conceived, how they might be "redescribed." . . . A comparison is a disciplined exaggeration in the service of knowledge, . . . an active, at times even a playful, enterprise of deconstruction and reconstitution which, kaleidoscope-like, gives the scholar a shifting set of characteristics with which to negotiate the relationships between his or her theoretical interests and data stipulated as exemplary.[14]

To conclude, then, it is possible for comparative studies, and more specifically comparative religion, and most specifically comparative mythology, to steer a middle course—between the universalism of our modernist forebears and the nihilism of certain of our postmodernist contemporaries—through the opening afforded by the cognitive activity of reading and interpretation. We may legitimately compare other people's myths not only because this is what we ought to be doing as scholars of religion, but also because when we do so we know that we are comparing relations and aspects rather than things. Finally, there is the matter of the term "history" in the history of religions. Our discipline has, on this side of the Atlantic, generally failed to incorporate an analysis of the role of historical development and change within its comparative enterprise. Following the examples of such scholars as Dumézil, Duby, and J. Z. Smith, we must effect this important shift in our methodology, from the morphological to the historical, if the comparative method within the history of religions is to be a meaningful and legitimate one.

Notes

1. Jacques Derrida, *Marges de la philosophie* (Paris: Éditions de Minuit, 1972), p. 254.

2. Thomas Docherty, *Introduction to Postmodernism: A Reader* (New York: Columbia University Press, 1993), p. 11, summarizing Jean-François Lyotard, *La condition postmoderne* (Paris: Éditions de Minuit, 1979), pp. 7–9.

3. Ibid., p. 11.

4. A favorite topic of historians of religion, particularly of the Indo-Europeanist variety: see, for example, Wendy Doniger O'Flaherty, *Women, Androgynes, and Other Mythical Beasts* (Chicago: University of Chicago Press, 1980), especially pp. 149–280.

5. David Eckel, "The Ghost at the Table: On the Study of Buddhism and the Study of Religion," *Journal of the American Academy of Religion* 62 (winter 1994): 1106.

6. Antoine Meillet, *La méthode comparative en linguistique historique* (Oslo: H. Aschehoug, 1935), p. 2.

7. Ibid., p. 1.

8. Ibid., p. 1.

9. Marcel Detienne, *L'invention de la mythologie* (Paris: Gallimard, 1981), pp. 131–32.

10. Georges Duby, *Les trois ordres ou l'imaginaire du féodalisme* (Paris: Gallimard, 1978).

11. David Gordon White, *Myths of the Dog-Man* (Chicago: University of Chicago Press, 1991).

12. Docherty, *Postmodernism*, p. 7, citing Stanley Fish, *Self-Consuming Artifacts* (Berkeley: University of California Press, 1972).

13. Jonathan Z. Smith, "The Wobbling Pivot," first read as a lecture at the University of Notre Dame in 1971, and published as the fourth chapter of *Map Is Not Territory* (Leiden: E. G. Brill, 1978), pp. 88–103.

14. Jonathan Z. Smith, *Drudgery Divine: On the Comparison of Early Christianities and the Religions of Late Antiquity* (Chicago: University of Chicago Press, 1990), pp. 50–53.

CONTESTED IDENTITIES

The Study of Buddhism in the Postmodern World

MALCOLM DAVID ECKEL

According to Charles Jencks, the postmodern era in architecture began in St. Louis at 3:32 P.M. on the fifteenth of July 1972.[1] No, it was not connected with the Annual Meeting of the American Academy of Religion. The meeting of our professional organization took place that year in Los Angeles, and many would, in any case, have avoided the chore of traveling to St. Louis in the summertime. The event that marked this moment in American architectural history was the demolition of one of the great monuments of high modernism, Minoru Yamasaki's Pruitt-Igoe Housing Development. The development had been built in the early 1950s amidst much fanfare about the clarity, rationality, and salubrious simplicity of its modern design. During its short life, the development had been vandalized repeatedly by its inhabitants and, despite the infusion of millions of public dollars, finally had to be put out of its misery with a few well-placed charges of dynamite. With it fell a confident tradition of modernist design, in which the traditional diversity of defensible, private spaces had been sacrificed in favor of a grand conception of public order.

Is it hyperbolic to think that the same implosion has taken place inside the grand systems of comparative religion? When I take my old copies of the phenomenologies of religion down from the shelf and thumb through their pages, I feel as if I were walking through the halls of abandoned buildings. My graduate school notes lie heavy in the margins, like scrawls of graffiti on the walls, attesting to the fact that human hearts and minds once contested these spaces. I wonder, each time I close one of these volumes and put it back on the shelf, whether the puff of dust that rises from its binding is not a reminder that systems are built to crumble, and the grander the system, the more spectacular the fall. It is inspiring to read Ninian Smart's foreword to the recent reprint of van der Leeuw's *Religion in Essence and Manifestation* and note his invitation to Buddhists and Hindus to write their own phenomenological classifications of religion,[2] but we know that few Buddhists would undertake such an anachronistic act, and if they did, their efforts would be unlikely to find their way to publication.

What has reduced the great tradition of comparative classification to such a ruined state? Certainly one of the reasons is the respect we now accord to the concept of difference. You do not need to spell this word with an "a" to know that an awareness of difference pervades the field we used to call "comparative" studies. A generation of scholars has grown up committed to the idea that each microculture or community has distinctive traditions, and these traditions need to be understood in their own terms, without subsuming or homogenizing them into the dominant culture. And this is true whether the dominant culture belongs to the outside interpreter or to some authoritative strand of the indigenous tradition itself. This concern for difference in the act of comparison is evident in many corners of religious studies, but seldom more clearly than in the theoretical works of Jonathan Z. Smith. His essay on "Fences and Neighbors: Some Contours of Early Judaism" in the volume called *Imagining Religion: From Babylon to Jonestown*, undermines the concept of a single, normative "Judaism" and argues in favor of a polythetic classification of multiple "Judaisms."[3] The next essay, "In Comparison a Magic Dwells," strips away the aura of "science" that has shrouded the notion of comparison since the time of Max Müller and argues that the "similarities" so beloved of comparativists have no more epistemic validity than the "similarities" out of which J. G. Frazer developed his theory of magic.

Does this argument about the epistemic validity of concepts of similarity remove the need for comparative analysis? Smith argues that it does not, although it does make the comparative process more problematic. In his final essay, on the mass suicide by the followers of Jim Jones at Jonestown in Guyana, Smith argues that scholars of religion have an obligation to "remove from Jonestown the aspect of the unique, of its being utterly exotic."[4] How is this done? By setting Jonestown next to two apparently similar phenomena: a cargo cult in the New Hebrides and the Dionysiac festival recounted in Euripides' *Bacchae*. I am not aware that the comparative procedure in this article has been given a name, but I am inclined to say that Smith proceeds in a style of "imaginative and ironical juxtaposition," in which dramatically different phenomena are set down side by side in such a way that they suggest common features. How "real" are these common features? That is unclear. But they are a useful imaginative device to remove the sense of uniqueness that makes the events at Jonestown seem unintelligible. This process of investigation is "magic" transmuted into understanding (if not into science) by the use of the "imagination."

The fascination with difference in postmodern discourse is sometimes taken to be a form of cultural nihilism in which all cultural relations are reduced to the play of power and domination. There is no doubt that "difference" has a critical and destructive side. Without discernible patterns of congruity and similarity, structures break down, whether they are structures of concrete and steel or structures of thought. It is easy to lose, amidst the rubble, the positive values that are struggling for expression. Charles Jenck's story of the decline of architectural modernism is not simply about the destruction of rationality; it also has to do with a discovery that what passed for a rational structure simply failed to reflect the needs of the people who lived in its spaces. The postmodern impulse in architecture is an attempt to listen to these needs and reappropriate, often in an eclectic or ironic way, precisely the same traditional elements that had been discarded in favor of the modernist project. There is an echo of this point in Lyotard's definition of postmodernism as "the loss of credulity in metanarratives."[5] It may be painful to see the concepts of "progress" or "Enlightenment rationality" fall from their foundations, but their absence makes room for other, more particular narratives. It is as if a multitude of cultures were on the couch and could learn for the first time to tell their own stories, released from all the internalized narratives that had imprisoned them and prevented them from making a distinctive and free appropriation of their own past.

I doubt that I am saying anything surprising or new when I sketch these features of the postmodern situation. All of us are acutely aware of the epistemological dilemmas we face when we cross the boundaries between traditions. But the same problems apply to internal acts of comparison within a single tradition. "Unity" and "identity" are problematic concepts in any tradition,[6] and nowhere are they more problematic than in the Buddhist tradition, a tradition that prides itself on exploring the absence of continuity and identity in things, including itself. It should come as no surprise if I say that Buddhist scholars have been going through their own therapeutic struggle to shake off the remnants of the modernist dream—the totalizing narratives and the unified visions—to achieve a more accurate understanding of the diversity and contradictions of their chosen object, the object that some, at least, still call by the name "Buddhism."

One of the myths that has recently come under attack is the myth that Buddhism conveys a teaching that is down-to-earth, tolerant, reasonable, and accessible to confirmation through direct experience. This myth has been given classic expression in the English writings of the Sri Lankan scholar and monk Walpola Rahula. In his popular introductory text, *What the Buddha Taught*, Rahula tells us that "almost all religions are built on faith—rather 'blind' faith it would seem. But in Buddhism emphasis is laid on 'seeing', knowing, understanding, and not on faith, or belief."[7] According to Rahula, Buddhism has no need and no place for the inspiration of a god or other supernatural being. It stems from a human experience of liberation and calls not for faith but for empirical confirmation in the experience of each of its adherents. In Rahula's tradition of interpretation, it is not uncommon to hear that Buddhism is not a religion at all, but a philosophy or simply a way of life.

Where does Rahula's interpretation come from? Gananath Obeyesekere has traced Rahula's construction of the Buddhist tradition to a series of intellectual and religious struggles that took place in Sri Lanka at the end of the nineteenth century.[8] At a time when the Buddhist Saṃgha was on the defensive under the combined pressure of Christian missionaries and the British colonial administration, there was a movement to reformulate the teaching of the Buddhist tradition and turn the tables on the Christian missionaries. The catalysts for this movement were an unlikely pair of Theosophists from America. Madame Blavatsky and Colonel Henry Steele Olcott arrived in Sri Lanka in 1880, took the five precepts that incorporated them formally into the Buddhist community, and set about advancing the Buddhist cause. They established a number of crucial organizations, including a Buddhist Theosophical Society, and developed an interpretation of the Buddha's teaching that was designed to turn the tables on the tradition's Western critics.

Olcott's reading of the tradition is most clear in *The Buddhist Catechism*, published in 1881, only a year after his arrival in Sri Lanka. He was aware that Christian apologists had treated Buddhism as a "dark superstition,"[9] and he responded in two ways. He argued first that whatever "superstitious" practices were present in the tradition needed to be purified and purged by returning to the teaching of the Buddha himself. His catechism asks, "Are charms, incantations, the observance of lucky hours, and devil dancing a part of Buddhism?" The answer is, "They are positively repugnant to its fundamental principles. They are surviving relics of fetishism and pantheism and other foreign religions." But Olcott also went beyond the defense of a purified Buddhism to turn the tables on the missionaries and draw attention to the "superstitious" elements in their own teaching:

Q: What striking contrasts are there between Buddhism and what may be properly called "religions"?

A: Among others, these: It teaches the highest goodness without a creating God; a continuity of line without adhering to the superstitions and selfish doctrine of an eternal, metaphysical soul-substance that goes out of the body; a happiness without an objective heaven; a method of salvation without a vicarious Saviour; redemption by oneself as the Redeemer, and without rites, prayers, penances, priest, or intercessory saints; and a *summum bonum*, that is, Nirvana, attainable in this life and in this world by leading a pure, unselfish life of wisdom and of compassion to all beings.

Obeyesekere has pointed out the irony in these words. From Olcott's catechism grew a tradition of Buddhist ambivalence (if not outright hostility) toward the concept of religion, but his catechism had a religious origin in Olcott's own liberal Protestant Christian background. Olcott wanted to purify Buddhism by returning to the teachings of the founder as they were recorded in its authoritative scriptures. The teaching he found in these texts had much in common with the liberal Protestantism of the late nineteenth century. It was opposed to "superstitious" practices, suspicious of miracles and the supernatural, and respectful of the canons of reason. Olcott made a particular point of noting that Buddhism was consistent with the teachings of modern science. Olcott's reading of the tradition has come to be called "Protestant Buddhism," and the label has stuck.

Some of the most important Buddhist scholarship in the last few years has attempted to trace the influence of these modernist, Protestant assumptions in the interpretation of Buddhism, both inside and outside the tradition. Obeyesekere has argued that the effort within the Sri Lankan Buddhist community to "purify" Buddhism of elements that could be considered miraculous, mythological, or supernatural has cut Sri Lankan Buddhism off from its emotional depths and stripped it of its conscience. His argument has powerful relevance to the ethnic conflicts that now afflict the island. Stanley Tambiah has shown, in exquisite historical detail, how the ideological movement to create a modern, purified Buddhism has been implicated in the political movement to "purify" Sri Lanka of Tamil influence, a movement that has fed the cycle of ethnic violence.[10] Gregory Schopen has argued that historical studies of Indian Buddhism have been distorted by a Protestant, textual bias.[11] Schopen has attempted to redress the balance by examining the evidence of Indian epigraphy and archaeology. Among other important examples of the same critical process in contemporary Buddhist studies, one of the most notable is Bernard Faure's brilliant dismantling of the myth of Zen immediacy.[12] The picture we get of the Buddhist tradition from scholars (and from others who work in a similar style) is more local, more concerned with ritual, myth, and the supernatural, and more subject, in its contemporary form, to the ideological fissures and conflicts that afflict religious traditions in other parts of the globe. In short, the picture is much closer to Jonathan Z. Smith's amorphous and contradictory "Judaisms" than it is to Olcott's clear, rational, unified account of the Buddha's teaching.

Two thoughts occur to me as I survey the ruins of the modernist myths in Buddhist studies. First, we do not need to weep for the loss of the modernist accounts of the Buddhist tradition. One reason (as Obeyesekere shows so vividly) is that the modernist construction of Buddhism was about as friendly to the complexities and depth of Sri Lankan religious life as the Pruitt-Igoe Housing Development was to the complexity of life in a major American city. To encourage its gentle implosion is an act of compassion and liberation. Another reason to choke back our tears is that the modernist project to clarify the nature of Buddhism and discern the patterns and influences that affect its development is quite capable of rising anew from the ruins. Like much of postmodern criticism, Obeyesekere's critique of the rational organization of Protestant Buddhism does not constitute the abandonment of Enlightenment rationality as much as the substitution of one form of rationality for another. In Obeyesekere's case this involves the displacement of Olcott by Freud in the service of a more complete understanding and appreciation of the Sri Lankan psyche.

This leads me to my second point. Obeyesekere and others have criticized earlier Buddhist scholarship for a mistaken attempt to identify and promote an "essential" Buddhism. The concept of an "essence" is not a neutral category: it suppresses differences and leads, in the wrong hands, to cultural arrogance and exclusion. But by contesting essentialist, "Protestant" conceptions of Buddhism, Obeyesekere cannot avoid taking a position about features of Buddhist life in Sri Lanka that is "essential" in another sense. I have argued elsewhere that there is no lexical reason why the word "essential" needs to be taken in a reified or substantial sense: it can simply mean "necessary."[13] If I understand Obeyesekere correctly, he is arguing that there are *necessary* features in Buddhist life that the Sri Lankan Buddhist community needs to rediscover if it is going to fashion an effective, compassionate response to its ethnic and political conflicts. It is tempting to call this a "new essentialism," based not on a concept of substantive identity but on a pragmatic sense that certain features of a tradition are necessary to the healthy survival of the community. But the terms are unimportant. The interesting point is that Obeyesekere and others have been drawn back into the old modernist conflict about the nature of "Buddhism" itself.

Is this simply a way to smuggle the old myths of "reason," "progress," and "identity" back into the study of the tradition and once again to deflect the force of the postmodern critique? Perhaps. But it is precisely this uneasy, hybrid character in postmodern scholarship that makes it so intriguing. Modernist myths are broken, but they do not go away. They coexist instead with the rediscovery of traditional patterns of life and thought that were considered long since out of date. In the complexity, eclecticism, and irony of this situation I find much cause for hope, as I do in the complex, ironical, and serious work of scholarship that goes on today in the circles of Buddhist studies.

Notes

1. Charles Jencks, *The Language of Post-Modern Architecture*, 5th ed. (New York: Rizzoli, 1987).

2. Gerardus van der Leeuw, *Religion in Essence and Manifestation*, trans. J. E. Turner (Princeton: Princeton University Press, 1986), pp. xvii–xviii.

3. Jonathan Z. Smith, *Imagining Religion: From Babylon to Jonestown* (Chicago: University of Chicago Press, 1982).

4. Ibid., p. 111.

5. Jean-François Lyotard, *The Postmodern Condition: A Report on Knowledge*, trans. Geoff Bennington and Brian Massumi (Minneapolis: University of Minnesota Press, 1984), p. xxiv.

6. Should we take the word "tradition" to refer to the *traditum*, the thing that is handed on, as Edward Shils does in his masterful study, *Tradition* (Chicago: University of Chicago Press, 1981), or should we interpret it, as its Latin source suggests, as the act of "delivery," "surrender," or "handing down"

(OED)? Either way, "unity" is problematic, in one case foundering on the instability of the object, in the other on the instability of the subject.

7. Walpola Rahula, *What the Buddha Taught*, 2d ed. (New York: Grove Weidenfeld, 1974), p. 8.

8. Gananath Obeyesekere, "Buddhism and Conscience: An Exploratory Essay," *Daedalus* 120 (1991): 219–39.

9. Ibid., p. 224.

10. Stanley Jeyaraja Tambiah, *Buddhism Betrayed? Religion, Politics, and Violence in Sri Lanka* (Chicago: University of Chicago Press, 1992). Tambiah gives a particularly revealing account of the relationship between Walpola Rahula's construction of a modernist, rational Buddhism and the mobilization of monastic organizations to promote a program of Buddhist "religio-patriotism."

11. Gregory Schopen, "Archaeology and Protestant Presuppositions in the Study of Indian Buddhism," *History of Religions* 31 (1991): 1–23.

12. Bernard Faure, *The Rhetoric of Immediacy: A Cultural Critique of Chan/ Zen Buddhism* (Princeton: Princeton University Press, 1991).

13. Malcolm David Eckel, "The Ghost at the Table: On the Study of Buddhism and the Study of Religion," *Journal of the American Academy of Religion* 63 (1995): 1085–1110.

POST-MODERN AND -COLONIAL
-STRUCTURAL COMPARISONS

WENDY DONIGER

It may at first appear that anyone engaged in the poststructural comparison of religious texts (and I use the word to denote primarily, but not only, verbal discourses), particularly of religions situated in any part of the world that has been colonized, must fight a war on two fronts: against both the postcolonial and the postmodern critique. I wish to argue that this need not be so, that the glass is half full, not half empty—or at least both half full and half empty.[1] For the comparativist, post-modernism is both a problem (to the extent that the monolithic emphasis on *différance* would rule out any comparison) and a solution (to the extent that the open-ended approach to texts encourages a wider range of comparisons than had hithertofore been imagined). So, too, the post-colonial critique is both a problem (in inspiring a guilt that, again, when monolithic, excludes European scholars from the study of postcolonial areas) and a solution (in inspiring new areas of awareness, new consciousnesses, in the comparative enterprise). That is, each of these schools has its own double fronts, one, the earlier wave, harmful and the other, the later wave, helpful to the comparative enterprise. Let us consider them one by one.

Postcolonialism and Comparison

In the discipline of the history of religions, scholars have, by and large, abandoned universalist comparative studies of the sort that Mircea Eliade once made so popular, as had the triumvirate of Frazer, Freud, and Jung before him. Structuralist morphologies fall prey to the same attacks, leaving would-be structuralists nowhere to stand but on tattered poststructural grounds. There are theoretical, methodological objections to these approaches, but the postcolonial critique argues primarily on a different level: it argues that they are politically unhealthy. Postcolonialism emphasizes the political dimensions of the perennial methodological issue within the field of comparative religion: the problem of the same and the different.

There is, I think, some irony in the fact that the modern comparative study of religion was in large part designed in the pious hope of teaching our own people that "alien" religions were like "ours" in many ways. (By "ours" we usually meant "Protestantism," like Mr Thwackum in Fielding's *Tom Jones*: "When I mention religion, I mean the Christian religion; and not only the Christian religion, but the Protestant religion; and not only the Protestant religion, but the Church of England."[2]) The hope was that if we learned about other religions, we would no longer hate and kill their followers; that "to know them is to love them." Emmanuel Levinas argues that the face of the other says, "Don't kill me."[3] This is the face that the comparative enterprise strives to illuminate. A glance at any newspaper should tell us that this goal has yet to be fulfilled in the world at large.

But the academic world, having gone beyond this simplistic paradigm, now suffers from a post-postcolonial backlash, inspired in large part by Edward Said's *Orientalism*. In this age of multinationalism and the politics of individual ethnic and religious groups, of identity politics and minority politics, to assume that two phenomena from different cultures are "the same" in any significant way is regarded as demeaning to the individualism of each, a reflection of the old racist, colonialist attitude that "all wogs look alike."[4] Moreover, in the present climate of anti-Orientalism, it is regarded as imperialist of a scholar who studies India, for instance, to stand outside (presumably, above) phenomena from different cultures and to equate them. Merely by emphasizing their commonalities, we are implicated in what Rolena Adorno has called "the process of fixing 'otherness' by grasping onto similarities."

We must beware, however, of leaping from the frying pan of imperialist universalism into the fire of an academic essentialism that can result from contextualizing a religious phenomenon in one cultural group. The emphasis on individual cultures, when reduced to the absurd (as it too often is), may lead to problems of infinite regress, first in the ever-broadening comparisons of contexts and ultimately in the ever-narrowing contexts themselves. This emphasis tends to generate a smaller and smaller focus until it is impossible to generalize even from one moment to the next: nothing has enough in common with anything else to be compared with it even for the purpose of illuminating its distinctiveness. The radical particularizing of much recent theory in cultural anthropology, for instance, seems to deny any shared base to members of the same culture, much less to humanity as a whole.[5]

But any discussion of difference must begin from an assumption of sameness; Wilhelm Dilthey has said that "interpretation would be impossible if expressions of life were completely strange. It would be unnecessary if nothing strange were in them."[6] If we start with the assumption of absolute difference, there can be no conversation, and we find ourselves trapped in the self-reflexive garden of a Looking-Glass ghetto, forever meeting ourselves walking back in through the cultural door through which we were trying to escape.[7] Even the most relentless of French deconstructionists could not, I think, compare the text of a Greek tragedy and, say, the text of an instruction manual for Word-Perfect for Windows, 1998; there is no common ground, no sameness. But any comparativist worth her pay could compare that Greek tragedy with many a story from the New York Times in 1998. If all stories on a given theme were the same, any study of them would make a very short book: one text, and a very long footnote. But if they were all entirely different, incomparably, incommensurably different, not only would there be nothing to compare but we would never be able to understand any story but our own. Maintaining this balance is particularly difficult in an age like ours when the extremes of globalization and diversification have come to power simultaneously and continue to egg one another on.

Similarity and difference are not equal, not comparable; they have different uses. We look to similarity for stability, to build political bridges, to anchor our own society, while we spin narratives to deal with our uneasiness at the threat of difference. Either similarity or difference may lead to a form of paralyzing reductionism and demeaning essentialism, and thence into an area where "difference" itself can be politically harmful. For, where extreme universalism means that the other is exactly like you, extreme nominalism means that the other may not be human at all.[8] Many of the people who argued (and continue to argue) that Jews, or blacks, or any other group defined as "wogs" were all alike (that is, like one another) went on to argue (or, more often, to assume) that they were all different (that is, different from us white people, us Protestants), and this latter argument easily led to the assertion that such people did not deserve certain rights like the rest of us. Essentialized difference can become an instrument of dominance; European colonialism was supported by a discourse of difference.

The members of a single cultural "group" may be very different, and it is just as insulting to say that all Japanese are alike as to say that the Japanese are just like the French. (The same goes for fin de siècle types: the essentialism of time can be just as harmful as the essentialism of place.) I applaud the art historian Sir Ernst Gombrich, who resists categories like "Renaissance man" or "Romantic psychology" as one would resist claims for "Aryan man" or "German physics."[9] The culturally essentialized position is in itself both indefensible and politically dangerous. Yet it is often assumed in "culturally contextualized" and historically specific studies: "Let me tell you how everyone felt at the fin de siècle in Europe and America." The focus on the class or ethnic group, if monolithic, can become not only boring, but racist.

I am unwilling to close the comparativist shop just because it is being picketed by people whose views I happen, by and large, to share. We must be sensitized to the political issues, but they need not ultimately damn the comparative enterprise. We need not submit to what Umberto Eco has nicely termed "textual harassment." I am not now, and have never been, a card-carrying member of the British Raj. But I refuse to stop reading and translating texts edited by people who were. There is much in the colonial scholarship on India that is worth keeping; I am unwilling to throw out the baby with the bath water. As the irrepressible Lee Siegel put it recently, "Those hegemonic, imperialist, Euro-centric colonialists were such amazing writers, and they knew so much more about India than all of us. They could ride horses, too."[10]

But there is also much in the postcolonial critique that is worth keeping; indeed, we can no longer think without it. We have learned from postcolonial discourse that the texts scholars publish have an impact on the people they write about, not entirely unlike the more obvious impact of participant-observer anthropologists. It has also taught us to be aware of how our texts have come to us; these texts now say to us, like third-world immigrants in England, "We're here because you were there."

Colonialism is no longer the political force it once was, but it is still there, especially if we use a word like "imperialism" instead of "colonialism," and bear in mind the aspects of our scholarship that still invade the countries that we study, like the Coke bottle that intrudes into the lives of the Bushmen in the (racist) film, *The Gods Must Be Crazy*.[11] In particular, the postcolonial critique has made us aware of how deeply evolutionist ideas are embedded in the history of comparison, and how hard we must work to overcome them.

But we can overcome the negative fallout from evolutionism; we don't have to go on doing it like that. The very fact that we have been made aware of these problems should make it possible for us to avoid them, at least to some extent. There are sharks in the waters of comparison, but now that we know they're there, we can still swim—a bit more cautiously, perhaps. We now realize, for instance, that the cultures that we are comparing have compared, too, that they are subjects, like us, as well as the objects of our study. Herodotus compared his ancient Greeks with the Egyptians; a number of recent studies have documented the attitudes of the ancient Chinese, Hindus, and others toward the Others on their borders.[12] In this way we can switch focus: the text we look at becomes a text we look through; the mirror becomes a window. The history of the ways in which Others have compared their own Others shows not only that our colonialism was not the first colonialism, but that comparison has long been an imperial enterprise. We need to know this, so that we can stop doing it the way they did it and start doing it the way we do it. This is, by the way, a good instance of the use of comparison to defamiliarize our own methods: when we compare ourselves, as comparativists, with the ancient comparativists, we notice things about ourselves that we had overlooked.

In pursuing the multivocal, multicultural agenda, we must face the implications of the fact that we use other peoples' stories for our purposes. The political problem inheres in the asymmetry of power between the appropriating culture and the appropriated. Thus, if Europe has dominated India, it is deemed wrong for a European to make use of an Indian text. But it seems to me that there are very different ways of using other peoples' texts, some of them fairly innocuous,[13] and that the usual alternative to appropriating a foreign text (however inadequate, or exploitative, or projective that appropriation may be) can be even worse: ignoring it or scorning it. Moreover, the European appropriation need not supplant the Indian version; the native voice can be heard even above the academic clamor of the foreign voice.

The gift that the postcolonial critique has given us is a heightened awareness of what we are doing, why, and the dangers involved. But the gift sours when the giver takes it back by arguing that these dangers are so great that we cannot do it at all. We should use the postcolonial consciousness not to exclude Western scholars from the study of non-Western texts, which merely contributes to the ghettoization of the Western world of ideas, but to show how texts (and the comparative study of texts) can be used as ghetto-blasters in our own society as well as in the world at large—that is, to blast apart the ghettoes of ideology. I want to argue against the present trend of studying only one cultural group—Jews, blacks—or only one gender. I would also challenge the trend of limiting those who study that group to those within the group—women studying women, Jews studying Jews—a trend which, if followed slavishly, would automatically eliminate not only my tiny, precious world of cross-cultural comparison but the more general humanism of which it is a part. This is a trend fueled, in large part, by the high moral ground assumed by disciplines, such as feminism and cultural studies, that argue, or imply, that their subject matter (racism, sexism, the class struggle, genocide) has such devastating human consequences that there is no room for error, or playfulness, or the possibility of more than one answer. But surely it is possible to bring into a single (if not necessarily harmonious) conversation the genuinely different approaches that several cultures have made to similar (if not the same) human problems. In this way we might hope to supplement the tunnel vision of identity politics with the wide screen of cross-cultural studies.

And the postcolonial critique itself furnishes us with the tools, more precisely the weapons, with which to do this. My objections above apply primarily to the first front, the earlier wave, of postcolonialism, which still casts its discouraging shadow over too much work in the field of history of religions. But the second front is more hopeful. This is the cohort of James C. Scott, Sarah Saleri, and the later Edward Said himself (in *Culture and Imperialism*[14]), who shift the emphasis away from the study of subalterns as victims and redirect it toward the mechanisms of resistance, the "weapons of the weak," as Scott has taught us to call them.[15] These scholars have revived our interest in texts that their postcolonial predecessors taught us to regard as irretrievably retrograde, sending us back to those texts in search of voices of subversion.

The old postcolonial critique was ideological in the worst sense of the word, reductive: white guys screwing black guys. Now it is much more nuanced, questioning not just power *tout court* but the power of resistance. Yet, to the extent that it is still about power, it is a Johnny one-note. And here is where postmodernism sounds a most welcome note—indeed, a cacophony—of its own.

Postmodernism and Comparison

The postcolonial agenda is compatible with some agendas of postmodernism, the age that rejects metanarratives and argues for the infinite proliferation of images.[16] The problem of the same and the different is crucial not only for comparative religion and postcolonialism, but for the self-definitions of postmodernism. For postmodernism, sameness is the devil, difference the angel; the mere addition of an *accent aigu* transforms the modest English word into the magic buzzword for everything that right-thinking (or, as the case may be, left-thinking) men and women care about: *différence* (or, buzzier yet, *différance*). From Paris the new battle-cry rings out: *Vive la différance!* The deconstructionist myth of Difference is what Joel Fineman, citing René Girard, has called "a story, always a story, by means of which societies resolve and ward off a catastrophe of order that Girard labels the crisis of 'No Difference' and that he defines as a loss of cultural distinctions so profound as to spell cultural suicide."[17]

But the postmodern critique has not solved the problem of cultural difference, as Eve Sedgwick has pointed out:

> Every single theoretically or politically interesting project of postwar thought has finally had the effect of delegitimating our space for asking or thinking in detail about the multiple, unstable ways in which people may be like or different from each other. This project is not rendered otiose by any demonstration of how fully people may differ also from themselves. Deconstruction, founded as a very science of diffEr(e/a)nce, has both so fetishized the idea of difference and so vaporized its possible embodiments that its most thoroughgoing practitioners are the last people to whom one would now look for help in thinking about particular differences.[18]

Yet there is a crucial difference between premodern constructions of difference and postmodern *différance*.[19] Early postmodernism compounded the felonies of postcolonialism; Foucault's overemphasis on power distorted the readings of many texts and played into the dark side of postcolonialism, while the argument that there was no text seemed to render irrelevant the traditional philological methods that were the foundation of traditional comparative studies. But the second wave of postmodernism, the later Foucault and most of Derrida, broke open the text in new ways that were particularly useful for scholars interested in using multiple variants, popular as well as classical, and in finding multiple meanings in them. Equally important, it restored a playfulness and even (dare I say it?) an aestheticism to a discipline that early postcolonialism had rendered grim and humorless.

Deconstructionism, in particular among aspects of postmodernism, has promoted the concepts of multivocality and multiple interpretations that are essential to the comparative method. That is to say, the postmodern comparativist eschews grand theories and imperialist metanarratives; allows several meanings/patterns to emerge; compares phenomena within a focused frame that aims at developing insights into the phenomena that are compared (rather than a grand theory); shows how the study of others is self-involving and becomes both personal and objective; accords prominence to local linguistic/knowledge contexts, but shows that their meaning transcends the local; allows all local voices/ interpretations to play a role; and centers the interpretive activity on a genuine intellectual/personal dialogue with the materials.[20]

And deconstruction has sharpened our awareness of our unexamined assumptions about individual authors. For we may apply to anonymous religious texts contemporary literary critics' insights into both the products of popular culture and canonical works of literature. Though both of these narrative forms have, as some of our ancient texts do not have, known social contexts, some works of popular culture (particularly, but not only, those from nonliterate cultures) share with many myths the lack of known or individual authors and hence come within the mythologists' camp (and I do mean camp). Films, for instance, like camels in the old joke, are often created by a committee. So, too, the hermeneutics of suspicion renders irrelevant the problem of the intention of the individual author of a great work of literature, making that, too, fair game for mythologists.

This focus takes the call for difference very seriously indeed, and follows it to the ultimate case, the case of the individual whose insights transcend her particular moment and speak to us across time and space. The emphasis on the individual balances the move outward, from culture to cross-culture, with a move inward, from culture to the individual author. The focus on individual insight leads us to a variety of what Paul Ricoeur called a second naïveté, positing a "sameness" that only superficially resembles a quasi-Jungian universalism but is actually based on a pointillism formed from the individual points of individual authors.

This emphasis upon real people, arguing from the bottom up, obviates the sorts of problems that arise when we argue from the top down and posit a transcendental agent as the source of cross-cultural congruences. And these real people are not merely political agents; they are the authors of texts with many different agendas, including aesthetic, philosophical, and especially religious agendas that postcolonial critique too often ignores. We can thus anchor our cross-cultural paradigms in an investigation of the unique insights of particular tellings of our cross-cultural themes, to focus on the individual and the human on both ends of the spectrum—one story, and then the human race—thus not so much ignoring the problematic cultural generalizations in the middle as leaping over them altogether.

Joan Scott has described the uses of individual names in furthering the apparently opposite feminist wish to designate groups by name in the construction of various sorts of histories:

> We insisted that the names of individual women be added to the lists of scientists, inventors, politicians, and artists. It was, in fact, the individualizing of women that offered the best way out of the ahistorical category of the group. It was an uncomfortable strategy to me at first, for it seemed to bow to the conservative critique that rejects all group categorization as antithetical to individuality. I finally decided that this was not the case because the inclusion of differently marked individuals deprived the abstract individual of his singularity and universality.[21]

That is, the inclusion of a number of individuals prevents the concept of the ideal individual (male and white, in the case that Joan Scott is arguing) from becoming the standard.

Those who would regard universalism as a colonialist debasement of the integrity of the ethnic unit might also regard such an emphasis upon individual creativity as an élitist debasement of the democratic unit. But surely this need not be the case. It is just as foolish to assume that an emphasis on the individual will be élitist as it is to assume that the opposite emphasis, on the entire human race, will be fascist. The emphasis on individual storytellers is élite only in the very narrow sense of the word—that some are "chosen" out of the group—but not in its broader implications—that those who are chosen have a particular social or cultural advantage. It acknowledges the unequal distribution of talent (in this case, storytelling talent), but does not assume that talent will be found in some places and not in others. Searching for our individual artists not merely in the bastions of the Western canon but in the neglected byways of oral traditions and rejected heresies, paying homage to the Tolstoys among the Zulus, Prousts of the Papuans (to respond to Saul Bellow's notorious challenge[22]), and artists of the graffito and the B-film, argues not for a narrow range of cultural excellence but, on the contrary, for a wider construction of inspiration that may be found in any culture. It may well be true that there are no Tolstoys among the Zulus, but we now know of Zulu heroic epic poems composed by some pretty rare individual talents, and probably others that we outsiders just haven't discovered yet. More to the point, it is also proper to ask how many Tolstoys there are among the Russians; such highly original individuals are rare both in groups that have writing and in those that do not. The question of Tolstoys among the Zulus is a question about who decides what works and authors are "good," and on what basis. My emphasis upon the individual at all levels of society, from high culture to popular culture, is designed in part to address this question as well as the deconstructionist objection to universalism and to the sort of humanism I am advocating, namely, that humanism falsely universalizes an ideological fiction based on the interests of the privileged. This position also argues ultimately for that particular flash of difference that is best illuminated by the context of sameness. And where the emphasis on the characteristics of a whole class or culture fails to take into account not only parallels in other cultures but originality in any culture, the emphasis on one individual (in comparison with other, less inspired individual tellers) can at least pinpoint the moment of inspiration, if not account for it. These arguments for pointillism are designed to counter naïve claims about novelty and to stress the creative dimension of thinking.

The postmodern critique thus helps us to avoid some of the distortions that result, on the one hand, from a certain kind of concentration on individual authors, and, on the other, from essentializing culture in the wake of the first wave of postcolonialism. In this way, second-wave postcolonialism and postmodernism complement one another, each compensating for and limiting the excesses of the other (particularly of the first wave of the other), like the lame man perched on the shoulders of the blind man. By emphasizing different aspects of difference, each keeps the other from retreating into a paralyzing nominalism; their competing essentialisms temper one another's reductive tendencies and carve out a space where historians of religions can engage in a more nuanced and self-aware cross-cultural comparison.

Notes

1. Portions of the following have been developed out of the discussion in my book, *The Implied Spider: Politics and Theology in Myth* (New York: Columbia University Press, 1998).

2. Henry Fielding, *Tom Jones*, ed. John Bender and Simon Stern, with an introduction by John Bender (Oxford: Oxford University Press, World's Classics Paperback, 1996), bk. 3, chap. 3, p. 109. First published as *The History of Tom Jones, a Foundling* (London, 1749).

3. Emmanuel Levinas, *Totality and Infinity: An Essay on Exteriority*, trans. Alphonso Lingis (The Hague: Martinus Nijhoff, 1979 [*Totality et Infini*, 1961]), pp. 198–99.

4. See Wendy Doniger, "Myths and Methods in the Dark," *Journal of Religion* 76 (October 1996): 531–47.

5. I am indebted to Sarah Caldwell for this cogent summary, in her introduction to my lecture at Ann Arbor on 7 February 1997.

6. Wilhelm Dilthey, *Pattern and Meaning in History* (New York: Harper Torchbooks, 1961), p. 77.

7. See Lewis Carroll, *Through the Looking-Glass*, chapter 2.

8. In fact, nominalism is the basis of both extreme difference and universalism, but that is another story.

9. Sir Ernst Gombrich, *The Essential Gombrich: Selected Writings on Art and Culture*, ed. Richard Woodfield (San Francisco: Phaidon Press, 1996).

10. Personal communication from Lee Siegel, 28 October 1996, regarding Lockwood Kipling's *Beast and Man in India*.

11. *The Gods Must Be Crazy* (1980), written and directed by Jamie Uys.

12. See, for instance, David Gordon White, *Myths of the Dog-Man* (Chicago: University of Chicago Press, 1991).

13. Wendy Doniger O'Flaherty, *Other Peoples' Myths: The Cave of Echoes* (New York: Macmillan, 1988; Chicago: University of Chicago Press, 1995).

14. Edward Said, *Culture and Imperialism* (New York: Knopf, 1993).

15. James C. Scott, *Weapons of the Weak: Everyday Forms of Peasant Resistance* (New Haven and London: Yale University Press, 1985).

16. I am indebted to David Tracy for the little that I know about postmodernism.

17. Joel Fineman, "Fratricide and Cuckoldry: Shakespeare's Doubles," *Psychoanalytic Review* 64 (1977): 409–53, citing René Girard, "Myth and Identity Crisis in *A Midsummer-Night's Dream*," Colloquium at State University of New York, Buffalo, winter 1969.

18. Eve Kosofsky Sedgwick, *The Epistemology of the Closet* (Berkeley: University of California Press, 1990), p. 23.

19. Jacques Derrida, "Violence and Metaphysics: An Essay on the Thought of Emmanuel Levinas," in *Writing and Difference* (Chicago: University of Chicago Press, 1978), pp. 79–153.

20. This was Ben Ray's useful formulation, in a personal communication, December 1997.

21. Joan W. Scott, "Gender and the Politics of Higher Education," inaugural talk for the Center for Gender Studies, University of Chicago (18 October 1996), ms., p. 15.

22. Charles Taylor discusses this statement, often attributed to Saul Bellow, in his *Multiculturalism and "The politics of recognition": an essay* (with commentary by Amy Gutmann, editor, Steven C. Rockefeller, Michael Walzer, and Susan Wolf [Princeton, NJ: Princeton University Press, 1992]), p. 42: "When Saul Bellow is famously quoted as saying something like, 'When the Zulus produce a Tolstoy we will read him,' this is taken as a quintessential statement of European arrogance, not just because Bellow is allegedly being *de facto* insensitive to the value of Zulu culture, but frequently also because it is seen to reflect a denial in principle of human equality." Taylor added a footnote, which also says what I want to say (p. 42, n. 18): "I have no idea whether this statement was actually made in this form by Saul Bellow, or by anyone else. I report it only because it captures a widespread attitude, which is, of course, why the story had currency in the first place." Bellow later denied having said this, but James Atlas, who first quoted it in his profile of Allan Bloom in *The New York Times*, insisted on it again in his profile of Bellow in *The New Yorker*, "The Shadow in the Garden" (3 July and 26 July 1995), pp. 74–85, p. 84.

Part Two

CASE STUDIES: CRITICAL ISSUES IN THE HISTORY OF RELIGIONS

WHAT'S BEYOND THE POST?

Comparative Analysis as Critical Method

BARBARA A. HOLDREGE

Is comparative study still possible in this era of "posts," in which postmodern, poststructural, and postcolonial critiques have attained ascendancy in the academy? The critiques that certain scholars of religion have made in recent years of the comparative study of religion resonate with the critiques that postmodernists and poststructuralists have made of idealist, essentialist, and foundationalist trends of scholarship, and to a certain extent they call into question the validity of the entire comparative enterprise. I would like to pose a question eloquently framed by my colleague Charles Long: What's beyond the post?[1] Is there a place for the comparative study of religion beyond the post? I would respond to this question with an emphatic yes—there is and has been and will be a place for comparative study pre- and post- and post the post. Indeed, I would argue, along with Jonathan Z. Smith, that the process of comparison is itself a constitutive aspect of human thought and an inextricable component of our scholarly methods. Smith writes:

> The process of comparison is a fundamental characteristic of human intelligence. Whether revealed in the logical grouping of classes, in poetic similes, in mimesis, or other like activities—comparison, the bringing together of two or more objects for the purpose of noting either similarity or dissimilarity, is the omnipresent substructure of human thought. Without it, we could not speak, perceive, learn, or reason. . . . That comparison has, at times, led us astray there can be no doubt; that comparison remains *the* method of scholarship is likewise beyond question.[2]

After surveying and critiquing four basic modes of comparison—ethnographic, encyclopedic, morphological, and evolutionary—together with their more recent variants, Smith concludes that none of the proposed methods is adequate. Yet he suggests that the comparative enterprise should not thereby be abandoned, for questions of comparison are critical to the task of the scholar of religion.

> We must conclude this exercise in our own academic history in a most unsatisfactory manner. Each of the modes of comparison has been found problematic. Each new proposal has been found to be a variant of an older mode. . . . We know better how to evaluate comparisons, but we have gained little over our predecessors in either the method for making comparisons or the reasons for its practice. . . . So we are left with the question [posed by Wittgenstein], "How am I to apply what the one thing shows me to the case of two things?" The possibility of the study of religion depends on its answer.[3]

As a comparative historian of religions specializing in Hindu and Jewish traditions, I am a vigorous exponent of the compelling, necessary, and indeed inevitable role of comparative analysis within the academic study of religion. At the same time I share with Smith a concern to develop responsible methods of comparative analysis that can counter the critiques of scholars who would condemn the comparative study of religion to a premature demise. In this essay I would like, first, to consider briefly a method of comparative historical analysis that can redress some of the problems found in past comparative studies. I will then turn to a consideration of the critical role of comparative analysis in the construction and critique of our categories and models in the academic study of religion.

Redressing the Comparative Method

Among the various modes of comparative analysis, the morphological approach in particular, especially as represented in the structural phenomenological studies of scholars such as Gerardus van der Leeuw[4] and Mircea Eliade,[5] has come under attack from a number of different perspectives. Three types of problems, which are closely interconnected, can be isolated. (1) *Insufficient attention to differences.* Such studies tend to be concerned with the common features and structural similarities among religious phenomena drawn from various religious traditions and consequently do not pay sufficient attention to the differences that give each tradition its unique character and integrity.[6] (2) *Insufficient atten-*

tion to the diachronic dimension. In their search for similarities and continuities, such studies are concerned primarily with synchronic structures and thus tend to disregard the diachronic dimension of religious phenomena. Religious phenomena are abstracted from history and treated as static, timeless structures, and hence the dynamic, changing nature of religious manifestations is ignored.[7] (3) *Insufficient attention to context.* Such studies thus fail to give adequate attention to the distinctive contours of each specific religious manifestation as shaped by the particular context—textual, historical, cultural, social, and/or religious—from which it emerges.

I have developed a method of comparative historical analysis that attempts to redress these problems by giving proper attention to differences as well as to similarities and to diachronic transformations as well as to structural continuities. This method involves three principal phases of analysis: (1) history of interpretations, (2) comparative analysis, and (3) cultural interpretation. For a detailed description and application of this three-phase method of analysis, one may refer to my book *Veda and Torah: Transcending the Textuality of Scripture*, which is a comparative historical analysis of the status, authority, and function of scripture as a constitutive category of brahmanical Hinduism and rabbinic Judaism.[8] The study is concerned in particular with the manner in which Veda and Torah, as the authoritative scriptures of these textual communities, assume the role of encompassing, paradigmatic symbols that incorporate and at the same time transcend the textuality of scripture.[9] For the purpose of this essay I will highlight briefly the central features of my comparative historical method.

Phase 1: History of Interpretations

The first phase of my comparative historical method is tradition-specific and involves analyzing each network of symbols separately, within the context of its respective tradition. I call this phase "history of interpretations" in that the analyses are undertaken within a diachronic framework and involve tracing the history of certain symbolic complexes through the core texts of each tradition. The history with which this phase is concerned is not *Entstehungsgeschichte*, a history of origins and cause-effect relations, but rather *Wirkungsgeschichte*, a history of effects, understood as the tradition of successive interpretations of particular symbolic complexes in the core texts of the traditions.

The history of interpretations phase of my study of Veda and Torah is of necessity focused on textual representations because of the distinctive nature of the traditions with which my comparative work is concerned. Both the brahmanical and rabbinic traditions constitute textual communities that have self-consciously defined the parameters of their respective traditions through compiling a set of discrete documents as a textual repository of normative values and practices and investing these documents with the authoritative status of a canon. Any sustained study of the brahmanical and rabbinic traditions thus must inevitably have its basis in texts. Two other factors necessitate reliance on normative texts as the primary source of our knowledge of the brahmanical and rabbinic traditions. First, these traditions are attested principally by textual evidence, and the texts that constitute the evidence are for the most part self-referential in that they form part of the canons of the traditions themselves. Our knowledge of the formative periods of the brahmanical and rabbinic traditions is thus limited primarily to the testimonies of the texts authorized by the brahmanical and rabbinic elite, with almost no independent sources of corroboration. Second, in the case of both brahmanical and rabbinic sources we are dealing with texts that were in most cases compiled by an anonymous, corporate authorship over long periods—sometimes hundreds of years—and that contain layers of accretions that may derive from different sociohistorical milieus. This fact precludes our ability to place such texts within strictly delimited historical contexts, and any such attempts constitute at best speculative reconstructions that are reliant almost exclusively on the testimony of the texts themselves. The consequence of these factors is that the most we can hope to arrive at is a history of interpretations of textual representations, not historical actualities. We can trace, for example, certain symbolic complexes that are used in the various strata of brahmanical texts to represent the status and authority of the Veda, and we can map the epistemological shifts in the discursive framework that dominates each textual stratum, but we cannot thereby definitively determine the actual sociohistorical conditions that generated these complexes and epistemological shifts.

A useful model for the history of interpretations phase of my comparative historical method is stratigraphy in geology. Stratigraphy involves examining and classifying the properties of individual strata and cross-correlating the different strata in order to discern regular patterns and recurrences of species as well as changes in species from stratum to stratum. Similarly, this phase is concerned with examining the symbolic complexes found in the core strata of texts in each tradition and cross-correlating the various strata in order to discern structural continuities as well as diachronic transformations from layer to layer.

In my study of Veda and Torah, this phase entails unearthing the symbolic formulations of Veda in the core strata of the brahmanical tradition, beginning with the oldest layers of Vedic literature—Saṃhitās, Brāhmaṇas, Āraṇyakas, and Upaniṣads—and proceeding through the more recent layers of post-Vedic literature—Manu-Smṛti, Mahābhārata, Harivaṃśa, and selected Purāṇas—to the philosophical speculations of the Darśanas, with particular emphasis on Pūrva-Mīmāṃsā and Advaita Vedānta. The Judaic portion of the analysis similarly involves excavating the symbolic configurations in which Torah is embedded in the earliest layers of pre-rabbinic speculation—wisdom literature of the Hebrew Bible, wisdom literature of the Apocrypha, and the Alexandrian Jewish philosophers Aristobulus and Philo—through the various strata of rabbinic literature—Mishnah, Tannaitic Midrashim, classical Amoraic Midrashim, Babylonian Talmud, and selected post-Talmudic Midrashim—to the speculations of certain medieval kabbalistic texts, with particular emphasis on the Zohar and the theosophical Kabbalah of thirteenth-century Spain.

The history of interpretations phase of my comparative historical method is particularly concerned with analyzing documentary contexts and the ways in which certain symbolic complexes are reshaped and reformulated in different textual environments in accordance with the epistemological framework of each stratum of texts. This phase of the analysis also attempts to illuminate the ways in which these differences in textual perspective may reflect competing or shifting sectional interests based on changing sociohistorical factors.

The final step in the history of interpretations phase involves re-embedding the symbolic complexes in their larger religiocultural matrices through an analysis of related practices. In my study of Veda and Torah, this step entails an examination of the practices involved in the transmission, study, and appropriation of the Vedic Saṃhitās and the Sefer Torah.

Phase 2: Comparative Analysis

The second phase of my comparative historical method moves from a tradition-specific history of interpretations to comparative analysis. This phase is concerned not only with delineating the structural similarities between the symbol systems and practices of the traditions, but also with highlighting the significant differences that give each tradition its distinctive character.

For example, the comparative phase of my study delineates a number of structural similarities between the symbol systems associated with Veda and Torah.[10] More specifically, my comparative analysis brings to light a multileveled model of scripture in which Veda and Torah are each represented as (1) the totality of the Word, which is the essence of the ultimate reality; (2) knowledge or wisdom, which is identified with the creator principle as the immediate source of creation; (3) divine language, which constitutes the archetypal plan or blueprint from which the creator structures the forms of creation; and (4) a concrete corpus of oral and/or written texts. At the same time my comparative analysis highlights significant points of divergence between the conceptions of language that underlie the symbol systems and practices associated with Veda and Torah, particularly with reference to (1) oral vs. written channels of language; (2) auditory vs. visual modes of perception; and (3) phonic vs. cognitive dimensions of language.

Phase 3: Cultural Interpretation

The last phase of my comparative historical method is concerned with cultural interpretation. The purpose of this phase is to examine the significance of the similarities and differences between the symbol systems and practices in light of the broader religiocultural matrices in which they are embedded. For example, in the cultural interpretation phase of my study of Veda and Torah, I consider the extent to which the specific parallels in the manner in which the categories of Veda and Torah are constructed reflect the more fundamental affinities shared by the brahmanical and rabbinic traditions as representatives of a distinctive paradigm of religious tradition. I also critically evaluate the extent to which my findings corroborate or contradict certain fundamental distinctions between oral and written cultures that have been delineated by anthropologists, literary historians, psychologists, and linguists.

This method of comparative historical analysis seeks to redress the three types of problems outlined earlier in that (1) it preserves the integrity of the individual religious traditions through first analyzing each symbol system separately, within the context of its respective religious tradition, before attempting to delineate the structural similarities as well as differences between the symbol systems; (2) it incorporates synchronic analyses within a diachronic framework that can serve to illuminate transformations as well as structural continuities; and (3) it is concerned with the ways in which symbolic complexes are reshaped in different documentary contexts, which may in turn reflect distinctive sociohistorical milieus.

Comparative Analysis as Critical Method

Having discussed briefly one example of "how" comparative historical analysis can be fruitfully approached, I will now turn to the question of "why" such comparative studies are important to the academic enterprise. In this context I would like to return to Jonathan Z. Smith's observation that the process of comparison is "a fundamental characteristic of human intelligence" and "*the* method of scholarship." More specifically, I will reflect briefly on the role of comparison in one fundamental aspect of our scholarship—the construction and critique of our categories and models in the study of religion. I will examine the role of comparative analysis, first, as an inextricable component of the process through which we construct and apply our scholarly categories and models, and, second, as a heuristic tool through which we can continue to test, reassess, refine, deconstruct, and reconstitute these categories and models.

Scholars of religion use a variety of categories to select, analyze, classify, and interpret religious phenomena. Categories such as symbol, myth, ritual, scripture, law, ethics, and mysticism have historically assumed a central role in the discourse of religious studies. Indeed, we find entire program units of the American Academy of Religion devoted to the discussion of these and other categories: the Ethics Section, Ritual Studies Group, Mysticism Group, Ascetic Impulse in Religious Life and Culture Group, and so on.

Comparative analysis is intrinsic to the process through which we construct and apply such categories. We use categories as instruments of inclusion and exclusion by means of which we classify religious phenomena according to whether they share or do not share certain properties. We construct and define the category "scripture" and then we survey and compare a range of potential candidates—the Hebrew Bible, the Vedic Saṃhitās, the Qur'ān, the *I Ching*, and so on—to determine whether they are sufficiently comparable to be included within the category thus defined. Jacob Neusner, who has reflected extensively on the problem of category formation, has emphasized the role of comparison in determining the usefulness of our categories.

> One of the criteria for the use[fulness] of forming a category is that category's effect in facilitating analysis, hence, comparison and contrast. . . . Should we discover that we are comparing things that are not sufficiently alike to warrant comparison, we may learn that our original principle of category-formation was awry. If, on the other hand, our comparisons and contrasts prove illuminating, so that we compare comparables and therefore find distinctions among them, gaining perspective on the context and meaning of the whole, then the original principle of category-formation finds solid vindication.[11]

The process of comparison involved in the formation and application of categories is inherently evaluative and hierarchical in that it establishes a standard against which particular phenomena are judged for inclusion or exclusion and are ranked as marked or unmarked taxa. The "politics of comparison" has been emphasized by Paul Morris, who comments on William Hazlitt's remark that "comparison is odious":

> [Hazlitt] considered it [comparison] to be scandalous and detestable because it compares two or more things against the standard of one thing, producing a hierarchical scale. Hazlitt was of course right, and on two accounts. First, one cannot compare two or more things without first constructing a heuristic scale or scales, consisting of one or more comparators, that allows one to identify the two things as comparable in terms of some given category. Secondly, the choice of scale is a "political" decision in that the given comparator is inherently evaluative.[12]

The politics of comparison in the study of religion extends beyond the construction of particular categories to the development of encompassing classificatory systems constituted by these categories and their interrelations. These classificatory schemas have at times served as models of religious tradition in our scholarly discourse. These models or paradigms are themselves inherently hierarchical, establishing evaluative scales according to which their constitutive categories are positioned and ranked in relation to one another. The hierarchy of taxonomies becomes the "tyranny of taxonomies"[13] when certain paradigms of religious tradition are accorded a privileged status as the dominant discourse over against which specific religious traditions are to be judged and hierarchized.

Up until recently the academic study of religion has been dominated by paradigms of religious tradition that arose out of a specific and discernible Protestant Christian context. The Protestant legacy of the academic study of religion in Europe and America, and its links to Enlightenment discourse and colonialist projects in the history of the modern West, is evident in the way in which the prevailing paradigms tend to privilege certain categories while marginalizing others. These paradigms emphasize a series of hierarchical dichotomies between such categories as sacred and profane, belief and practice, doctrine and law, individual and community, universalism and particularism, and tradition and modernity. This hierarchizing of categories can be seen, for example, in a number of persistent trends in religious studies scholarship: first, the tendency to emphasize the distinction between sacred and profane and, as a corollary of the separation of church and state, to compartmentalize religion as something distinct from culture; second, the tendency to define religion as a "belief system" and to give priority to categories such as faith, belief, doctrine, and theology while underprivileging the roles of practice, ritual, and law; third, the tendency to give precedence to the individual over the community as the locus of religious life and consequently to give less emphasis to the social and cultural dimensions of religion; and, fourth, the tendency to define religious identity in terms that privilege universalism over particularism and hence reflect a missionary model of religious tradition. While recent developments in the fields of ritual studies and cultural studies have provided important correctives to such tendencies, the Protestant legacy still lingers—albeit unconsciously—in the work of many scholars of religion.[14]

The Protestant subtext of the dominant paradigms provides the implicit standard against which other religious traditions are compared and evaluated. While perhaps appropriate for the study of some religious traditions, such paradigms, together with the hierarchical taxonomies they perpetuate, become a straitjacket when applied to other traditions. One of the important tasks of the comparative study of religion in this context is to test and critique the prevailing paradigms, expose their inadequacies, and generate a range of possible models to account for the multiplicity of religious traditions. My own comparative research, for example, emphasizes how two of the world's major religious traditions—Hinduisms and Judaisms—defy the classificatory schemas associated with the prevailing paradigms. These traditions construct other categories and taxonomies that bring to light different sets of relationships, such as those between religion and culture, ethnic identity and religious adherence, observance and nonobservance, and purity and impurity. Such relationships are obscured by the application of the prevailing models. In contrast to the Protestant-based paradigms, in which precedence is given to belief, doctrine, and theology, and tradition-identity is rooted in the missionary character of Christian traditions, Hinduisms and Judaisms provide alternative paradigms of religious tradition, in which priority is given to issues of practice, observance, and law, and tradition-identity is defined primarily in terms of ethnic and cultural categories that reflect the predominantly nonmissionary character of these traditions.

Among the array of Hinduisms and Judaisms, brahmanical Hinduism and rabbinic Judaism in particular share significant affinities. Indeed, my work suggests that—contrary to the stereotypical characterization of Hindu and Jewish traditions as representing opposite ends of the spectrum of the world's religions—the brahmanical and rabbinic traditions constitute two species of the same genus of religious tradition: as elite textual communities that have codified their respective norms in the form of scriptural canons; as ethnocultural systems concerned with issues of family, ethnic and cultural integrity, blood lineages, and the intergenerational transmission of traditions; and as religions of orthopraxy characterized by hereditary priesthoods and sacrificial traditions, comprehensive legal systems, elaborate regulations concerning purity and impurity, and dietary laws. I term the brahmanical and rabbinic traditions "embodied communities" in that their notions of tradition-identity, in contrast to the universalizing tendencies of missionizing traditions, are embodied in the particularities of ethnic and cultural categories defined in relation to a particular people (Indo-Aryans, Jews), a particular sacred language (Sanskrit, Hebrew), and a particular land (Āryāvarta, Israel). These ethnocultural systems share an abiding concern for the body as a site of central significance that is the vehicle for the maintenance of the social, cosmic, and divine orders. The body is the instrument of biological and sociocultural reproduction that is to be regulated through ritual and social duties, maintained in purity, sustained through proper diet, and reproduced through appropriate sexual relations. In their roles as "peoples of the body"[15] the brahmanical and rabbinic traditions provide the basis for developing alternative paradigms of religious tradition to the Protestant-based models that have tended to dominate the academic study of religion.

One of the important tasks of comparative study—and in particular of the comparative study of Hinduisms and Judaisms—is thus to challenge scholars of religion to become more critically self-conscious of the Protestant legacy that lingers in our categories and taxonomies and to reconfigure our scholarly discourse to include alternative paradigms.[16] Comparative analysis is not only intrinsic to the process through which we construct and apply categories in the study of religion, it can also serve as an important corrective to the strategies of domination through which we privilege certain categories and models over others in our academic discourse. Comparative analysis can serve as a heuristic tool not only to establish taxonomies but also to critique and dismantle their tyrannies. Understood in this way, the comparative study of religion is accorded its rightful place as a viable postmodern and post-postmodern approach.

Notes

1. This question was posed by Charles Long in the course of a personal exchange we had concerning the current trends of scholarship that identify themselves as "post."

2. Jonathan Z. Smith, "Adde Parvum Parvo Magnus Acervus Erit," chapter 11 of his Map Is Not Territory: Studies in the History of Religions, Studies in Judaism in Late Antiquity, vol. 23 (Leiden: E. J. Brill, 1978), pp. 240–41.

3. Jonathan Z. Smith, "In Comparison a Magic Dwells," chapter 2 of his Imagining Religion: From Babylon to Jonestown (Chicago: University of Chicago Press, 1982), pp. 19–35, esp. 35; 40–41. Smith gives a more detailed critical analysis of these four modes of comparison in "Adde Parvum Parvo Magnus Acervus Erit." The latter essay also contains a brief bibliographical survey of recent studies on the comparative method by historians of religions and anthropologists.

4. Van der Leeuw's phenomenology of religion is concerned with the religious phenomenon qua phenomenon—that is, with "what 'appears' " to "someone"—and does not make judgments about the reality, or noumenon, that lies behind the manifest appearance, the phenomenon. His phenomenological analysis begins by classifying similar types of religious phenomena, drawn from a wide variety of religious traditions, into groups by name—sacrifice, prayer, myth, and so on. The phenomenologist, through the double movement of empathy (Einfühlung) and epochē, then seeks to grasp the "essence" (Wesenheit) of a particular phenomenon and the structural relations (verständliche Zusammenhänge) that constitute the phenomenon in order to arrive at an understanding (das Verstehen) of the "ideal type" (Idealtyp). Van der Leeuw's monumental work, Religion in Essence and Manifestation, is essentially a phenomenological typology that explicates the nature, structure, and meaning of the ideal types that he has arrived at through his phenomenological method. The meaning of the religious phenomena that he explicates inevitably extends beyond the meaning for any particular group of believers. For a discussion of van der Leeuw's method, see "Epilegomena," in his Religion in Essence and Manifestation, vol.

2, trans. J. E. Turner, with Appendices . . . incorporating the additions of the second German edition by Hans H. Penner (1938; reprint, Gloucester, MA: Peter Smith, 1967), pp. 672–95; idem, "Some Recent Achievements of Psychological Research and Their Application to History, in Particular the History of Religion," "On Phenomenology and Its Relation to Theology," and "On 'Understanding,' " in *Classical Approaches to the Study of Religion: Aims, Methods and Theories of Research*, ed. Jacques Waardenburg, vol. 1, Religion and Reason 3 (The Hague: Mouton, 1973), pp. 399–412.

    5. Smith views Eliade's work as "a massive exemplar in religious studies" of the morphological approach to comparative analysis. See Smith, "In Comparison a Magic Dwells," pp. 25, 29; 29, 34. Although Eliade designates himself a historian of religions rather than a phenomenologist of religion, he makes use of a structural phenomenological approach in his explorations of "patterns in comparative religion." Like van der Leeuw, in his studies 'of myth, symbol, and ritual Eliade draws his examples from a wide range of religious traditions—with particular emphasis on small-scale societies and Asian traditions—and seeks to grasp the universal structures that underlie and unite the particular historical manifestations of a religious phenomenon. In his analyses of religious symbols he begins by examining and comparing, through morphological analysis and classification, a considerable number of specific manifestations of a particular religious symbol from different historical-cultural contexts. Amidst the diverse valorizations of the symbol, he gradually deciphers the "structure of the symbol" and grasps the core of essential meaning that interconnects all of the particular meanings. This meaning is not limited to those meanings of which a particular group of believers were fully conscious, for in Eliade's view religious symbols have an autonomous, coherent structure that is independent of the religious person who uses them. Unlike van der Leeuw, who seeks to grasp the essence of the phenomenon but does not inquire concerning the reality that underlies the appearance, Eliade makes normative assertions concerning the ontological status and existential value of religious symbols and maintains that they are revelatory of reality, disclosing the structures of human and cosmic existence. For Eliade's delineation of his approach to the history of religions, see in particular his "Methodological Remarks on the Study of Religious Symbolism," in *The History of Religions: Essays in Methodology*, ed. Mircea Eliade and Joseph M. Kitagawa (Chicago: University of Chicago Press, 1959), pp. 86–107; *The Quest: History and Meaning in Religion* (Chicago: University of Chicago Press, 1969). For a critical analysis of Eliade's phenomenological approach, see Douglas Allen, *Structure and Creativity in Religion: Hermeneutics in Mircea Eliade's Phenomenology and New Directions*, Religion and Reason 14 (The Hague: Mouton, 1978). For critiques of Eliade's method by anthropologists and historians of religions, see Guilford Dudley III, *Religion on Trial: Mircea Eliade and His Critics* (Philadelphia: Temple University Press, 1977), and, more recently, Jonathan Z. Smith, "In Search of Place," chapter 1 of his *To Take Place: Toward Theory in Ritual*, Chicago Studies in the History of Judaism (Chicago: University of Chicago Press, 1987), pp. 1–23. See also William E. Paden, *Religious Worlds: The Comparative Study of Religion* (Boston: Beacon Press, 1988), who addresses some of the limitations implicit in the phenomenological ap-

proaches of van der Leeuw and Eliade and proposes the concept of "religious worlds" as an alternative framework for the comparative study of religion.

6. Smith points out that the issue of difference has been ignored not only by the morphological mode of comparative analysis but by the comparative enterprise in the human sciences generally: "*[C]omparison has been chiefly an affair of the recollection of similarity. The chief explanation for the significance of comparison has been contiguity* [italics Smith's]. . . . The issue of difference has been all but forgotten." Smith attempts to counter this trend by emphasizing that questions of difference are constitutive of the very process of comparison. "[C]omparison is, at base, never identity. Comparison requires the postulation of difference as the grounds of its being interesting (rather than tautological) and a methodical manipulation of difference, a playing across the 'gap' in the service of some useful end." See Smith, "In Comparison a Magic Dwells," pp. 21, 35; *25–26, 40.* Smith reiterates this point in his critique of Eliade in chapter 1 of *To Take Place*, pp. 13–14.

7. In his critique of the various modes of comparative analysis, Smith maintains that the morphological is "the only mode to survive scrutiny" and yet is also "the one which is most offensive to us by its refusal to support a thoroughly historical method and a set of theoretical presuppositions which grant sufficient gravity to the historical encapsulation of culture." While he recognizes the importance of patterns and structures as devices for interpretation, he insists that they must be grounded in historical processes. "The responsible alternative," he suggests, is "the integration of a complex notion of pattern and system with an equally complex notion of history." See Smith, "In Comparison a Magic Dwells," pp. 26, 29; *30, 34.*

8. See Barbara A. Holdrege, *Veda and Torah: Transcending the Textuality of Scripture* (Albany: State University of New York Press, 1996). For an overview of the results of my longer study, see "Veda and Torah: The Word Embodied in Scripture," in *Between Jerusalem and Benares: Comparative Studies in Judaism and Hinduism*, ed. Hananya Goodman (Albany: State University of New York Press, 1994).

9. It is not within the scope of the present analysis to enter into the scholarly debate concerning the meaning of the term *symbol*. In my book I use the term in accordance with Paul Ricoeur's characterization of a symbol as having a double intentionality. The first-order meaning is the primary, literal signification, which points beyond itself to a second-order meaning that functions as a potentially inexhaustible "surplus of signification." Veda and Torah each functions as a symbol in this sense, in that each has a primary signification as a delimited corpus of texts, which opens out to a second-order meaning that explodes these circumscribed limits and assimilates to itself a network of significations. For Ricoeur's analysis of the nature and function of symbols, see his *The Symbolism of Evil*, trans. Emerson Buchanan (Boston: Beacon Press, 1969), pp. 10–18, and his subsequent reflections in *Interpretation Theory: Discourse and the Surplus of Meaning* (Fort Worth: Texas Christian University Press, 1976), pp. 53–63.

10. The structural similarities delineated in my study are phenomenological. By "structure" I do not wish to imply the binary structures of structuralist

analysis, the archetypal structures of Jungian psychology, or the ontological structures posited by Mircea Eliade. Eliade's perspective is discussed in n. 5.

11. Jacob Neusner, *Ancient Judaism and Modern Category-Formation: "Judaism," "Midrash," "Messianism," and Canon in the Past Quarter-Century*, Studies in Judaism (Lanham, MD: University Press of America, 1986), p. 25. See also Robert D. Baird's discussion of the role of categories in the study of religion in his *Category Formation and the History of Religions*, Religion and Reason 1 (The Hague: Mouton, 1971).

12. Paul Morris, "The Discourse of Traditions: 'Judaisms' and 'Hinduisms' " (paper delivered at the Annual Meeting of the American Academy of Religion, San Francisco, 1992).

13. This expression derives from Bruce Lincoln's illuminating article, "The Tyranny of Taxonomies," *Occasional Papers of the University of Minnesota Center for Humanistic Studies* 1 (1985).

14. A number of scholars have raised issues in recent years concerning the persistence of Protestant presuppositions and categories in the academic study of religion. See, for example, Neusner, *Ancient Judaism and Modern Category-Formation*, pp. 13–17; Gregory Schopen, "Archaeology and Protestant Presuppositions in the Study of Indian Buddhism," *History of Religions* 31 (August 1991): 1–23. See also Frits Staal's more general critique of Western paradigms of religious tradition, which he argues are inappropriate for the study of Asian traditions, in his *Rules without Meaning: Ritual, Mantras and the Human Sciences* (New York: Peter Lang, 1989), pp. 387–419.

15. Howard Eilberg-Schwartz uses this designation for the Jews in his edited collection *People of the Body: Jews and Judaism from an Embodied Perspective*, SUNY Series, The Body in Culture, History, and Religion (Albany: State University of New York Press, 1992). See also Daniel Boyarin, *Carnal Israel: Reading Sex in Talmudic Culture*, The New Historicism: Studies in Cultural Poetics (Berkeley: University of California Press, 1993). For a discussion of Hindu discourses of the body, see Barbara A. Holdrege, "Body Connections: Hindu Discourses of the Body and the Study of Religion," *International Journal of Hindu Studies* 2 (December 1998).

16. The significance of the systematic comparison of Hinduisms and Judaisms as the basis for constructing alternative paradigms of religious tradition has been emphasized by my colleague Paul Morris. Morris has stressed in particular the heuristic value of positing two discrete models—missionary traditions (Christianities, Islams, Buddhisms) and nonmissionary traditions (Hinduisms, Judaisms)—in order to elucidate the notion of religious tradition. See Morris, "The Discourse of Traditions: 'Judaisms' and 'Hinduisms.' " See also Barbara A. Holdrege, "What Have Brahmins to Do with Rabbis? Embodied Communities and Paradigms of Religious Tradition," in *Judaism and Asian Religions*, ed. Harold Kasimow, *Shofar* (special issue) 17 (spring 1999): 23–50.

The recent upsurge of interest in the comparative study of Hindu and Jewish traditions among scholars of religion is evidenced by the establishment of a number of forums to foster sustained discussions of the historical connections and cross-cultural resonances among these traditions: the American Academy of Religion Comparative Studies in Hinduisms and Judaisms Group (1998); the

American Academy of Religion Comparative Studies in Hinduisms and Judaisms Consultation (1995); the Society for Indo-Judaic Studies (1993); the journal *Indo-Judaic Studies* (1994); and the World Heritage Hindu-Judaic Studies Series (1995). Mention should also be made of the recent collection of essays *Between Jerusalem and Benares*, ed. Goodman, which represents one of the first efforts by a group of scholars of Judaica and Indology to explore the affinities among these traditions. Goodman's introduction provides a brief survey of previous studies that have attempted to delineate connections among Hindu and Jewish traditions.

THE CONTEXTUAL ILLUSION

Comparative Mysticism and Postmodernism

JONATHAN R. HERMAN

The purpose of this essay is to explore new directions for the comparative study of mysticism, in light of the various challenges which may or may not be correctly labeled "postmodernist." As is the case in many other branches within the study of religion, the study of mysticism has recently been steered away from a comparative agenda because of the primacy that most scholars now place on "context," that is, the concern that mysticism, like any other religious phenomenon, can only be understood when it is examined in its historical, cultural, social, and, perhaps most important, linguistic contexts. The one methodological wrinkle unique to this area is that mysticism has ordinarily been understood to be a matter of "experience"—as opposed to doctrine or praxis—and the question persists as to whether experience in general, and mystical experience in particular, is in some way independent of or intellectually abstractable from its context. The dominant (though by no means unanimous) view, identified most with Steven Katz, Robert Gimello, and others, is that there is no epistemological basis for positing a "pure" uninterpreted or unmediated experience, and that all experience—even mystical experience—is contextually bound and thus only intelligible contextually. It is even occasionally suggested that the significance of mysticism is found not in experience itself, but in the relationship between the mystical path and the existing social or cultural norms.[1]

I am not inclined to dispute the prevailing epistemology, but it should be noted that this particularistic approach does lend itself to two overly severe corollaries. The first is that mysticism does not exist as an auton-omous, *sui generis* category—Hans Penner writes of the "mystical illu-sion," the idea that "mysticism" is a romantic and ill-conceived reifi-cation which lumps together numerous distinct phenomena like Jewish mysticism, Buddhist mysticism, and so forth.[2] The second is that an understanding of a particular historical occurrence of mysticism cannot reveal anything of importance about a separate, contextually unrelated occurrence. Taken together, these points render somewhat suspect the entire enterprise of a "comparative" study of mysticism. Clearly, if the juxtaposition of two or more distinct phenomena cannot produce either an extrapolation about a general case or new information about the particulars, then the process of comparing would indeed be gratuitous.[3] Thus, the discipline is rapidly becoming recognizable not as a single enterprise concerned with synthesis, but as a collection of independent, meticulously regionalized enterprises. The "comparative" study of mys-ticism, it would seem, is being replaced by the "cumulative" study of mysticism.

Nevertheless, there are some instances where a comparative approach is helpful and, in fact, necessary. For the balance of this essay, I will examine one particular historical example that seems to undermine the aforementioned corollaries and then consider the theoretical and meth-odological implications of this "anomaly." The case involves two ap-parently unrelated texts, separated by vast time and distance: *Chuang Tzu*, the ancient Chinese Taoist classic, and *I and Thou*, Martin Buber's modern Jewish classic. Despite the seeming incongruity, a sensitive read-ing of these documents does reveal some strong resonances, particularly in how both authors develop a kind of affirmative existentialism. Chuang Tzu and Buber both emphasize a dialectic between utilitarian and relational orientations toward reality, the significance of presence and reciprocity, and the potential meeting of the absolute in even the most mundane worldly act. Still, there has been little incentive in either the Sinological or Buberian communities to subject these two works to rigorous comparative analysis, as it was generally assumed in both do-mains that there was no historical or conceptual basis for such an en-deavor, that there was no shared context from which one could produce a meaningful comparison. Complicating matters further has been the obvious problem of academic logistics; few scholars have possessed the dual competence necessary to comment on both texts with confidence. Regionalization has sometimes been due to very pragmatic concerns.

But what creates the imperative to bring these two works together into one scholarly conversation is a fascinating though much overlooked morsel of religious history: the fact that Buber had actually published a German translation of and commentary on *Chuang Tzu* more than a decade before he wrote *I and Thou*.[4] The details of Buber's Taoist volume are quite complex, and I have discussed them at length elsewhere,[5] though they can be summarized through a schematic overview of four significant moments, four distinct fruits, of Buber's encounter with *Chuang Tzu*. First, under the influence of the "romantic" *verstehen* interpretive school in general and a personal association with Wilhelm Dilthey in particular, Buber develops a unique hermeneutic—one that has since been unintentionally echoed by several Sinologists—where textual "meaning" is identified not with the reconstructed intent of the author, but with the self-transformation of the reader inspired by his or her engagement with the text. Thus, a faithful interpretation would not explicate simply what the text *says*, but would demonstrate what it *inspires*. Importantly, Buber understands this not as a general hermeneutic, but as an interpretive model most appropriate to the peculiar demands of the *Chuang Tzu* text.

Second, once Buber establishes this unusual hermeneutic, he implicitly offers most of the commentary portion of his work—the actual textual interpretation—both as a legitimate response to *Chuang Tzu* and as a statement of his own self-consciously transforming view of reality. This hypothesis is validated when one observes that Buber's principal interpretive themes—oneness within transformation, continuous regeneration of self, the existential sphere as the locus of meaning—simultaneously reflect a defensible reading of the *Chuang Tzu* and are philosophically compatible with Buber's other works of the period, notably *Daniel* and various essays on Judaism.[6] Thus, to view Buber's commentary as either a Sinological document or a projection of his own changing religious propensities exclusively is simply to ignore the scope of the work's historical significance.

Third, in both Buber's text translation and commentary, one can detect the germination of his I-Thou principle, a recurring motif that I have labeled "proto-dialogical" thought. That is to say, there is tremendous thematic continuity between Buber's recasting of *Chuang Tzu* and the mature dialogical position that he would later express in *I and Thou*. When taken in tandem with the established hermeneutic, this connection might suggest that the process of transformation begun through Buber's original encounter with *Chuang Tzu* was continued in his self-conscious formulation of dialogical philosophy in *I and Thou*. In fact, Buber's famous contemplation of a tree,[7] a vivid description of loosening subject-object experience and being drawn into relation, is surely a reflection on Chuang Tzu's own meditations on the "use of the useless tree."[8] In a manner of speaking, *I and Thou* can be imaginatively conceived, at least in part, as a subsequent layer of Buber's interpretation of *Chuang Tzu*. Or, in more familiar Buberian language, the Taoist volume is the chrysalis to the butterfly emerging in *I and Thou*.

Fourth, the previous claim could certainly be dismissed as postmodernist sophistry were it not demonstrable that Buber's dialogical principle does, in fact, bring much to an understanding of *Chuang Tzu*, that the terminology and spirit of *I and Thou* provide a valid and creative lens through which one may reexamine the original Chinese. Specifically, the new interpretive framework provides an important conceptual link between Chuang Tzu's complex philosophical repartee on theoretical relation—for example, his discourse on equalizing things[9]—and his playful mystical vignettes illustrating personal relationships, which otherwise appear to be tenuously related. For example, Chuang Tzu's memorable account of the ox-carver who discerns the configurations of matter and energy so keenly that he never has to sharpen his blade is indeed one of Buber's "strange lyric and dramatic episodes, seductive and magical,"[10] which gives an allegorical clue as to how one can live in the "present."[11]

What these four points together suggest is that the respective studies of Buber and *Chuang Tzu* are not really as separable from each other as one might previously have imagined. A complete account of Buber's I-Thou principle would require not simply an acknowledgment of Taoist influences, but an understanding of *Chuang Tzu* itself and the nature of Buber's transformative encounter with it. Conversely, an intellectually responsible study of *Chuang Tzu* would be well served to consider the voice that Buber brings to it, both in his intentional commentary on the text and in his implicit commentaries in *I and Thou*. Moreover, the resonances between Chuang Tzu's model of mystical fulfillment—what Sinologist Lee Yearley calls an "intraworldly mysticism"[12]—and Buber's model—what Buber scholar Maurice Friedman calls a "mysticism of the concrete and the particular"[13]—are so strong as to suggest a single typology of mystical experience. Indeed, here is a case where it would seem that one type of comparative project both enhances the understandings of the particulars and raises provocative questions about the general category. What is most important about this is that it follows not from *a priori* assumptions about the nature of mysticism but from a close attention to context (albeit not the most immediately obvious context) and a willingness to allow the context to determine the appropriate methodologies.

Now to return to the theoretical implications of this argument, I am not suggesting that every time one wishes to engage in comparative study one must first locate the forgotten evidence that one mystic had studied another. Rather, I am presenting this as a case in point as to how the "new comparativism" can be constructed without circumventing the demands of contextual study, but also without yielding to the prevailing suppositions about context. At a lively public discussion of mysticism several years ago, Huston Smith asked Steven Katz if he felt that the mediation of experience divided or united people, that is, whether the experiences produced through differing contexts were shared or unique. Katz replied that this question did not really matter to him, that his main concern was the adoption of the particularistic epistemology, and that he was not invested in whether contextualization produced similarities or differences.[14] I have no reason to doubt Katz's sincerity, but this issue does merit closer scrutiny, as any existing epistemological paradigm certainly involves a set of expectations as to what kind of information one will find and what the significance of that information will be. The fact that comparativists are frequently accused before the fact of dilettantism, perennialism, essentialism, or relativism, the fact that a comparative study of Buber and *Chuang Tzu* was tacitly deemed unnecessary (and is still sometimes viewed with suspicion) by the academy, demonstrates that there is a widespread presupposition that *phenomena belonging to observably different contexts are self-evidently unrelated to one another.*

But more important than the issue of continuities and discontinuities between and among contexts is the positivism that often determines precisely how contexts are identified or constructed. One immediate problem is that many scholars simply assume that their subject's cultural, institutional, and linguistic-conceptual contexts are primary. Buber is invariably described first and foremost as an early twentieth-century German Jewish intellectual; Chuang Tzu is described as a fourth-century B.C.E. Chinese philosophical Taoist. But these characterizations are not purely objective; they involve a methodological choice. Feminist theorists may argue that gender is the primary context, family psychologists that birth order is primary, sociologists and economists that class is primary. It is hardly self-evident that Buber's being Jewish is more instructive than his being male or his being white, although it is always tempting for the researcher to overlook the contexts he or she does not entirely understand or value. This point was made ironically clear during a recent roundtable discussion on the newly emerging field of Hindu-Jewish studies, when one panelist spoke of shared Hindu and Jewish perceptions of scripture, another of the day-to-day life of Jewish communities in India, and another of the encounter with Hinduism stimulating his own Jewish self-understanding. Nevertheless, one participant argued that there was not, in fact, any context that would allow for a meaningful comparison between Hinduism and Judaism.[15] As my colleagues in feminist theory frequently remind me, the construction of context often involves a political agenda or a power dynamic. It is one thing to state that there is no context that allows for a meaningful comparison; it is quite another to acknowledge that the contexts we habitually privilege do not allow for a meaningful comparison.

Another problem is that contextualization frequently entails some type of reification or totalization, that it does not always account for differences *within* the "same" context. If we examine it closely, I doubt that I and members of my own family or of my inherited tradition really mean the same thing when we use the word "God," though each of us would be superficially classified in the same category. I doubt that any five randomly chosen scholars in this discipline mean the same thing when they use the word "religion." As I mentioned earlier, Hans Penner writes that mysticism is an "illusion . . . the result of an abstraction which distorts the semantic or structural field of a religious system."[16] I would take this a step further and suggest that too often particularistic study is guided by the "contextual illusion," the mistaken belief that "religious systems" and "cultural contexts" are not heuristic constructions, but objective realities. This deconstruction of context, so to speak, is not intended as evidence that context is ultimately not important. Rather, it is a plea that if our intention is to rescue the study of mysticism from the entropy of philosophical speculation and return it to its rightful place within the "history of religions," then it is essential to recall Wilfred Cantwell Smith's landmark observation that these "religions" should be thought of not as discrete, easily compartmentalized entities, but as living historical complexes that are in constant interaction with one another, often overlapping in unusual and unanticipated ways.[17] It may, in fact, be appropriate to "regionalize" the study of mysticism and the study of religion in general, but it is equally important to recognize that a number of factors are involved in informing and determining each "region." Contexts are ordinarily configured by the observable demarcations defined by geography, religious tradition, and language, yet there are many other options. Robert Gimello, for example, who is identified closely with the particularistic approach, chooses to organize his data in terms of "conceptual, practical, discursive, and institutional contexts,"[18] which may be human contrivances but may also be "vehicles for the transmission of what might be called the influence of the transcendent."[19] And Chuang Tzu and Martin Buber, given the roles of intellectual influence and textual interpretation, are inextricably part of each other's hermeneutic-historical contexts.

To summarize and to generalize somewhat, I would argue that the best hope for a rigorous comparative study of mysticism is to work within the prevailing—and I believe, well-placed—concern for context, but to do so with a renewed methodological self-consciousness and a receptivity to the types of resonances that may indicate connections buried beneath the surface. That is to say, when one wishes to develop a single discourse which integrates two or more distinct phenomena, it is indeed necessary that there be a historical or conceptual basis for comparison, but it is most likely incumbent upon the researcher to locate or to construct the appropriate context, to determine the methodologies salient to that context, and to draw conclusions that do not exceed the scope of the context or the methods. In private correspondence, Steven Katz stated that particularistic study of mysticism does, in fact, allow for a comparative study, but only if it is done in a "careful and thoughtful way."[20] I offer the Buber/Chuang Tzu project as one concrete example of this type of work, and as a vehicle through which to establish some workable parameters for future study.

Notes

1. This position is expressed in a comprehensive series of volumes edited by Steven T. Katz: *Mysticism and Philosophical Analysis* (New York: Oxford University Press, 1978); *Mysticism and Religious Traditions* (New York: Oxford University Press, 1983); and *Mysticism and Language* (New York: Oxford University Press, 1992). It appears to be a self-conscious response to the once-pervasive "perennial philosophy" or "perennialist" approach to the history of religions. Though associated primarily with Aldous Huxley, Frithjof Schuon, Huston Smith, and several others, the perennialist label has also been applied anachronistically to scholars like Mircea Eliade, Carl Jung, and anyone else whose disposition seems to resonate with the principal ideology. Those influenced either directly or indirectly by this approach were more likely to emphasize

the similarities among religions, as they viewed all of the "major" religious traditions as variants of one generic type of truth-seeking, with certain recognizable patterns that occupy similar positions throughout the world and across the centuries. Of this background, Robert Gimello writes:

> The academic study of mysticism is a relatively new undertaking, born (insofar as it had a determinable birth) not more than a hundred years ago. Unfortunately, it cannot boast of an entirely admirable pedigree. One of its several parents, for example, was a kind of romanticism which combined arrogant dismissal of traditional, plebeian, institutionalized religion with affection of an aristocratic spiritual individualism. Some of the early students of mysticism, for example, were men and women who would have little truck with mere "religion" but who yearned to join an imagined company of mystical illuminati, a trans-cultural and trans-historical brotherhood of "seers" and spiritual heroes who were thought to feed—not on the meaty and pungent but quite common food of doctrine, faith, revelation, scripture, church, ritual, and commandment—but only on the distilled "essence of all religions," an elixir of "pure (or at least 120 proof) mystical experience." Such attitudes have not vanished, by the way. They are still very much in the air—in works by the likes of Frithjof Schuon, for example, whose theory of "the transcendental unity of religions" the great theologian and historian of religion Henri de Lubac rightly called "esoterically pretentious." Much the same might be said of the too many works by the insufferable Joseph Campbell, and of the current epidemic of enthusiasm for the "new age."

See Gimello, "Remarks on the Future of the Study of Mysticism" (unpublished manuscript presented at the annual meeting of the American Academy of Religion, November 1990), pp. 1–2. The modern alternative to this position is discussed in *The Problem of Pure Consciousness: Mysticism and Philosophy*, ed. Robert K. C. Forman (New York: Oxford University Press, 1990).

2. See Hans Penner, "The Mystical Illusion," in *Mysticism and Religious Traditions* (Oxford: Oxford University Press, 1983), pp. 89–116.

3. This assertion is predicated on the perhaps postmodernist assumption that comparative study is not simply the observation of continuities and discontinuities, similarities and dissimilarities between and among religious phenomena. Comparison is only heuristically useful when some *significance* can be drawn from such observations, when something is revealed—about either the particulars or the general case—that would not be readily accessible through regionalized area studies.

4. Martin, Buber, *Reden und Gleichnisse des Tschuang-tse* (Leipzig: Insel-Verlag, 1910).

5. See Jonathan R. Herman, *I and Tao: Martin Buber's Encounter with Chuang Tzu* (Albany: State University of New York Press, 1996) or, for a more brief introduction to the subject, "I and Tao: Buber's *Chuang Tzu* and the Comparative Study of Mysticism," in *Martin Buber and the Human Sciences*, ed. Maurice Friedman (Albany: State University of New York Press, 1996).

6. See Martin Buber, *Daniel: Dialogues on Realization*, trans. Maurice Friedman (New York: McGraw-Hill, 1965) and "The Spirit of the Orient and Judaism," in *On Judaism*, trans. Nahum Glatzer (New York: Schocken Books, 1967), pp. 57–78. *Daniel—Gespräche von der Verwirklichung* was originally published in 1913; "Der Geist des Orients" was presented in 1912 and first published in 1915.

7. Martin Buber, *I and Thou*, trans. Ronald Gregor Smith (New York: Charles Scribner's Sons, 1958), pp. 7–8.

8. See Chuang Tzu, *Basic Writings*, trans. Burton Watson (New York: Columbia University Press, 1964), pp. 29–30 and 60–62.

9. See Chuang Tzu, *Basic Writings*, pp. 31–45.

10. See Buber, *I and Thou*, p. 34.

11. See Chuang Tzu, *Basic Writings*, pp. 46–47.

12. See Lee Yearley, "The Perfected Person in the Radical Chuang-tzu," in *Experimental Essays on Chuang-tzu*, ed. Victor H. Mair (Honolulu: University of Hawaii Press, 1983), pp. 125–39.

13. See Maurice Friedman, "Martin Buber and Asia," *Philosophy East and West* 26 (1976): 415–16.

14. This exchange occurred during a panel discussion at the 1990 meeting of the American Academy of Religion in New Orleans.

15. This discussion occurred at the 1993 meeting of the American Academy of Religion in Washington, DC. Panelists included Nathan Katz, Purushottama Bilimoria, David Blumenthal, Ashok Gangadean, Hananya Goodman, Barbara Holdrege, Harold Kasimow, Dan Lusthaus, Kana Mitra, Paul Morris, Braj Sinha, and Bibhuti Yadav.

16. See Penner, "Mystical Illusion," p. 89.

17. See Wilfred Cantwell Smith, *The Meaning and End of Religion* (New York: Harper & Row, 1962).

18. See Robert M. Gimello, "Mysticism in Its Contexts," in *Mysticism and Religious Traditions*, ed. Katz, p. 84.

19. Gimello, "Remarks on the Future of the Study of Mysticism," pp. 17–18.

20. Personal correspondence from Steven Katz, 17 November 1991.

DISCOURSE ABOUT DIFFERENCE

Understanding African Ritual Language

BENJAMIN CALEB RAY

"How am I to apply what one thing shows me to two things?" Wittgenstein's question, quoted by Jonathan Smith at the end of his essay "In Comparison a Magic Dwells," neatly poses a central problem in the comparative study of religion. How can the scholar who has perceived something in terms of the religious language of one culture translate this perception into the language of another, especially if that language is the discourse of the Western secular academy, and be sure that she conveys the same meaning? It is a Wittgensteinian puzzle of cross-cultural perception and scholarly reflexivity that requires decisions about similarity and difference and about the discourse of interpretation, and these decisions are crucial to the outcome.

Some ethnographers of African religions, such as Edith Turner and Paul Stoller, whose works I shall discuss below, have tackled this puzzle by refusing to "translate" African religious terms into Western concepts of social scientific rationality. Both believe that the difference is too great and that meaning would be lost. Instead of the language of so-called ethnographic realism, with its functionalist analytical categories and generalizing style, they have chosen a more humanistic and subjective mode of discourse: the first-person, self-involving narrative. For them, the first step was to accept the intelligibility of African conceptual terms in which their fieldwork experiences were given. Then they went about fashioning an appropriate discourse to communicate their experience. What previous anthropologists have regarded as unintelligible and incomparable in rituals of healing and sorcery, Turner and Stoller have shown to be both intelligible and comparable.

In both cases, this involved the difficult task of explaining the efficacious or *performative* force of ritual language—how ritual words make things happen in people's lives. Their struggle to apply what they understood in one language to discourse in another resulted in personalized narratives that enable readers to enter into new religious worlds, thus broadening our understanding of the African religious life.

I

Before taking up Turner's and Stoller's work, I want to comment on a postmodern argument that would cast suspicion on their achievement and undermine the possibility of comparative religion. It is the argument of cultural particularism—the view that different societies are culturally unique and hence fundamentally unknowable by outsiders and incomparable.

The problem of cross-cultural intelligibility is the central question of the essays in *Writing Culture: The Poetics and Politics of Ethnography* (1986), edited by James Clifford and George E. Marcus.[1] In various ways, the authors of these essays express well-justified doubts about the validity of older ethnography. At issue is the question whether anthropologists can still claim to represent other cultures, once it is recognized—as all anthropologists now do—that all cultures are diverse, contested, multivocal, and linguistically complex, and that ethnographic writing is consequently best conceived as a form of literature rather than as scientific observation.

One view is that of Stephen A. Tyler, who claims that ethnography should not attempt to represent anything objectively but rather try to be more like poetry. It should attempt only to evoke a "fantasy of a possible world of commonsense reality." Rejecting the "observational" and "theoretical" language of old-style ethnography as inadequate, Tyler proposes that ethnography become more poetic and less rational, "a reality fantasy of a fantasy reality. That is to say, it is realism, the evocation of a possible world of reality already known to us in fantasy."[2]

Insofar as this view is coherent, it is an argument for cultural particularism cast in the form of an attack upon older ethnographic modes. Here the operative words are "fantasy" and "reality." By using this dichotomy, Tyler implies that there is no way the outsider can portray another culture except by creating a "fantasy" account of it, for some-how the other culture's "reality" is intrinsically inaccessible and un-knowable. Ethnographers can strive only to produce better forms of fantasy or a "reality fantasy," as Tyler calls it. Ethnographic discourse, he argues, has no referential validity and never makes contact with the other's separate world; it can only "evoke" it, never adequately describe it. The ethnographic enterprise of representing the "other" is just too laden with Western concepts to offer a real connection.

This, of course, is a self-defeating argument for cultural solipsism. How is it, we might ask, that Tyler can refer so confidently to the other culture's "reality" that underlies an ethnographer's "fantasy," and yet deny that any outsider, including himself, can gain any genuine knowl-edge of it? It should be obvious that Tyler uses the terms "reality" and "fantasy" in ways that are self-contradictory. To call something a "fan-tasy" makes sense only if we know the reality upon which the fantasy is based and can distinguish between the two. Tyler's denial that this can be done undermines the reality/fantasy distinction that is the premise of his argument. To reject Tyler's view, however, is not to disagree that there have been many bad ethnographies and that their problems have often stemmed from anthropologists' cultural prejudices, lack of lin-guistic ability, and the taint of Western power relationships.

The issue here is not epistemological, as Tyler believes, but moral and political. Other contributors to *Writing Culture* fall into the same error. They convert their well-founded claims about the mistakes and pretenses of Western anthropologists into philosophical arguments about the in-comparability of cultural worlds. While it is essential to recognize that all cultures constitute complex linguistic, political, and social domains, sometimes difficult for the outsider to understand, it is only confusion to argue that we can never comprehend each other, and hence can only "represent" each other more or less poorly.

In an important essay, "Representation and Reality in the Study of Culture," John Bowlin and Peter Stromberg take issue with this post-modern anthropological view.[3] They point out that in rejecting old-style ethnographic realism, postmodern anthropologists have mistakenly ad-vocated their own brand of philosophical antirealism based upon "the epistemic authority of 'local truths,' 'multiple subjectivities,' 'discursive regimes,' and the like." They reject the popular anthropological adage that cultural difference "goes all the way down" as merely a popular exaggeration. "Culture," they conclude "is not a language, scheme, or domain" through which the world is apprehended but a construct created to facilitate thinking about cross-cultural inquiry. Today, they suggest, it is a concept that may need some rethinking.

The basic problem is the widely held assumption that cultures constitute independent epistemic domains with their own languages and standards of meaning and truth. Outsiders should not talk of truth or engage in moral evaluation of other cultures because that would only privilege the outsider's cultural domain. Anthropologists should only talk about meanings and intentions, not truth and belief. Thus, all that anthropologists can actually do is "represent" other cultures because their language cannot adequately connect with the other's "world."

Given this view of culture, no wonder anthropologists feel there is a "crisis of representation" at the heart of their discipline. Hard as they try to get things right, their account will never correspond to the other's reality. For the contributors to *Writing Culture*, it is, in fact, a philosophical bind that cannot be escaped; no essay in this volume provides a workable solution because none can be created.

The difficulty, again, is with the notion of culture as something that constitutes a separate, conceptually unique domain or scheme of thought and experience. To reject this view does not require accepting the philosophical realist's theory that only "our" Western language, or some perfected version of it, say, the language of social science, corresponds to reality "out there" and that other languages don't. The realist is simply wrong in supposing that we can jump out of the world and check. We can only check our *understanding* of other people's languages by living in their society, developing linguistic competency, and assessing their statements about the world. We do not have to share all their beliefs about the world or all their feelings. But in learning their language well enough, we will come to recognize that we share an enormously large part of the world in common.

Take Evans-Pritchard's famous example of the falling granary that causes injury among the Azande of Central Africa. Zande village granaries are large heavy structures made of wooden beams and clay. When they fall down upon people sitting beneath them, serious injury often results. Everyone knows that in the course of time termites will eventually eat through the tall support posts of the granary and that the granary will fall down and have to be replaced. Azande also know that everyone sits beneath their granaries in the heat of the day to talk and socialize and play games. Consequently, it sometimes happens that people are injured when a granary collapses. The question is not why a particular granary collapsed, but why it collapsed and injured this or that particular person. Azande call this the "second spear" of witchcraft. They do not deny that termites eat the supports of granaries; Zande witchcraft beliefs do not exclude natural causation. In the case of the fallen granary, termites are the "first spear," and witchcraft is the "second"; it explains why a falling granary injures or kills someone. And a witchcraft investigation will begin. Azande refuse to accept the notion of chance occurrence in such cases.

As outsiders, we can understand a great deal of Zande discussion of such events, because we share a wide range of beliefs about the world as the basis of our understanding: the whole spectrum of natural causes and effects concerning the granary, its collapse, and the injuries involved. The particular witchcraft belief is something we can also understand, although we may not accept it. Evans-Pritchard claimed that he understood it well enough to live among the Azande by using this belief in his everyday affairs. But without the large foundation of shared beliefs about the rest of the world, which Bowlin and Stromberg rightly emphasize, Evans-Pritchard wouldn't have been able to comprehend Zande witchcraft beliefs and participate in witchcraft discourse. His refusal to accept the validity of these beliefs, however, did not make him the smugly self-confident anthropologist that he was. Although politically left-wing, his professional arrogance was part of the imperialist scholarly culture that he was unable to shed. His brilliance as an ethnographer stemmed rather from his compassion and adaptability, and especially from his insight that there was a great deal of human sameness about the world, despite the few differences, a view his ethnography helped to justify. Indeed, as Clifford Geertz points out, the effectiveness of Evans-Pritchard's accounts involves a "dialectical approach to ethnography [that] validates the ethnographer's form of life at the same time as it justifies those of his subjects."[4]

Thus, Bowlin and Stromberg argue that to accept Paul Rabinow's view that different cultures constitute "specialized domains," means that cross-cultural talk of meaning and truth would have to cease. This is because, as Richard Rorty reminds us, talk of truth is nothing more than talk about the world.[5] It is not talk that is constantly qualified by theories; it is talk about how things are, about what is and what is not the case. Similarly, to accept Talal Asad's view that all inquiry and criticism is culturally relative and power-tainted means that ethnography can only be ethnocentric and vitiated at every turn. This view Bowlin and

Stromberg call "tragic ethnocentrism." Good ethnography, however, proceeds with linguistic competence and epistemic humility, as well as maximum openness to new experiences and truths about the world.

Hence, Bowlin and Stromberg call upon postmodernists to reexamine their philosophical assumptions. Intentions and beliefs, meanings and truths are not separable in the way postmodernists suggest. They are all given together wherever we encounter them. Bowlin and Stromberg end their essay by affirming anthropologist Michelle Rosaldo's simple, yet profound observation that "because no human world is utterly unlike the things we know, the translation of particulars is at once a way of probing a distinctive though not wholly unfamiliar form of life and an exercise in the comparative study of human societies."[6]

Cross-cultural understanding is always difficult, especially in the complex domain of religious experience, in which language competency and a high degree of personal involvement are basic requirements. The works of Turner, Stoller, and others demonstrate that this approach can succeed. Their humanistic mode of writing is not everyone's style of ethnography, but then not all forms of nonfiction writing are appealing to everyone. By this remark, I do not intend to reduce the issue of cross-cultural understanding to a matter of taste but only to emphasize that truthful and realistic ethnography may come in several forms.

Despite the postmodern shift in ethnography from scientific observation to personal narrative, some anthropologists seem to think they are getting better at it, especially now that the people they write about are able to read and review their books. James Clifford concludes his introduction to *Writing and Culture* with the optimistic assessment: "May not the vision of a complex, problematic, partial ethnography lead, not to its abandonment, but to more subtle, concrete ways of writing and reading?"[7]

II

To return to the ritual studies of Turner and Stoller, I would urge that these relate directly to the issue of cultural particularism. Their ethnographic accounts demonstrate that African ritual performances can be adequately understood largely in their own terms, and can be shown to possess their own intellectual integrity. Turner and Stoller came to accept the reality of the African spiritual world that they experienced, and they struggled with questions of ethnographic description and interpretation in order not to distort it.

In the 1950s, the renowned ethnographer Victor Turner was able to explain the therapeutic value of Ndembu healing ceremonies, called *ihamba*, by stripping off their "supernatural guise," as he called it, and translating their procedures in terms of social and psychological concepts.[8] As a result, Turner's account implied that the *ihamba* priests were skillful therapists—talented manipulators of sacred symbols and social dynamics. But unfortunately, as Edith Turner indicates, his account, like other ethnographic accounts of shamanistic healing at the time, portrayed the healers as charlatans nonetheless, as well-meaning sleight-of-hand artists. This is especially true of the *ihamba* priests, because the ritual requires them to dramatically "remove" the invisible spirit from the patient's body and place it in a container of sacrificial blood. The priest then triumphantly "lifts" out the spirit in the form of an animal tooth for all to see. For Victor Turner the tooth was an effective "symbol" of the back-biting envy of the villagers, nothing more. Turner's functionalist approach did not accord reality to the *ihamba* spirit and was not framed in the language of the people's experience of it. His well-intended interpretation could only suggest that the priests deceivingly "extracted" the nonexistent spirit from the patient by an act of professional trickery.

Thirty years later Victor Turner's wife, Edith Turner, returned to the same Ndembu village and took another look at the *ihamba* rites. This time she took part in the ceremonies as a fully engaged participant. She became personally caught up in its social and psychological dynamics and opened herself to experience the Ndembu spiritual world. The results were revolutionary, as she herself points out. She records her experience of *ihamba* healing rites in a detailed account, *Experiencing Ritual: A New Interpretation of African Healing* (1992).

During the *ihamba* ceremony, relatives and friends of the patient are required to voice aloud their personal grudges and feelings of anger toward each other and the suffering patient, and the patient too must express her anger and resentments. The participants' forceful songs and angry "words" attract the attention of the *ihamba* spirit and awaken it, so that it will leave the patient's body. The spirit's departure relieves the patient of his troubles. The procedure is a type of exorcism in which the spoken feelings of the participants expel the afflicting spirit. The priest's job is to identify the spirit, command its attention, encourage the participants to speak out, and, finally, to catch the spirit in a cupping horn or container.

He leads the singing of aggressive songs and stirs up people's feelings so that they will say what is in their hearts. The participants' "words" are regarded as the active agent of the process, as Turner indicates: "This expression, *words*, connected a certain action of prime importance to the success of the *ihamba*, the act of 'coming-out-with' whatever was secretly bothering the patient about her fellows, or bothering any member of the community."[9] As Turner explains it, a spirit had become trapped inside the patient "stoppered up by the stopping up of words and grudges" (138) which the people had to express for the spirit to hear, thus unplugging it from the patient's body, and so it would depart.

The climax of one of the ceremonies was reached when Turner herself was provoked into uttering angry words of her own. Her words, it turned out, expressed the last of the conflicted relationships to be voiced at the ceremony, and they had the effect of releasing the troubling spirit. Annoyed and angry at the misdeeds of some of the people involved, Turner shouted out: "OK, OK, OK, so it *is*. And it's woe. That's it." Immediately, Meru, the patient, fell down into a state of trance, and the ceremony reached its climax. At this point, Turner was emotionally drained from the hours of singing, dancing, and drumming, and from the fervent intensity of the process. She was also feeling the effects of the medicines ingested by herself and the priests. Tears flowing down her face, clapping her hands "like one possessed" in time with the heady rhythm of the mortar and drum, Turner watched the patient lose consciousness and fall onto the ground in a trance state.

Then, she writes, "I felt the spiritual motion, a tangible feeling of breakthrough going though the whole group. Immediately the patient fell" (149). The priest pressed on her back to guide out the afflicting spirit. Turner, like all the others, had reached an enhanced state of consciousness, and "a kind of collective Pentecost experience" occurred. There was instantaneous joy at the successful outcome. All shared a common perception of what happened:

> Suddenly Meru raised her arm, stretched it in liberation, and I *saw* with my own eyes a giant thing emerging out of the flesh of her back. This thing was a large gray blob abut six inches across, a deep gray opaque thing emerging as a sphere. The gray thing was actually out there, visible, and you could see [the priest] Singleton's hands working and scrabbling on the back—and then the thing was there no more. Singleton had it in his pouch. (149)

Turner's self-involving narrative is able to show the connection between the ritually spoken words and their psychosomatic results. As she explains it, the people's words of anger literally brought about an internal spiritual change in the patient, which later became manifested in the symbol of the extracted ivory tooth.

Turner was puzzled, however, by the question of her own objectivity. What did she see? Acting herself as a priest, did she see the same thing the other priests saw? Afterwards, Singleton, the leading priest, said, "The thing we saw, we were five." This statement, which Turner did not wish to probe under the circumstances, confirmed that they saw the same thing, the *ihamba* spirit exiting the patient's back. Turner explains that she also took the uniformity of the priests' reactions to the event to indicate that they all saw approximately the same thing. What she saw was something culturally objective, but not everyone saw it, only a few.

How, then, could she explain the meaning of this phenomenon without betraying her conviction about its validity? She decided to "[allow] the dialogue with the people in the field to assume to the full its potential importance to the ethnographer and his or her readers" (163). Thus, she provides the reader with a full account of the ritual dialogue that shaped the events she experienced. She was able to convey the full meaning of this dialogue because she herself had engaged in it, and her experience of the "event" of the spirit's appearance that was shaped by its discourse. In wrestling with the problem of how to interpret it she became, in a sense, her own informant. In the context of the healing ritual, she and the cultural "other" had become one. She became "other" to herself, and strove to understand what she experienced. "In this treatment of Ihamba I am taking statements of the protagonists as truth, and now I have become accustomed to it, it looks strange that anthropologists do differently" (172). By keeping her mind fixed on that "truth," she interprets the meaning of this discourse in Western language. In her own words,

> [W]hen the psychosocial body [of the ritual participants] was ready for some unseen triggering—even perhaps including that of the white stranger's frustration and tears—all of a sudden the soul of the whole group was delivered of its oppression and the patient's brain, negated by trance, allowed her body to open and provide the outlet for the spirit to escape—the opaque mass of plasma—into the air, to be stuffed into the homey mongoose skin pouch. (165)

Following Turner's example, we might say that the language of ritual experience can be successfully translated into Western discourse only by someone who has become fully conversant in that language and has shared the experiences expressed in it. Only in this way could Turner make the two discourses approximately equivalent to each other. The result is that the Ndembu ritual experience has become cross-culturally intelligible—without its being reduced to something different by the concepts of a more "scientific" language—the alternative that Turner refused to accept. We may not accept the reality of the Ndembu world she describes, but this is not because she has failed to make it intelligible. Nor is this a matter of imposing the categories of our world upon it.

What Turner has succeeded in showing us is the performative power of ritual language, its ability to rearrange people's feelings and command psychological forces to make things happen in people's lives. "The Ndembu doctors, by focusing, seem to facilitate the organizing into palpable existence of the thing that is troubling the patient, then they get rid of it" (72).

As for the ivory tooth supposedly removed from the patient's back which the priest later pulled out of his container, Turner wondered if this was just a conjuring trick. Other anthropologists, such as Lévi-Strauss, had been content to believe it was, leaving us to wonder about the healer's honesty. "How does he retain his faith in the system?" Lévi-Strauss asked.[10] He concluded that the native shaman in question was both an impostor and a great shaman. Turner agrees that when looking at the ivory tooth produced at the end of the ritual in a Western cause-and-effect sequence, it is impossible to conceive of it as the actual cause of the patient's suffering. "In the West the only words for such a process are 'trickery,' 'sleight-of-hand,' and the like" (169). By staying within the discourse of the *ihamba* priests, who refer to the spirit inside the patient and the ivory tooth with the same word, *ihamba,* Turner emphasizes that the two are the same thing. The shaman is aware of two realities, and the language he uses embraces both. The tooth, Turner concluded, is more than a symbol, more than a mere metaphor for the troubles in the village. It is the manifestation of an invisible reality made visible in the world, the "outward and visible sign of an inward and spiritual being," in the discourse of Western theological language (82). Thus Turner asserts, "[H]ere symbols and their meanings and the effect of them were one, not one *standing* for the other" (73). Invisible spirit and visible tooth are both *ihamba.* To explain it otherwise would violate Ndembu discourse, make impostors out of healers, and consequently cloud our understanding.

Unlike Turner, we may choose not to believe in the reality of the *ihamba* spirit. We do not, however, have to substitute "more veridical" Western psychological theory to understand the efficacy of Ndembu ritual words.

It is important to remember, of course, that Turner, the priests, and the patient drank the ritual medicines, and only they saw the phenomenon. An altered state of perception might have been involved. That, however, does not obscure the point that the words of the ritual brought about a change in the patient's disposition, healing her troubles. Not to believe in the reality of the spirit is not a failure of our understanding. It does not mean that we belong to different epistemic worlds, nor it is a criticism of the Ndembu.

Paul Stoller relates a similar problem describing the efficacy of ritual language among the Songhay of Niger. In his study of Songhay sorcery techniques, *In Sorcery's Shadow* (1987), Stoller rejected what he calls the "Evans-Pritchard option" of sending informants to learn about sorcery techniques, as Evans-Pritchard did in his study of Zande witchcraft. Stoller undertook to apprentice himself to a well-known sorcerer. The process included learning incantations, eating special foods of initiation, ingesting protective powders, wearing protective objects, and trying out sorcery techniques. He also suffered the effects of sorcery attacks, in the form of physical paralysis, from other sorcerers. Only in this way, Stoller believed, was he able to "penetrate a world that few Songhay know directly." This involved repeated fieldwork trips over a period of seventeen years, the sorting out of initially misleading information, and identifying his own interpretive errors. Eventually, Stoller "crossed the invisible threshold of Songhay sorcery," via the route of personal experience. "Now," says Stoller, "I knew the fear of facing my own mortality. Now I knew the exultation of repelling the power of a great sorcerer. I could no longer be a dispassionate observer of Songhay society. I had become more deeply involved in things Songhay than I could have ever imagined."[11] As a result of entering the world of sorcery, Stoller confesses that "my unwavering faith in science vanished." Like Turner, Stoller came to believe in the invisible powers that he was learning about. Like Turner, he also sees that meaning, belief, and truth are all linked together. The anthropologist does not just "represent" reality; he or she must describe how things are actually experienced.

Stoller relates a series of curing procedures performed by his teacher Sorko Djibo for a Muslim man who suffered from an undiagnosed illness. The man complained of chronic lethargy, aching joints, and nausea. He turned to the *sorko* after consulting a local Islamic healer, a local state nurse, a regional physician, and, finally, the doctors at the national hospital in the capital of Niamey. No one could diagnose his illness or treat him successfully. Since the man was a pious Muslim, it was out of desperation that he requested the help of Sorko Djibo, a well-known sorcerer in the town.

As soon as Djibo saw him, he pronounced him to be bewitched. The man resisted at first, saying that he did not believe in the sorcerer's "devils." But he soon relented, fearing that if he did not do something he would eventually die. The *sorko* promised to cure him after three days.

For the next two days, Stoller assisted his friend Djibo in fumigating the patient with the smoke of a special root and carefully rubbing the smoke into the man's ears, armpits, navel, and other joints and orifices. On the third day, the man began to suffer intensified fever and pain. This time the *sorko* recited an incantation over a gourd which contained a mixture of twigs, perfume, and water. Stoller describes the procedure:

> The words of the incantation, Djibo told me, would infuse the liquid with the force of the heavens. Through the text, which is called "water container," Djibo spoke to Ndebbi, the intermediary between human beings and Iri Koy, the High God of the Songhay cosmos. He sang about his ancestors and their power and how their power has been passed down through generations, father to son, father to son. He spoke of the world of the eternal war, the world of sorcery in which men have thirty points (crossroads) of misfortune and women have forty points of misfortune. He described the inhabitants of the world of eternal war: witches, evil genies, the evil Songhay spirits, sorcerers, and Iblis, the Islamic devil. When innocents come upon their points of misfortune, they are in a space between the spirit and the social worlds and are vulnerable to attack. But when the evil witches, genies, spirits, sorcerers, or Iblis attack an innocent, the innocent can sometimes repel them. The agents of evil can be misled. They can be overcome. They can be defeated.[12]

The *sorko* recited the text three times, each time spitting into the ablution. "In this way," the *sorko* explained, "the force of the heavens, which is embodied in words, enters the potion."[13] He left instructions for the man's wives to wash him with the ablution, especially the joints of the body, and the ears, nose, and mouth.

Then the *sorko* and Stoller left the compound to search for the sick man's spiritual "double," which, according to the *sorko*, a witch had stolen. The smoke had prepared the man's body to receive back its double; it had to be found, the *sorko* explained, before the witch transformed it into an animal and cut its throat. Locating a large pile of millet husks on top of a sand dune by the river, where the wives of the compound winnowed the chaff from the millet seed, the *sorko* knelt down and sifted through the chaff in search of the man's missing double. Suddenly, he jumped to his feet, and cried out excitedly, "Wow! Wow! Wow! Wow!" He immediately turned to Stoller and asked whether he had seen the double. Stoller replied that he had not. The *sorko* asked if he had felt or heard the man's double. Again Stoller had to deny that he had felt or heard anything. He also wondered "whether Djibo had feigned his 'discovery.' " "How," Stoller asked, "could he see, feel, and hear something which had eluded my senses?"[14]

Upon returning to the compound, the two were greeted by the patient himself, striding towards them across the courtyard, fully recovered and extravagantly praising the *sorko* and his spirits. Delighted, Djibo turned to Stoller and said, "The words were good for this one."

Stoller's account shows that, as in the Ndembu ceremony, the efficacy of the ritual consists in linking together sacred words with the spirit world and the patient's psychological state. Uttering the words had the desired effect of joining together the patient and his spiritual double. By contrast, the Ndembu words accomplished the opposite result of separating a spiritual element from the patient. In both cases the performative force of the words brought about a transformation within the suffering patient. Although in the Songhay case the words were spoken in the privacy of the patient's compound, they were directed at the invisible spirits. In both cases, properly empowered words, like the shamans and sorcerers themselves, are held to reach across the two realities, the spiritual and the social, to gain their effect.

In the epilogue to this account Stoller indicates that it was only through his experience of invisible realities that he "stepped in the world of Songhay sorcery," and "understood it well—from a Songhay perspective." For this reason, Stoller, like Turner, resisted the translation of sorcery ritual into Western psychological concepts, which would have misrepresented both his experience and that of the Songhay. Stoller and Turner recognized that the word and experience are inextricably entwined—how people experience the world is inevitably expressed in the words they use. By translating them into the rationalistic concepts of Western psychology, we not only change their meaning, we obscure the experience we are trying to comprehend. Why not try to write under the influence of this experience using its categories and knowledge to expand our understanding?

Like Turner, Stoller decided to include his reflections in his ethnography, recognizing that this was going against the tradition of an author's personal absence from the text. For better or for worse, Stoller declares, "every ethnographer is a character in the story of his or her fieldwork." Reflecting upon his ethnographic style, Stoller emphasizes that while cultural difference plays a key role in his textual construction, he constructs a personal narrative with which his readers can identify. By including his own self-reflection in the ethnography, he enables the reader to become receptive to descriptions that would otherwise appear implausible. This, he indicates, allows the events of the field to penetrate the reader: "In this way the anthropological writer, using evocative language, brings life to the field and beckons the reader to discover something new—a new theoretical insight, a new thought, a new feeling or appreciation."[15]

III

It might be supposed, however, that these closely observed and reflexively written ethnographic narratives undermine the possibility of comparative study from one society to another. Does not their highly situated perspective frustrate any effort at cross-cultural comparison? Just the opposite is true. The richer the contextual and historical detail, the more explicit the ethnographer's intellectual and personal perspective, the better grounded comparison can be.

While situated in different cultures, Turner's and Stoller's accounts of the efficacy of ritual language reveal the logic and meaning of this widely practiced ritual technique. The Songhay sorcerers say that it is the sound of the incantation that carries across the visible and invisible worlds; it is the sound and tone of the incantations, not the words themselves (which can sometimes be meaningless) that is the action and creates the desired effect.[16] For the Ndembu it is not the sound but the meaning of the words that creates the effect, that "unstoppers" the afflicting spirit and compels it to leave the patient's body.

But in this difference lies a profound similarity: in both cases ritual words perform healing acts. It is the ritual speech act, the power of words, that transforms and heals the patient. For Ndembu and Songhay, the spirits must "hear" the words for the results to occur, yet it is the words that perform the action. This is what is meant by the performative, or "perlocutionary," force of words, as J. L. Austin called it.[17] Whether the hearers are human or spiritual matters not to the linguistic act and its performative force. To comprehend it, as Austin showed, is to comprehend the conditions of the speech act, which Turner and Stoller describe in such detail. Performative force is the ability of words to "do" things, not just "say" things. It is not a feature of language that belongs only to the Ndembu and Songhay "world." It is a common feature of the human linguistic world, and it would be strange if African languages lacked it.

It has been said that the great potential of postmodernism is its capacity to "decenter experience," to enable us to experience and comprehend other cultures as much as possible in their own terms. In the two examples I have described, the ethnographers have "decentered" themselves from Western social scientific concepts and have described their experience in terms of a discourse that is shaped by the "other." In this way, they have taken something culturally different and found an effective way of expressing it in a Western humanistic mode of discourse, without reducing it to something that is only part of our world. In doing so they enable us to gain insight into another realm of experience, and thus they have expanded our world.

Scholars who have tried to understand how and why ritual words operate in a performative fashion, it turns out, are those who have become personally engaged in the forms of life in which such actions occur. I do not see how it could be otherwise. I am not advocating that comparative religionists must "go native" and join the ranks of the religions they seek to understand—neither Turner nor Stoller did. I am suggesting that they need to become more like the writers of good nonfiction narratives by becoming self-conscious of their craft and by using a more personal, poetic, and self-involving style of writing that is influenced by the world they are writing about. When this is done successfully, there is no need to "strip away the supernatural guise."

Writing in this mode springs from the author's solidarity with a living community or, in the case of the past, a once living community. This solidarity is both personal and moral. It is based on trust and long-term acquaintance. Again, I do not see how it could be otherwise. In keeping with this kind of ethnography, I would propose that the purpose of comparative religion is both intellectually heuristic and morally engaged. It is based upon intellectual and moral involvement with religious communities (past or present) and with the community of scholars who study them. Its aim is not to identify transcendent universals but to discover enriching insights into shared aspects of human experience, and thus to advance the conversation of humankind. Insights gained through comparison should enable people of different cultures and religions to enter into dialogue, to gain mutual understanding, and to build important religious bridges and political relationships.

Notes

1. James Clifford and George E. Marcus, eds., *Writing Culture: The Poetics and Politics of Ethnography* (Berkeley: University of California Press, 1986).

2. Stephen A. Tyler, "Postmodern Ethnography: From Document of the Occult to Occult Document," in ibid., p. 139.

3. John Bowlin and Peter G. Stromberg, "Representation and Reality in the Study of Culture," *American Anthropologist* 99, no.1: 123–34.

4. Clifford Geertz, "Slide Show: Evans-Pritchard's African Transparencies," in *Works and Lives* (Stanford: Stanford University Press, 1988), p. 70.

5. Richard Rorty, "Pragmatism, Davidson, and Truth," in *Objectivity, Relativism, and Truth*, vol. 1 (Cambridge: Cambridge University Press, 1991), pp. 126–50.

6. Bowlin and Stromberg, "Representation and Reality," p. 132.

7. Clifford and Marcus, *Writing Culture*, p. 25.

8. Victor Turner, "A Ndembu Doctor in Practice," in *The Forest of Symbols: Aspects of Ndembu Ritual* (Ithaca: Cornell University Press, 1967).

9. Edith Turner, *Experiencing Ritual: A New Interpretation of African Healing* (Philadelphia: University of Pennsylvania Press, 1992), p. 60. This work is hereafter cited in text by page numbers in parentheses.

10. As quoted in Turner, *Experiencing Ritual*, p. 165.

11. Paul Stoller and Cheryl Olkes, *In Sorcery's Shadow: A Memoir of Apprenticeship among the Songhay of Niger* (Chicago: University of Chicago Press, 1987), p. 153.

12. Ibid., p. 69.

13. Ibid., p. 70.

14. Ibid., p. 70.

15. Paul Stoller, *The Taste of Ethnographic Things: The Senses in Anthropology* (Philadelphia: University of Pennsylvania Press, 1989), p. 54.

16. Ibid., p. 120.

17. J. L. Austin, *How to Do Things with Words* (London: Oxford University Press, 1962).

AMERICAN RELIGION IS
NATURALLY COMPARATIVE

WINNIFRED FALLERS SULLIVAN

The study of American religion occurs in the context of a highly politicized and polemical local public debate concerning the interpretation
of the First Amendment to the United States Constitution and the appropriate location of religion in contemporary American life.[1] An analogous debate is occurring throughout the world. It is urgent that these
debates—both in the United States and elsewhere—be informed by serious comparative scholarship about religious pluralism and about the
legal contexts in which religion happens. The American conversation
has been plagued by attitudes of American exceptionalism and determined to some extent by the culture of American constitutional debate.
A comparative perspective would give needed perspective to the internal
American debate and refine understanding of the American example for
comparison with other countries in which multiple religious communities subsist within a secular state.

I will begin by briefly summarizing my understanding of Jonathan Z.
Smith's articles on comparison[2] and then speak in more detail about
comparison and American religion. I take it from the many references
to Smith in the essays collected here that there is general agreement that
he has practically patented "comparison" for the purposes of religious
studies today. While "comparative religions"—at least as formerly practiced—has come to be regarded as impossibly compromised, for the
various reasons described by Smith and by many of the scholars in this
volume, comparison, at least as defined by Smith, remains an urgent and

necessary part of studying religion. Smith emphasizes the importance of comparing religions or religious phenomena, however, neither out of multicultural enthusiasm nor because he perceives a natural unity among them. I take him to mean what he says in the very beginning of his essay on the subject in *Map Is Not Territory*: "The process of comparison is a fundamental characteristic of human intelligence."[3] To do scholarly work is to compare. It is how our minds work. The challenge for us is not, if we wish to think about religion, whether or not to compare, but whether we can do a good job of it. Thinking about anything is, for Smith, a very serious business. It is our work, and the labor of it involves constant comparison. We cannot think or write about religion without comparing.

Smith's reflections on the characteristics of human intelligence could be dismissed as an unnecessary truism, as an excuse for returning to business as usual. But that is not how he sees our work. While comparison is inescapable, we still need to be self-conscious about how we go about it. Smith admits, for example, of different kinds of comparison— the ethnographic, the encyclopedic, the morphological, and the evolutionary—each useful in its own way for understanding the products of human culture. Furthermore, in studying religion, in particular, Smith urges the necessity for a combination of methods which makes possible both the development of patterns and a faithfulness to history. The goal is to historicize morphology.[4]

As I understand Smith, ours is a reflective and self-consciously constructive scholarly enterprise, a creation rather than a discovery. His call for the use of deliberate craft in the construction of models of religion is, in part, I think a response to excessive naturalizing in religious studies—the illusion that religious data have natural shapes that we need only notice and common features that offer themselves for comparison and categorization. On the contrary, understanding the religiousness of human beings is, Smith suggests, an unnatural enterprise, one that demands sophisticated technique and a complex notion of history, one that aims not at discovering the natural religion of mankind but that aims at thinking carefully about constructing the scholarly category of religion so that we can better understand human culture. Comparisons are valid only insofar as they further that end.

I take as emendations of Smith's description of our job the suggestions made by Benjamin Ray and Jonathan Herman, both of which I think Smith would admit as reasonable, even necessary, clarifications of his own understanding. Ray reminds us that there is no "raw data," that all data is already interpreted,[5] and Herman, that there is a give-and-take between data and theory, that we must have "a willingness to allow the context to determine the appropriate methodologies."[6] Smith ends his first essay on comparison with the image of a spiral as a description of change in scholarly method, taken from an article by Paul Mercier commenting on the use of comparison in anthropology:

> "If anthropology returns to the comparative method, it will certainly not forget what it has learned meanwhile in general and what it has learned about the limitations of the method in particular. It will return only in that spiral-like movement, so characteristic of scientific thought, arriving after half a century at the same point but at a higher level. It will know better how and what to compare than it knew fifty years ago." This applies to our discipline as well.[7]

So, we too, humbled, return to comparison.

The 1996 AAR panel on comparison in New Orleans was the second conversation in which I was asked to participate in which the assignment was jointly to lament the descent of the study of religion into area studies and collectively to promote a return to comparative studies or history of religions[8]—to a *new* comparative religious studies committed to categories and issues that reach across religious traditions while retaining a serious attention to the particularities of history. It is also the second in which I have been the only one trained primarily in American religion or in Christianity. For a historian of religions who studies either American religion or Christianity, this call to arms finds us in a rather different place from the rest of religious studies. The reasons for this displacement are related and have resulted in an inversion, in a way, of the theoretical concerns seen by scholars of religion who study the religion of other traditions and other countries.

Theological reflection within and scholarly investigation of Christianity has had a somewhat tangential relationship to the development of the modern study of religion, generally, for reasons of disciplinary boundaries, of institutional location, and of apologetics.[9] While historical-critical study of the Bible and theological developments were fundamental to the invention of the new discipline for the comparative study of religion, comparativists today for the most part do not study Christianity. It has been set apart. There are complicated reasons for this. Many early comparativists were interested in origins; Christianity was seen either as the culmination and end of an evolutionary development or as a different phenomenon: the truth as opposed to error. The development of a vocabulary and methods for the study of religion was different for Christianity. There appeared to be less need to justify the terms than there was in the study of non-Christian religions.

The study of post-Constantinian Christianity[10] has been done principally by historians, who, for the most part, at least until recently, have been suspicious of comparative categories.[11] The establishment of chairs in European universities apart from theological faculties tended to isolate Christianity from the study of other religious traditions, while separatist interpretation of the First Amendment to the United States Constitution has meant that the study of American Protestantism was left to church historians and denominational historians, rather than being studied by "secular" scholars. These areas of study might be said to suffer from too great an emphasis on history, not too little. History has been the way to study "us";[12] anthropology or history of religions the way to study "them."[13] Thus, American religion has been studied by historians, while other religions have been studied as reified ahistorical systems.

So while the prejudice in Christian studies has been for historical method, for a certain segment of the religious studies community there is a sense in which Christianity has not been included in the category of "religion." Even today, in some graduate departments, Christianity is seen as being insufficiently "other" to be studied anthropologically.[14] The reasons are several. As David Eckel asserts, Barbara Holdrege implies, and Jonathan Z. Smith has argued, Protestant Christianity has been excluded because it has been thought to be a part of the method, a source of theory, not a part of the data.[15] Catholicism, on the other hand, was studied by proxy in the study of pre-Christian and primitive traditions.[16] American religion, Christian and otherwise, was simply not serious or interesting enough, or perhaps it was not understood to be "real" religion.[17] Many of the people who study Christianity and American religion happily go to different professional meetings and write in different journals from those scholars of religion who study other religious traditions.

If the invention of area studies is understood, as it is in this volume, to have been in response to a certain kind of ahistoric and agenda-laden comparative study, the problems associated with area studies do not really exist in the study of Christianity and American religion. Historians of post-Constantinian Christianity and American religion are discovering comparison for the first time. There *are* problems of parochialism and of American exceptionalism in American religious studies. The study of American religion today, however, is in many ways a vital comparative exercise, one that is, at its best, well-informed by history. This is so, I think, for a number of interesting reasons. I am going to divide my discussion of comparison and American religion into two parts: comparison within American religion and comparison with American religion.

Comparison within American Religion

The study of American religion has now, for some years, been moving out of a narrow church-history perspective; it has nevertheless had to struggle against a powerful story in which American and Protestant identities were carefully intertwined.[18] Before about 1950, for apologetic reasons, for political reasons, and for reasons of institutional location, American religion was studied as the history of the Protestant Church in America.[19] American Protestantism *was* American Religion. The story began with the Puritans of New England. It continued with a meticulous sorting out of the theological differences between and among Calvinists: Presbyterians and Congregationalists, mostly. It starred such luminaries as Anne Hutchinson and Cotton Mather and included doctrinal debates such as the antinomian controversy and the Half-Way Covenant. In this story the middle states, when they appeared, were supporting characters, early experiments in tolerance and diversity, but the tolerance and diversity were primarily among Protestants. The small communities of Jews and Catholics in Philadelphia and Maryland did not fit into the story and were largely ignored. The Southern states had an even more passive role. They featured the transplanted Anglicans, a weak establishment with Tory priests that would give way to Enlightenment deism and pietistic evangelization in the Great Awakening—beginning with George Whitefield, the Grand Itinerant.

The story of the Protestant Church in America continued after the Revolution with the flourishing of Methodists and Baptists as the West was won. The hero here was the circuit preacher, braving the weather to make his round and bring religion to the backwoods and the frontier. Beginning with the Cane Ridge Revival in Kentucky, Protestant Christianity was shown to adapt successfully and creatively to the new conditions, tailoring its theology and its culture to fit new people and places. It reached its crescendo in the Righteous Empire, as Martin Marty has called it.[20] It is a story of growth and expansion.[21]

Roughly contemporaneously with the publication of Will Herberg's

Protestant, Catholic, Jew[22] in 1955, American religion was revised.[23] Two wars and the coming of age of immigrant communities had changed the religious landscape. More than a century after the first waves of Catholic and Jewish immigrants, it was now understood to come in three flavors, not just one. Herberg stressed, however, that it was the common features which were more distinctive than the divergent ones at mid-century: the true American religion was what Herberg called the "American way of life," the religion of Eisenhower's America. Herberg made an important point, not only about mid-century American religion but one that continues to be valid today. His account, however, did not fit important segments of the population—most notably African Americans, for whom the church played a different role.[24]

In the last twenty years, and beginning roughly with the work of Catherine Albanese,[25] the study of American religion has burst wide open. It is now about everyone. Now we begin with the Indian traditions, and we linger over them, partly in a gesture of recompense and reconciliation, but also because we have something to learn from them about what American religion is. What will become persistent American themes of humanity and nature, of immigration, of diversity, of cultural encounter and of historical adaptation and change can be discerned in the stories of these traditions. Their study enriches our understanding of American religion. The first Europeans in America are now Spanish conquistadors and Franciscan missionaries, French trappers and Jesuit priests, not English Puritans with their "godly ministers."

This different starting point makes very real differences. Where you start sets a standard for what follows later. It sets a benchmark. If you start with the Puritans, then it is their religious life which defines religion. If you start with the Navajo and the Iroquois, the Spanish and the French, religion suddenly looks very different. Religion is about symbol and myth, ritual and violence, sacred space and sacred time, as well as being about baptism and conversion and the work of the spirit. Religion is public, given, communal, and acted out, as well as being private, chosen, individual, and believed. The study of this riotous diversity has become a richly productive field benefiting eagerly and enormously from what might loosely be called religious studies approaches. What was once church history—Protestant church history—has become mostly a marvelously textured and sophisticated inquiry into the religious lives of Americans—an inquiry that not only includes non-Protestants but provides new understandings of Protestants. The achievements of American religious studies *can*, of course, be exaggerated. There has, at times, been an overcelebratory tone to some of this scholarship, a tone which tends to ignore hard questions about political contexts and about the deeply ambiguous nature of all religious reality. Religious studies categories have sometimes been borrowed without adequately assimilating the critique of those categories, or allowing the American material to provide a new critique of old categories.

All in all, though, perhaps those who are distressed by the ghettoization or overspecialization in area studies might take heart and find something useful in the American experience. The shift of perspective in American religious studies is really very dramatic and has revealed a fascinating array of religious data for the student of religion. What was once limited to the narrow and triumphal tale of the development of progressive Protestant theology is now almost overwhelmed by comparative possibilities.

Apart from the sheer diversity, American religion has some peculiar features which lend themselves to the comparative enterprise. It is not enough simply to notice the increased presence of non-Western religious traditions in American cities and countryside. American religion is "naturally" comparative in another sense. American religion is distinctive in form because of its history. It is not age-old. It is new—and proudly so. It has invented itself quite purposely from the ground up in a very short and specific historical context. American religion might be almost regarded as presenting itself as a controlled experiment in comparative religion. The study of American religion asks such questions as, What does disestablished diaspora religion look like? What happens to religion when it is separate from the state? What happens when it is separated from the places and the older religions of the places it inhabited? What happens when it shares space with all of the other religions of the world? As one looks across the parallel histories of the religious communities of the United States, one sees common themes—provoked by a shared history.

There have been a number of attempts to describe the peculiarities of American religion. By way of example, I will use here a classic and enduring one, that of Sidney Mead.[26] Sidney Mead has written about the corrosive effects of the new place and new politics on European Protestantism. Looking back from the mid-twentieth century, he found six characteristics of the peculiarly American "denomination": (1) a kind of historylessness which finds its source in the tendency of American sects to refer only to the early church for a pattern, dismissing all church history from the first century to the Reformation; (2) the voluntary principle, in which church membership depends on persuasion alone; (3) the mission enterprise, resulting in widespread ecumenical charitable efforts; (4) revivalism, leading to Arminianism and an undercutting of the importance of doctrine and practice; (5) pietism and anti-intellectualism; and (6) a competition among the churches which results in constantly shifting patterns of alignment and cooperation. These tendencies, Mead emphasized, are the direct result of, the price to be paid for, one might say, in Mead's eyes, disestablishment of the churches and the free exercise of religion. Importantly, while Mead set out to describe only Protestant Christianity in the United States, and while all of these characteristics derive from the histories of the sects of the left wing of the Reformation—those who might be said to have invented the separation of church and state, theologically speaking—all six can be seen to be descriptive of both other American Protestants, and of other American religions as well, at the end of the twentieth century.

Anyone who has studied American religion has noticed this tendency of new imports, as well as home-grown traditions, to conform themselves to the model Mead describes, so that first Catholics and Jews, and later even Hindus and Mormons, gradually come to look more and more like American sectarian Protestants. This change has happened not just because Protestants have held the political majority, but because the form of American Protestantism resulted from its negotiation with the legal structure under which it was created. Newer religious groups found a ready-made legal place for them, a legal place constructed of tax laws, zoning laws, employment laws, anti-discrimination laws, building codes, food and health regulations, and so on, a legal place that views them as voluntary, non-profit organizations and determines to a remarkable extent the religious forms they create. The shape of the place created for religion in the United States is so powerfully constructed that the distinctiveness of a new religious community in the United States, if it is to persist, requires the expenditure of enormous energy.[27]

The cross-cutting themes in American religion almost demand a comparative eye from the scholar. The competitive spirit Mead described means that American religious practitioners are constantly casting a comparative eye at one another. The voluntary principle means that the individual calls the shots. She can always go and join up somewhere else. There are other important cross-cutting themes: the immigrant experience; the construction of nature, race, and ethnicity; and the effects of three great wars, among others. The study of American religion is one of comparison from the beginning.

Comparison with American Religion

Studying American religion can also provide interesting comparative opportunities with religion outside the United States. It is less frequently done, but the hubris and isolationism of American studies makes it urgent. Furthermore, as more and more countries come to be secular states with multiple diaspora religious communities living within them, the contemporary political and legal experience of religious communities becomes more and more comparable and the example of the United States more relevant. What Mead saw in the American situation has interesting cross-cultural parallels and contrasts.

José Casanova has argued in his recent book, *Public Religions in the Modern World*,[28] that the relative political influence of different churches in Europe, South America, and the United States today is best explained by the prior presence or absence of an established church. Ireland and Poland remain more Catholic and less secular than France or Spain, Casanova argues, because Ireland and Poland never had caesaropapist state churches with the accompanying rabid anticlericalism:[29] "[C]onsistently throughout Europe, nonestablished churches and sects in most countries have been able to survive the secularizing trends better than has the established church."[30] Casanova discusses in detail various versions of the secularization thesis and then takes a series of case studies—from Brazil, Poland, and the United States and others—to argue that there is an inverse link between a prior legal establishment of religion and the continuing public persuasiveness of a particular religious tradition within a secular state today. Further comparative, historical, and morphological study of established, disestablished, and nonestablished religions is necessary to test and further Casanova's work, particularly outside Christianity.

American religion is disestablished and has always been disestablished. It was separate, in a sense, right from the beginning. This makes a real difference from most of the rest of the religion studied by religion scholars. All American religion has happened in a space constructed by American law. This is not only so from the time of the Constitution, after which the First Amendment defines the conditions for American religion. It is so from the beginning of European migration. Long before the drafting of the United States Constitution, the move across the Atlantic by European Christians can be understood as the beginning of what became and continues to be an ongoing disestablishment of religion in the Americas, a disestablishment that did not simply legally disconnect it more and more from the state but which profoundly changed its nature. The crossing itself—the change of place—made the first decisive difference.

The first American disestablishment, the actual physical move, supported by reformed and Anabaptist interpretations of Pauline theology, was the result of the uprooting of national churches from their largely geographically organized parishes in Europe. They were released to find a new form, divorced from "place," in Jonathan Z. Smith's sense.[31] Where you lived no longer determined who and how and where you worshiped. Where you lived was no longer sacred in the same way.

This new freedom from place gave rise in the United States to new theological and political arrangements as English Puritans[32]—and later Catholics and others—struggled to invent a new kind of society and a new kind of religion in a new land, a land unmarked by the sacralizing history and structures of the old. The land was, of course, strongly marked by soon destroyed sacralizing structures of existing Indian traditions. The holocaust that followed was too rapid and the iconoclastic inclinations of American Protestants too resistant in North America, however, for the syncretic interpenetration of religious life and practice that occurred in other mission fields, including New Spain. American religion developed in a different way. American religion became subject to law as religion is now becoming subject to secular legal construction around the world.

But the high wall of separation—the American version of disestablishment—is not the only way to do it. Americans are often surprised to find how casually Europeans take vestiges of religious establishments such as government support of religious institutions, public celebration marked by prayer and religious services, catechesis in public schools, and so on. The new Constitution of South Africa attempts to guarantee religious freedom while promising to enforce religious family-law codes. The Constitution of Japan, which also guarantees religious freedom, has been interpreted to permit government-supported apotheosis in Shinto ceremonies of war dead.[33] The wearing of veils by Muslim schoolgirls is differentially treated under British law and French law,[34] although both are committed to religious freedom. There are many fertile areas for comparison in the attempt to understand the contemporary accommodation between law and religion. To mention a few: the development of family-law codes, government subsidy of religious schools, symbolization and celebration of political power, religious nationalism, regulation of ritual behavior, zoning, the clash between international human rights and religious norms, taxation of religious institutions, the accommodation of historically oppressed minorities, the meanings assigned to "religion" in legal and constitutional schemes, the privileges of religious specialists in prisons and in the armed services, and the construction of religions in trial settings.

There is a loud and contentious debate in the United States today about the appropriate relationship between religion, law, and politics. It is conducted largely by those who unconsciously inhabit the religious reality described by Sidney Mead. It is urgent that this debate be informed by serious comparative scholarship. This is so not only because of its intractability but also because the categories used in religious studies have immediate political and legal currency in any state that constitutionally both disestablishes religion and undertakes to protect it.

Conclusion

Bringing together American religious history with the comparative study of world religions would bring a much needed cross-cultural comparative perspective to the study of American religion and law. It could perhaps provide an example in the call for better history and a more sophisticated understanding of the role of law in the formation of the world's other religious traditions. I hope that those of you who are busy creating historicized morphology will include American religion in your studies.

Notes

An earlier version of this article was prepared for the panel on "The Comparative Study of Religion: Contemporary Challenges and Responses (Part II)" at the 1996 Annual Meeting of the American Academy of Religion. I am grateful to Alexandra Brown and Frank Reynolds for reading and commenting on earlier drafts of this article.

1. In this article I use the phrase "American religion" to refer inclusively to the varied religious lives of all Americans. I use it in preference to "religion in America" in order to emphasize the important formative influence of American legal and political structures on the shape of religion in the United States.

2. Jonathan Z. Smith, "*Adde Parvum Parvo Magnus Acervus Erit*," in *Map Is Not Territory: Studies in the History of Religions* (Leiden: E. J. Brill, 1978) and "In Comparison a Magic Dwells," in *Imagining Religion: From Babylon to Jonestown* (Chicago: University of Chicago Press, 1982).

3. Smith, *Map*, p. 240.

4. Smith, *Map*, p. 264.

5. See Benjamin Ray's response to the panel "The Comparative Study of Religion: Contemporary Challenges and Responses," Annual Meeting of the American Academy of Religion, Philadelphia, 1995.

6. Herman, p. 96 in the present volume.

7. Smith, *Map*, p. 264. The upward spiral is a rather progressive image for these cautious times. Perhaps some will say that the spiral is broken in places or that it coils back on itself at times, arriving at a lower, rather than a higher level. Perhaps the multiple genealogies of religious studies are more aptly represented as a weaving or as a musical composition that returns to old themes but with significant variations. Nevertheless, while perhaps we do not learn and build on our knowledge with the clean sense of progression that a spiral suggests, and we almost certainly have forgotten critical discoveries, we surely return to old methods with new insights as to their proper use.

8. The other was a conference at Western Maryland College entitled "Reconstructing a History of Religions: Problems and Possibilities," 8–9 November 1996.

9. For two accounts of this history see Claude Welch, *Protestant Thought in the Nineteenth Century, vol. 2, 1870–1914* (New Haven: Yale University Press, 1985), pp. 104–45; and Eric J. Sharpe, *Comparative Religion: A History,* 2d ed. (La Salle, IL: Open Court, 1986). This history plays out in interesting ways in undergraduate curricula. Different locations for the study of Christianity and American religion exist—philosophy departments, history departments, and sociology departments for Christianity and American religion, and religious studies departments for the rest. The array of methods and disciplinary locations is confusing to undergraduates when they are selecting courses, although the interdisciplinary possibilities, if explicitly acknowledged, can be very exciting to them in the classroom.

10. Biblical studies and the study of the early Christian communities have had a somewhat different history than the study of medieval and modern Christianity. They have perhaps remained closer to comparative studies, in part because, as in the study of American religion, the religious landscape of the first century was so varied and competitive and the religious communities so highly conscious of the competition. The formation of identity in medieval and modern Christianity had a different dynamic—the debates were seen as internal, on the whole.

11. With some obvious and important exceptions like Peter Brown, Caroline Walker Bynum, and Catherine Albanese.

12. Or sociology—but sociology seems notably absent from this conversation. The sociological study of Christianity, indeed of religion generally, seems also to have a tangential relationship to the comparative study of religion, because of fears of reductionism. A renewed emphasis on history in comparative study might profitably be accompanied by a renewed interest in sociology.

13. See Johannes Fabian, *Time and the Other: How Anthropology Makes Its Object* (New York: Columbia University Press, 1983).

14. At the Divinity School at the University of Chicago, for example, Chris-

tianity and American religion have been studied in an area called History of Christianity, while other religious traditions are studied in an area called History of Religions. History of Religions did not welcome studies in Christianity. This disciplinary separation has been breached at the level both of individual dissertations as well as in cross-disciplinary conversation among faculty and students, but the institutional prejudice remains, there, and elsewhere. Christianity has also suffered by being "implicated" in the imperialist and colonialist projects, and is therefore suspect.

15. See Eckel, "Contested Identities," and Holdrege, "What's Beyond the Post?" in the present volume. See also Jonathan Z. Smith, *Drudgery Divine: On the Comparison of Early Christianity and the Religions of Late Antiquity* (Chicago: University of Chicago Press, 1990), showing the Protestant bias of biblical studies. Of course Protestant Christianity is far more diverse and complex than is allowed by these condemnations. We must not make the mistake of allowing ourselves to treat Protestantism as monolithic simply because some forms of Protestantism have enjoyed political hegemony.

16. See Smith, *Drudgery Divine*, in which Smith details the distorting effects of Protestant anti-Catholicism on the study of Early Christianity. He shows biblical scholars using "pagan" as synonymous with "Roman Catholic" when setting up a comparison of pure Christianity (Protestant Christianity) and pagan superstition (Roman Catholicism).

17. Perhaps it is not real religion, being disestablished. Real Christianity is European Christianity.

18. See the preface and chapter 1 of Sidney Ahlstrom, *A Religious History of the American People* (New Haven: Yale University Press, 1972), for a description of the history of American church history.

19. See, for example, Robert Baird, *Religion in America* (New York: Harper & Row, 1970; original edition 1844) and William Warren Sweet, *The Story of Religion in America* (New York: Harper & Brothers, 1930).

20. Martin Marty, *Righteous Empire: The Protestant Experience in America* (New York: Dial Press, 1970).

21. I borrow here from a typology of the stories told about American history in the Supreme Court, see L. H. LaRue, *Constitutional Law as Fiction: Narrative in the Rhetoric of Authority* (University Park: Pennsylvania State University Press, 1995).

22. Will Herberg, *Protestant, Catholic, Jew: An Essay in American Religious Sociology* (Chicago: University of Chicago Press, 1955).

23. The study of American Catholicism and American Judaism still remain somewhat ghettoized. Scholars in these fields belong to their own historical associations and write for different journals.

24. The story of African American religion is now being told in many places. Pioneering works are Albert Raboteau, *Slave Religion: The Invisible Institution in the Antebellum South* (New York: Oxford University Press, 1978) and Eugene Genovese, *Roll, Jordan Roll: The World the Slaves Made* (New York: Pantheon Books, 1974). For a recent overview of race and Southern Baptists, see Paul Harvey, *Redeeming the South: Religious Cultures and Racial Identities* (Chapel Hill: University of North Carolina Press, 1997).

25. Particularly the first edition of her *America: Religions and Religion* (Belmont, CA: Wadsworth, 1981).

26. Sidney Mead, *A Lively Experiment: The Shaping of Christianity in America* (New York: Harper & Row, 1963).

27. That energy can be seen on a large scale in the story of the maintenance of a parallel Catholic culture during the late nineteenth and the first half of the twentieth centuries and on a smaller scale in the struggle of small separatist groups such as those of Hasidic Jews.

28. José Casanova, *Public Religions in the Modern World* (Chicago: University of Chicago Press, 1994).

29. Ibid., p. 29. In the time since Casanova wrote, one can see the churches in both Ireland and Poland struggling to retain this advantage in a rapidly changing world. And the American Catholic Church struggles to remake itself, too. While the American Catholic bishops have an important public voice on moral issues, as Casanova notes, the institutions that produced that voice are changing very rapidly. For a lively portrait of the American Catholic Church in the nineteenth and twentieth centuries, see Charles R. Morris, *American Catholic: The Saints and Sinners That Built America's Most Powerful Church* (New York: Random House, 1997).

30. Casanova, *Public Religions*, p. 29.

31. Jonathan Z. Smith, *To Take Place: Toward Theory in Ritual* (Chicago: University of Chicago Press, 1987). See also Tod D. Swanson, "To Prepare a Place: Johannine Christianity and the Collapse of Ethnic Territory," *Journal of the American Academy of Religion* 62 (summer 1994): 241–63.

32. See Elizabeth Dale, "Conflicts of Law: Reconsidering the Influence of Religion on Law in Massachusetts Bay," *Numen* 43 (May 1996): 139–56, for one discussion of the transition from religion to law in the American colonies.

33. The Nakaya case, Showa 63 [1988] June 1.

34. Sebastian Poulter, "Muslim Headscarves in School: Contrasting Legal Approaches in England and France," *Oxford Journal of Legal Studies* 17 (1997): 43–74.

DIALOGUE AND METHOD

Reconstructing the Study of Religion

DIANA L. ECK

The fast-changing religious world of the twentieth century is a challenging context in which to reflect on the question of method in religious studies. How do we understand this word "religion"? And how do we approach the study of religion? In this essay, I would like to offer an interpretation of religion, looking at three critical perspectives I believe are important to the study of religion: comparative, historical, and dialogical. In each case, I will reflect on some of the tremendous movements and tumultuous changes in today's world as a way of illustrating the importance of each kind of work.

For many years, some of us have referred to our field of study as the "comparative study of religion" or the "history of religions." Twenty years ago, these terms signaled, though not very precisely, the kinds of work undertaken by scholars studying non-Christian or non-Jewish traditions. Today such a usage is clearly in need of revision as scholars in every field of the study of religion are called upon by colleagues and students to set their specialized work in the wider context of the historical and comparative study of religion. Indeed, this wider context is built into the structure of doctoral work both at Harvard University and the University of Chicago. It is simply no longer the case that the terms "comparative" and "historical" studies describe a subfield of the study of religion; rather, they designate intellectual perspectives to be cultivated in all fields of the study of religion. And it is certainly not the case that these terms "go uncontested," to borrow Derrida's phrase; postmodern thought, when applied to these perspectives, implies a profound challenge to the validity of their cultivation. However, I believe that the "wider context" of religions in all its reality today, in all its kaleido-scopic multidimensionality, and with all its shifting boundaries and con-tinual tendency toward their fluid transgression, is a worthy subject of postmodern contemplation. "Comparative" and "historical" are not the reifying approaches they are often described as being.

As for the dialogical perspective, the complexity of today's religious and scholarly worlds involves every student of religion in multiple con-versations, with many voices insistent on being heard on their own terms. This situation calls our attention to the question of "voice" in our work. In what contexts do we speak and write, and to whom do we address ourselves? From whom do we expect a response? What real or imagined community of colleagues participates in the discussion around the "table" as we work? How do we take account of our own multiple voices—academic, theological, political, civic—and of the mul-tiple tables round which we sit? I have sometimes been accused of being a boundary-crosser, even a trespasser, moving from the study of the religious life of India to reflections that would more properly be called Christian theology and, more recently, into the study of American reli-gious life. One of the many things I have learned in doing so is the importance of a dialogical perspective: being clear about my own loca-tion, intention, and voice—indeed, voices—both in my writing and teaching. The question of voice is critical in cultivating a dialogical per-spective in the study of religion.

A Comparative Perspective: The Interweaving of Traditions

A comparative perspective is hard to avoid today, for there is no place on earth where religion is simple or singular. Religious people and com-munities dwell in increasingly complex contexts, with political and eco-nomic forces and other religious communities challenging their assump-tions and identities. In the late twentieth century the migration of peoples both as refugees and immigrants has sharpened our awareness that traditions are not isolated from one another, but increasingly and inextricably interrelated. This is our new global, geopolitical, and, I would say, "georeligious" reality. There are mosques in the Bible Belt in Houston, just as there are churches in Muslim Pakistan. There are

Cambodian Buddhists in Boston, Hindus in Moscow, Sikhs in London, Muslims in Paris. Understanding the religious life of any city or region, or any religious community, inevitably involves the scholar in the study of religion in its multiplicity. This very multiplicity is one meaning of "comparative" study, for no tradition or community stands alone, but lives in the force-field of others. And no tradition or community speaks with a single voice, but contains its own inner disputations and multiple perspectives.

In the past three decades, the immigration of peoples has changed the religious demography of the world, creating a level of cultural interpenetration unprecedented in human history. On every continent there are complex "world cities" like Los Angeles, a city with a Latino population so large that it has been called a "Latino subcontinent" and with an Asian population that is a microcosm of all Asia, with substantial Chinese, Japanese, Korean, Cambodian, and Vietnamese subcultures, both Christian and Buddhist. Indeed, the range of Buddhist expression in Los Angeles may well make this city the most complex Buddhist city in the entire world. The city also has a strong and vibrant Jewish community, and substantial and vocal Black Christian and Muslim communities. Los Angeles has so many Iranian immigrants it has been called "Irangeles" or "Tehrangeles." And let us not forget the multitude of Christian churches—from the glass and glitter of the Crystal Cathedral to booming, quasi-denominational movements like the Vineyard Fellowship and Calvary Chapel. Like Indra's net of jewels, each linked to and reflecting the others, the religious communities of Los Angeles are each part of the life of a complex multireligious cosmopolis. They share this context, whether they choose to polish their own jewel, ignoring or rejecting the refractions of the others, or whether they choose to explore the meanings of this new multireligious reality.

In addition to transforming cities, migration has also created new universities, like Harvard University, for example, where it is common for Jewish, Christian, and Sikh students to share a rooming suite and where the baccalaureate service has come to include hymns from the Rig Veda and surahs from the Qur'ān. In 1997, this sea-change in Harvard's own demography was signaled publicly when Imam Talal Eid was the "chaplain of the day," offering an opening prayer before more than twenty thousand people at the commencement ceremonies in Harvard Yard. This lively pluralism has also presented new teaching challenges. For those of us who teach religion, the multireligious classroom environment makes vividly clear that there *is* no presumptive normative viewpoint; the language of the "other" is no longer applicable, for we are all other to one another.

These worldwide currents have created a new geography within as well. Our students and colleagues, and indeed we ourselves, may be Christians who read the *Gita*, Jews who sit Buddhist meditation, agnostics who religiously practice yoga. We know that there are immigrant Buddhists in Oklahoma City who keep a Buddha altar at home and go to church on Sundays, that there are Hindus in Louisville with Jewish and Christian sons-in-law. So how do we describe these border-crossings in our midst, in our families, in our minds, in our souls? Speaking as religious persons, how do we describe ourselves to ourselves? As Christian-Buddhists? As Jewish yogis? Speaking as scholars, how do we describe this phenomenon? Do we use terms like syncretism? Hybridization? Mongrelization? *Mestizaje*? Do we speak of conversion? Convergence? Or is it something else?

In short, today there is no way to study or attempt to understand the religious life of any part of the world, certainly our own, by seizing one particular strand and examining its textures, drawing it from the fabric of its cultural weave. The threads, however distinctive, are all woven together. In studying our own century, it is increasingly difficult to compartmentalize our work in customary ways as students of Jewish, Christian, Buddhist, Islamic, or Hindu traditions. To be a student of religion looking at the late-twentieth-century world is to recognize that religious communities do not exist in isolation, but in interrelation with one another, and must be studied in that dynamic interrelation.

If our habits of mind as scholars of religion are difficult to break, the problem is even more difficult when we encounter the new interest in "religion" on the part of colleagues in other fields of study, where the essentializing eye, especially as regards "religion," is still very much at work. In 1994, a prominent American political scientist, Samuel Huntington, described the post–Cold War geopolitical reality as the opposition of "the West and the rest," proposing that "civilizational identity" will have a major role in the coming political realignment.[1] He sees the "Confucian," "Islamic," and "Hindu" worlds as virtually monolithic forces to reckon with in the geopolitical arena and foresees a "clash of civilizations," especially between the "Islamic world" and the West. But in light of the migrations of these past decades, one would have to ask how it is possible to see a world of religiously based civilizational blocs, each based on its own broad consensus. A closer analysis reveals that "the Hindu world" is not only internally complex, but geographically dispersed—in Leicester, Durban, and Pittsburgh. The so-called Islamic world is also multivocal and internally argumentative, and it includes growing communities in Lyon, London, Hong Kong, and Houston. Islam is not a new "bloc," like the Soviet bloc, and it is not somewhere else, on some other part of the globe. Today, Chicago, with nearly seventy mosques and half a million Muslims, is part of the Islamic world.

It is precisely the interpenetration, proximity, and interrelation of ancient civilizations, with both the conflict and the transformation inherent in such proximity, that is the hallmark of the late twentieth century. This is our new "georeligious" reality. The map of the world cannot be color-coded as to its Christian, Muslim, Hindu identity. Each part is marbled with the colors and textures of the whole. Not incidentally, the inner world of much of humankind today inevitably participates in the marbling, mixing, and hybridization of this complex georeligious reality.

It is this new georeligious reality that surrounds and challenges us as scholars of religion today, requiring us to work the wide canvas of comparative studies. And yet we also know that this swirling interpenetration of cultures and religious traditions, while it may be more intense today, is far from historically unprecedented. Indeed the challenge of studying the postmodern world with all its plurality should alert us to the difficulty of studying any historical period as if its religious life could be color-coded, boundaried, and studied in separate units. What about the multiple currents of the Hellenistic world—Greek, Roman, Egyptian, Jewish, Christian? What about the complexity of north India in the second century B.C.E.—Vaishnava and Shaiva, Jain and Buddhist? Or third-century China—Taoist, Confucian, Buddhist? Much of the most important work in religious studies investigates the many ways in which the so-called boundaries of what we have come to call "traditions" or "religions" have been negotiated and re-negotiated. The Indian historian Romila Thapar reminds us of "the tyranny of labels," especially when terms like "Hindus" or "Muslims" are used to suggest monolithic religious identities, eliding the "infinite shades of difference" within each of them and the historical processes by which these terms came to be used.[2] As scholars of religion, we should critically investigate the labels of any religious taxonomy, suspecting that the equivalent of today's Jews practicing Buddhist meditation and today's Christians reading the *Gita* have been there all along.

A Historical Perspective: The Dynamic Change of Traditions

A second feature of the religious world today is the sheer energy of religious change, religious revolution, and religious resurgence: the chaotic revitalization of religious life in the former Soviet Union; the growth of a wide spectrum of Islamic movements, national and global; and the shift of the Christian majority population from the northern to the southern hemisphere. Changes of such consequence and significance remind us that religious traditions are historical, in the sense that they are dynamic movements. Religious traditions cannot be studied as if they were fixed entities that could easily be summarized and categorized, their so-called beliefs and practices catalogued and classified.

We can observe this dynamism right before our eyes in the United States. In the past decade, for example, an African American woman was consecrated an Episcopal bishop in Boston, an event that would have been unthinkable to the Anglican builders of Old North Church only two centuries ago, and the Central Conference of American Rabbis voted to support marriage for gays and lesbians, a move that would have astonished most American Jews even a generation ago. Also in the past decade, American Muslims have developed a fully American infrastructure, with annual conventions, public affairs organizations, youth summer camps, and Islamic leadership workshops, while American Hindu communities have formed temple societies, applied to the IRS for non-profit status, and raised the funds for dramatic new Hindu temples in the suburbs of Nashville, Atlanta, Cleveland, and dozens of other American cities.

The emergence of a distinctively American Buddhism is another dramatic new development. For the first time in history, Buddhist teaching lineages have crossed the Pacific Ocean, transmitted from Asian-born teachers such as the Korean Zen Master Seung Su Nim, the Japanese teacher Maezumi Roshi, and the Tibetan Chogyam Trungpa Rinpoche to American-born students who are now shaping a new American Buddhism. What will this new Buddhism become, with its distinctive psychological vocabulary, its focus on meditation practice, its move from monasticism to lay leadership, its prominent women teachers, and its absorption into American popular culture?

Some scholarly critics may insist that the teaching and practice popularized by American Dharma teachers and published each year in increasing numbers of popular books are not "Buddhism." But what if these scholars had been in China in the fourth century when the *Vi-*

malakirti Sutra became popular, reorienting monastic Buddhism toward the piety and wisdom of the laity? In a culture built upon Confucian traditions of family and filial piety, the Buddhist monk's renunciation of family had little popular appeal. But were the new lay-oriented traditions really "Buddhism"? And what if there had been scholarly observers in Japan when the devotional Jodo Shinshu movement began? Was this wholehearted devotion to Amida Buddha really "Buddhism"?

Again, an analysis of our present situation makes clear a broader principle of the study of religion: that the religious traditions we study are not boxes of texts, commentaries, and interpretations passed from hand to hand through the generations, but dynamic traditions, more like rivers, gushing, rolling, converging, branching out to water and transform new lands, or sometimes dying out completely in the desert sands. These traditions have always changed, sometimes gradually and sometimes in ways that would be considered quite revolutionary.

Studying "religion," then, is studying traditions and communities in motion. As Wilfred Cantwell Smith demonstrated nearly four decades ago, our English thing-ish noun "religion," which we use all too confidently, is of relatively recent usage and ill-suited to convey the dynamic, complex, historical movements that have come to be called "religions."[3] He suggests we might well abandon the term in favor of the cumulative phrase "religious tradition," a rendering which, he believes, preserves a greater sense of process and change—in relation to other traditions and in response to each era. In any case, the traditions that have come to be called "Christianity," "Buddhism," or "Hinduism" are not "systems" or circumscribed entities to which people "belong," but dynamic movements in which people participate, movements that often include within them vigorous debates and arguments. These movements are not best understood by uncovering their "origins," as interesting as that project may be, for as Smith puts it "time's arrow is pointed the other way." They should be studied in all their historical dynamism, multiplicity, and multivocality.

"Historical" study, in this sense, does not mean, as Max Müller put it, to "take the spade and shovel to see what there is left of old things," but rather to study traditions as dynamic, changing, in process. What has emerged in the course of the history of religious traditions is certainly as significant as what can be discerned of their beginnings—from Siddhartha Gautama to Roshi Bernie Glassman of Yonkers, from St. Paul to Troy Perry of the Metropolitan Community Church. The so-called history of religions is not over, after all, but is evolving before our very eyes. Looking at the dynamic change of today's traditions helps us to remember that the traditions we study were always in motion, transformation, even revolution.

A Dialogical Perspective: Attention to Voice

The geographical interrelation of traditions and the dynamics of religious change make plain both the comparative and historical dimensions of the study of religion today. But there is still more in the late twentieth century that alerts us to new possibilities in the academic study of religion: the heightened awareness that people of every religious tradition have of one another, an awareness that has produced new forms of intense religious chauvinism as well as new forms of interreligious cooperation.

Scholars of religion have rightly paid considerable attention to religious chauvinism and the hardening of religious "boundaries" in new forms of Christian fundamentalism, Hindu nationalism, and Islamist movements. But the bridging of religious communities through a multitude of interreligious movements, though less publicized, has also become a startling new fact of the late twentieth century. Globalization and interdependence in the economic, political, and religious realms today have begun to necessitate new forms of non-hegemonic mutual engagement or "dialogue." Any astute observer of the currents of religious change today must take note of the expansion, even explosion, of the intentional and casual interreligious relations that fall under the phrase "interreligious dialogue"—from formal meetings, to joint workprojects, to discussions over the back fence. These new forms of interreligious dialogue constitute a fascinating focus and field of study for scholars of religion today.

A century ago, the 1893 World's Parliament of Religion in Chicago was introduced by its Chairman John Henry Barrows as "the first school of comparative religion wherein devout men of all faiths may speak for themselves without hindrance, without criticism, and without compromise, and tell what they believe and why they believe it." While the planning and overall spirit of the Parliament still partook generously of universalist and Orientalist thinking, this notion of enabling people to "speak for themselves" did represent something new. The Parliament was all too zealously hailed as "the morning star of the twentieth century," but in one sense, it really was a harbinger. Now, a century later, there are multireligious parliaments and assemblies virtually every year on a variety of topics from human rights to the environment; there is a growing worldwide infrastructure of interreligious networks, such as the World Conference on Religion and Peace; and in the United States there are numerous new urban and suburban interfaith councils where Catholic, Protestant, Jewish, Muslim, Buddhist, Hindu, Jain, and Zoroastrian participants meet on a regular basis.

This new interfaith movement has also produced countless quasi-formal new relationships, such as the high-level liaison between the National Conference of Catholic Bishops and the American Muslim Council, now regularly issuing joint statements on social issues from religious violence to population policy. Theologians and philosophers meet to discuss *kenosis* and *shunyata*, sponsored by the Society for Buddhist-Christian Studies. Christian monastics and contemplatives of the Monastic Interreligious Dialogue arrange long intermonastic exchanges with their Buddhist counterparts. Benedictine monks settle down in Dharamsala, while Tibetan nuns take part in the life of the Benedictine Monastery and Ashram in Sand Springs, Oklahoma. Most important, perhaps, are the countless ways in which ordinary people live and work in daily relationship to their neighbors of other faiths—in offices at the Lotus Corporation, in the dormitory at Ohio State, or in a Dallas PTA meeting.

Some of us in the academic community will certainly study these new forms of encounter, for they are fascinating case-studies in the negotiation of religious difference and religious identities. After all, had we been scholars of religion in India in the 1570s with the opportunity to study the dialogues and disputations that took place in the Emperor Akbar's audience hall, would we not have leaped at the chance to do so? Would it not have been fascinating to hear what Akbar, the Vedantins, and the Jesuits of Goa all had to say to one another? Would we not have learned a great deal about the construction of religious identity from these dialogues? And the same is true today, in ways so prolix and mundane that they may even escape our attention. How do American Catholics and Muslims present themselves to one another? How does a framework of discourse develop among Protestants, Baha'is, Jains, Mormons, and Muslims in, say, the Metropolitan Washington, DC, Interfaith Conference? There is much to research, to observe, to study in these new developments.

But beyond being a subject of study, dialogue is also a method of study. The cultivation of a dialogical perspective, including critical and self-critical awareness, is increasingly important in the academic world. When Lord Curzon, the former Viceroy of India, envisioned the creation of the School of Oriental and African Studies at a conference in London in 1914, he described the institution as "part of the necessary furniture of Empire," where Englishmen could learn what they needed to know in order to rule responsibly and effectively.[4] The accumulation of knowledge about the colonized "other," knowledge that objectified the "other" without listening to the voice of the other, was the hallmark of what has come to be critiqued as Orientalism. Of course, "Orientalists" were no more monolithic than the traditions they attempted to study, define, and comprehend. Nonetheless, it would be fair to say that most paid little serious attention to the location of voice, either their own or that of the "other." Much Orientalist objectification did not hear an authentic voice in response, and the questions posed by the "other" went unheard, questions we now recognize as critical to the clarity of intellectual work. Today, the authority of the Orientalist voice is gone, and moving beyond Orientalism means moving into the methodological terrain of dialogue, a way of working in which both the voices of those we study and the voices of scholars situated in the contexts we study become integral to the process of understanding.[5]

For scholars of religion this means taking seriously the fact that there are people on both sides, all sides, of the process of understanding. Not only are the religious lives, texts, or phenomena we study situated in particular historical, geographical, intellectual, and cultural contexts, but so are we who attempt to understand them. Dialogue is the discipline of thought that enables us to gain clarity about our own situatedness, our own form of questioning our own position—whether methodological, political, religious, secular, even antireligious—so that our own subjectivity, our own language, and our own categories are not privileged and universalized unwittingly in our work. By a "dialogical" method, I do not mean that scholars of religion must participate in what has come to be called "interreligious dialogue," though some may choose to be explicitly involved, as I have. Rather, I mean that the study of religion is itself a form of dialogue involving not only encounter with our subjects of study, but continued reflection on the personal, religious, or intellectual presuppositions that shape the intention and direction of our own study.

I know that the term "dialogue" provokes considerable negative reaction among some scholars who associate it with amiable interfaith roundtables or the quest for religious harmony, which, they would argue, have no place in the academic study of religion. When Fredrich Heiler gave a major address at the 1958 meeting of the International Association for the History of Religion entitled "The History of Religions as a Way to the Unity of Religions," he was criticized as an "enthusiast" and "promoter" who brought "subjective" matters into the study of religion. His critics argued for the "objectivity" of the comparative study of religion, insisting that the promotion of values such as interreligious harmony or peace is always laden with particular theological premises and properly constitutes a form of "theology," as opposed to *Religionswissenschaft*. As Zwi Werblowsky put it in a similar critique of the work of Joachim Wach, the scholar of religion "eliminates his religion from his studies, whatever the 'religious' character of the motives and drives that make him study religion at all."[6]

Today, both sides of the argument that would pit "enthusiasts" against "objective" scholars are quite out of date. As for the so-called enthusiasts, anyone who studies or participates in "interfaith dialogue" in today's world knows that it is not about promoting the unity of religions as much as exploring the rocky terrain of deep differences in a world in which religious difference has been marked by misrepresentation, stereotype, and violent conflict. In any case, dialogue today is not a roundtable or a conference that scholars "promote," the implication being that if they did not promote it, it would not happen. Dialogue is already happening, under its own steam, in a multitude of ways, all over the world. And it will go on happening whether or not scholars study it, participate in it, provide leadership for it, or take no note of it at all.

On the other side, the so-called scientific study of religion and its notions of purely "objective" scholarship with no authorial viewpoint is increasingly understood to be intellectually naïve. As scholars such as Wilfred Cantwell Smith and Veena Das have repeatedly made clear, even the most "secular" of social scientists write out of a set of premises and to a community of readers, both of which invite investigation and critique. The hermeneutical discussion has advanced markedly in the comparative study of religion, in part because of much more extensive contacts among scholars from different cultures and traditions. Those of us from the West who study the Hindu tradition have friends and colleagues who are devout Hindus or who are Hindu scholars working critically on their own tradition and responding to our work. Most of us now have students who are Hindus, many of them undertaking the disciplined study of their own tradition, for the first time, under our guidance. So the issue of who "we" are as scholars of India's religious traditions, how we position ourselves in relation to our work, is not only our question, but legitimately theirs.

The burgeoning interreligious dialogue movement provides a context for thinking about dialogical method, though its purpose is distinct from that of the academic study of religion. As method, the ability to situate our own voice and viewpoint in one or another conversation or disputation is intellectually obligatory—whether we are "religious" or not, secular or not, feminist or not, Marxist or not. The mutuality and critical awareness that shape the give-and-take of dialogue are the very investigative tools that enable us to become more sharply aware of our own consciousness, ethics, and voice as scholars.

For those of us in the West who study the traditions of Asia there is no move beyond the authorial presumption of the Orientalist voice except a dialogical move. The scholarly community of conversation in which we participate is worldwide, with many voices engaged in discussion and mutual critique. Scholars whose traditions we, as Western academics, study are leading voices in the discussion. We respond to them and they to us. We in the largely English-speaking North American academy find that our questions are often the wrong questions, our methods in constant need of adjustment, our language and lexicon of scholarship inadequate to the traditions we study. We not only ask questions, we are ourselves interrogated. We are challenged and critiqued. In a postcolonial, post-Orientalist world, those of us who are Western academics know full well that there are people on all sides of the scholarly conversation: subaltern, secular, and pluralist; Hindu, Christian, and Muslim; American, European, and Indian. Therefore, to give a careful account of how we situate ourselves in the discussion is increasingly incumbent upon us all. A dialogical approach requires one important thing: our presence, our critically self-conscious presence in our work, interrogating our own viewpoint lest we become merely political or polemical.

Multiple Contexts, Multiple Voices

"Voice" includes the whole range of vocabulary, nuance, rhetoric, revelation, intention, reference, and authority that shapes the ways in which we speak or write in particular contexts. Our "voice" is always situated in a particular conversation, whether academic, theological, or public.

In the academy, we may speak of these conversations as discourses, a broad and polite word for these contexts of conversation which are often disputations, even heated arguments. Whether conversation or argument, discourse or disputation, each context of discussion has its own story or mythos, its own canons of authority, its own forms of evidence. Recognizing the multiplicity of our own voices as participants in multiple conversations is part of the challenge of teaching and writing.

For example, as a student of the religious traditions of India my voice is engaged with those of other scholars in this field, both textual scholars and fieldworkers—American, European, and Indian. In making a point or writing a paper, I cite the work of colleagues, I refer to Sanskrit textual sources. As a Christian thinker, I contribute to another related but very different conversation, more aptly an argument: the worldwide Christian argument about the relation of Christianity to other religious traditions. Here the authority to which I turn, the force and direction of my speaking and writing, the audience to whom I address myself is distinctively Christian. I will certainly be overheard by colleagues in Indian studies, but I have clearly signaled a different set of conversation partners. In making arguments, I cite Christian theological interpreters, I appeal to Christian scriptural sources. As a citizen, I find myself increasingly involved in public discussion on the role of religion in American life, and turn for authority not to my own scriptures, nor to the views of the religious traditions I study, but to the canons and covenants of citizenship. The conversation is likely to include Madison or de Tocqueville, Justice Scalia or Justice Brennan, the Constitution, and the Bill of Rights.

This is a simplified illustration of an important principle: whenever I write or speak, I must be clear about which argument I am currently participating in, which disputation or conversation I am involved in, for all of us are involved in many. We are, as my colleague Michael Sandel has put it, "multiply situated selves." We speak and write in multiple contexts—religious, academic, civic, familial. Recognizing this is what being aware of "voice" means. As teachers and writers, we must work to discern clearly the distinctive voices we ourselves speak; and when we shift lanes, we are obliged to use a turn signal.

We shift lanes all the time and adjust our voices accordingly. My voice is not the same in the discourse of a discussion group at Harvard-Epworth United Methodist Church, in the discourse of a meeting of the Faculty of Arts and Sciences at Harvard, in the discussion of a thesis prospectus with colleagues in Indian Studies, in conversations with Hindus in a hilltop temple in Madhya Pradesh, in meetings with Muslim leaders in Indiana, in a multireligious board meeting of the World Conference on Religion and Peace, and in a caucus of gay and lesbian faculty members. The rules of the road require the nuanced, often subtle, signals that indicate the particular voice I bring to a conversation or disputation. Being aware of "voice" means, likewise, being aware of the contexts of both my speech and my silences, as I decide whether or not to speak openly as a lesbian woman in professional conversations with Christian, Jewish, or Muslim leaders, for example, or whether or not to articulate an explicitly Christian response to a Jewish student's classroom question on Christian anti-Semitism. For multiply situated selves, voice is a matter of continual negotiation.

Voice has been an important issue for me in my writing as someone committed to a dialogical framework for comparative study. I began my academic work in religion as a student of the religious traditions of India. My first major project was a study of the city of Banaras, which I eventually published as *Banaras, City of Light* (1982). It was both a textual and contextual study of what that city has meant to Hindus for whom it has been so important for so many hundreds of years. I studied its multitude of Sanskrit texts, some of them a thousand years old; its Hindi texts, many of them the ephemera, the pamphlets published virtually yesterday; the text of the city itself, with its temples, ancient and modern; and the subtexts of its controversies and its interpreters, yesterday and today.

In the course of that work, I spent many months visiting temples, listening to Hindus talk about their religious life, learning as much as I could from pandits and pilgrims, asking in one way or another what this all means to Hindus. When Banarsi scholars from both the university and the city met to talk about my book one searing July day two years after it had been published, the thing I found most interesting was their astonishment that this book about a city so familiar to them had been written by an American scholar, not by a Hindu.[7] I realized that no Hindu would have written the book, organized the material, or used the interpretive voice that I used, and yet it was possible in that scholarly voice to articulate an understanding of Hindu religious life that Hindus themselves would recognize and find illuminating. Some Indian scholars would disagree with aspects of my work. They would say I listened to too many brahmins or put too much stock in Sanskrit Puranas, but even those who disagreed recognized that we were at the same table, so to speak, involved in the same argument.

I learned something else from the dialogical process of my work in India: that the scholarly lexicon I brought with me, including words many of us use quite readily as students of religion, was in need of revision. The terms "pilgrimage place" or "sacred place" do not have the same resonance as the term *tirtha*, "a ford, a crossing place." The terms "image" and "icon" were not quite adequate to convey the meanings of *murti* or *vigraha*, which imply a sense of divine embodiment. "Worship" overlapped only slightly with the semantic field of *darshan*, which meant something more like "seeing" or "beholding." I had the term "mysticism" in my lexicon, but what did that term refer to in this context: the interior journey of the yogi? The dialectical practice of *tantra*? The devotional songs of the *bhaktas*? The intellectual dialogue generated by immersion in another world of reference sets a challenging agenda for the historical, comparative, and dialogical study of religion. It also affects our voice as scholars: whether we use our language as if its meanings were obvious, or whether we pause to reflect on its analogical or problematic nature. Today we can reconstruct a vocabulary adequate to the study of religion only by scrupulous attention to the primary dialogical process of translation.

As a student of India, I also had another set of questions that many of my Western colleagues did not share. For me, however, they were critical questions, for I am not only a scholar, I am also a Christian, thinking about my own faith as I study Hinduism, reading the Bible by the Ganges, so to speak. I not only visit Hindu temples, but occasionally pray in them; I not only study with Hindu teachers, but touch their feet. What does this all mean? Can I give an honest, reflective, theological account of what it means to be a person of faith, immersed in the study of another tradition, and constantly engaged in the inner dialogue such study seems to require of me? And so I wrote another book—a very different book—addressed not to my colleagues in the academy, but to Christians who in one way or another have wrestled with these questions. *Encountering God: A Spiritual Journey from Bozeman to Banaras* (1993) explores a very different terrain than *Banaras, City of Light*. Here I ask not what Banaras means for Hindus, but what Banaras means to me; not what the intellectual dialogue of comparative study means for the study of religion, but what it means to the shape and language of my own faith. The disputation I enter here is about Christian theology and is an attempt to recast and articulate a pluralist Christian theological position shaped by the dialogical encounter with people of other faiths. It is a theology "with people in it," and one of those people is myself.

Every scholar of religion can supply personal examples of the count-less and complex ways in which religious, ethical, political, or intellec-tual commitments shape his or her research and teaching. What topics do we choose for our life's work? What do we decide to write or to teach? What do we assign students to read, and how do we navigate our way through the semester? Above all, how do we render an account of these choices to our readers and our students? It is this accountability that forces us to reflect in a more sustained and explicit way on the question of voice in our work—the many voices articulated and sub-merged in the societies and communities in which we live, the many voices articulated and struggling for articulation within the academy, and the many voices spoken and silent within ourselves.

Voice is always personal, but never merely personal. In articulating where we have come from, what questions have driven us, what we have learned, and what has changed us, we are not transgressors who muddy the otherwise clear waters of scholarly inquiry. We are rather developing our capacity to observe and name the various currents that already shape our lives and our work. In doing so we bring a more critical clarity to our intellectual encounter with people and scholars of other traditions. It is my contention here that becoming more self-conscious of the mul-tiple voices we inevitably have as scholars, as people of faith, as citizens, or as activists is essential to the truthfulness of our writing and teaching, and that encouraging students to recognize and become critically aware of their own multiple voices is part of the task of education. It is the submerged voices—unidentified, unacknowledged, unspoken—not the vocalized ones, that distort and impoverish the integrity of the academic enterprise.

Attention to voice is most certainly not a matter of being "confes-sional," somehow inappropriately personal in a public place. It is, rather, an important intellectual matter, recognizing that there is a per-son on both sides of the dialogical, deliberative conversation we call learning. To understand and begin to articulate someone else's point of view, someone else's worldview, requires that we understand and begin to articulate our own. But this is not a sequential process, as many educational critics like Allan Bloom and advocates of the "Western canon" have suggested, stressing the urgency of studying the classics of our "own" culture before tackling those of "other" cultures. As Charles Taylor has argued and as all of us who are teachers well know, under-standing is not sequential, as if we must learn "this" before we learn "that," but dialogical.[8] It is precisely the dialogue with what is "other" or "different" that begins to make us more aware of and interested in what we ourselves presuppose and take to be normative. And in America's fast-changing multicultural and multireligious context, the question of what "we" mean when we say "we," and how "our own" and "other" are constructed is high on the agenda of educational, public, and religious institutions.

Both as a pedagogy and a methodology of comparative study, cultivating a dialogical perspective involves the discipline of listening, learning, interacting with the "other" in a way careful and sustained enough to be able to see, and even to articulate, the other's point of view—both the others who are before us and the others whose multiple voices speak within us. As J. L. Mehta, an Indian philosopher of religion, has put it, "True dialogue . . . is a questioning of each other and it never leaves us where we were before, either in respect of our understanding of the other or of ourselves."[9] Gradually we become bilingual or multilingual, able to articulate the point of view of others accurately and sympathetically, and aware of our own shifting positions as scholars shaped by one mode of reasoning or another, or as religious persons involved in or estranged from our communities of faith, or as citizens engaged in or alienated from public affairs.

Taking our situatedness, our presuppositions seriously and attempting to become more clearly aware of them in the process of work; taking our response to what we study seriously; and taking the response of those whom we study seriously, even if we finally disagree with them—all this may seem like common sense. It is what Hannah Arendt refers to as "the soundless solitary dialogue we call 'thinking.' " But it is this dialogical dimension that we must explicitly appropriate, whether soundless and solitary, or vocalized and public.

One of my own teachers, J. L. Mehta (mentioned above), was a Hindu, raised in Banaras, who became fascinated with Heidegger, learned German, wrote on Heidegger, studied Indian philosophy, taught Hindu philosophy at Harvard Divinity School, and worked in his last years on the Rig Veda and the Mahabharata. Speaking of the task of understanding the "other"—that is to say, the West—from the Indian perspective, and of understanding the deep past of his own tradition, he wrote:

> Whether it is the forgotten past of my own traditional heritage or the otherness of a different religious tradition, in each case I am thrown back upon myself, to a reexamination of my own pre-conceptions, to an awareness of my own prejudices and their restrictive influence on my thinking. This to and

fro movement between myself and the other, between my present and the heritage of my past is also part of what is known as the "circle of understanding" which leads to a deepening and widening of my own self-awareness through the corrective circularity of understanding.[10]

Today "comparative studies" require this recognition of dialogical, critical self-consciousness as part of our fundamental scholarly apparatus. Such a dialogical model reshapes the very character of our investigation, constantly forming and transforming our categories of analysis, our language of interpretation, and our awareness of our own prejudices and their restrictive influence on our thinking. Comparison is a dialogical form of thinking and working in relationship. Like all thinking, like all relationships, it requires, above all, our attentive and constant presence.

Notes

1. Samuel Huntington, *The Clash of Civilizations and the Remaking of World Order* (New York: Simon and Schuster, 1996).

2. Romila Thapar, *The Tyranny of Labels* (New Delhi: Zakir Husain College, 1996).

3. Wilfred Cantwell Smith, *The Meaning and End of Religion* (New York: Macmillan, 1963).

4. Edward Said, *Orientalism* (New York: Vintage Books, 1979), p. 214.

5. Veena Das's article, "The Anthropological Discourse on India: Reason and Its Other," in *Assessing Cultural Anthropology*, ed. Robert Borowsky (New York: McGraw-Hill, 1994), is a response to Louis Dumont's work, aiming at providing space for a dialogue she finds to be absent in Dumont's way of working. She sees three kinds of dialogues composing the ethnographic text on India: "that with the Western traditions of scholarship in the discipline; with the Indian sociologists and anthropologists; and with the 'informant' whose voice is present either in the form of information obtained in the field or as the written texts of the tradition. It is the interrelationship between these dialogues that provides the methods for our understanding of the anthropological text."

6. The discussion about personal involvement and religious commitment in relation to the "science of religion" is summarized in Eric J. Sharpe, *Comparative Religion: A History* (New York: Charles Scribner's Sons, 1975). The chapter is called "Twenty Years of International Debate," and Werblowsky's contribution to this discussion is cited on p. 276.

7. The context here was an award ceremony held in July of 1984 on the occasion of Vyasa Purnima under the auspices of Maharaja Vibhuti Narayan Singh to present the Rai Krishna Das Prize of the Hanuman Samsthan of Calcutta.

8. Charles Taylor, *Multiculturalism and "The politics of recognition": an essay* (Princeton: Princeton University Press, 1992).

9. J. L. Mehta, "Problems of Intercultural Understanding in University Studies of Religion," in *India and the West: The Problem of Understanding* (Chico, CA: Scholars Press, 1985), p. 122.

10. J. L. Mehta, "Problems of Understanding," unpublished lecture, Harvard University Summer Institute, 13 June 1988, p. 3. These topics are also taken up in the series of essays in *India and the West* and in *Philosophy and Religion: Essays in Interpretation* (New Delhi: Mimshiram Manoharial, 1990).

Part Three

A REVISED COMPARISON: NEW JUSTIFICATIONS FOR COMPARATIVE STUDY

JUGGLING TORCHES

Why We Still Need Comparative Religion

KIMBERLEY C. PATTON

Is the comparative study of religion obsolete? Should it be? The school rooted in a rich and venerable heritage (Max Müller, James Frazer, Carl Jung, Rudolf Otto, Gerardus van der Leeuw, and many others) perhaps reached its definitive climax in 1959 with *History of Religions: Essays in Methodology*. This collection showcased, among that of others, the work of Joseph Kitagawa, Rafaelle Pettazzoni, Wilfred Cantwell Smith, and Mircea Eliade. In the wake of several decades of critique associated with or inspired by postmodern thought, including deconstructionism, comparative religion now often finds itself on the sidelines, dismissed by scholars both within and outside the discipline. Until now, there have been few serious, organized responses to the impact of postmodern thought upon the comparative study of religion.

For a number of years, comparative method in the study of religion has been under fire so heavy that there are very few of us left standing. Those who cling gasping to the spars are often unwilling to compare religious phenomena, theologies, or artifacts outside of footnotes or less heavily policed "epilogues." With philosophical roots in neo-Kantianism and Nietzsche, the largely European postwar doctrines of the past few decades insist on a kind of cultural incommensurability, on the hopelessness of any project of translation, and above all, on the "totalizing" intent and effect of any analysis that—by juxtaposing un-historically related phenomena, even playfully—strays beyond the strictly contextual boundaries of the local, the corporal, or, ironically, the "transgressive." Can we ever "see" religions in relation to one another? Do postmodernism's claims render any comparison in religious studies a form of distortion—obsolete, irresponsible; in other words, is the method a philosophical and epistemological impossibility?

Rightly or wrongly, comparison in our field used to be an unproblematic affair, roughly following the spirit of one of two models established by linguistics. As classicist Gregory Nagy explains in a recent study on the performative values of ancient poetry, "[C]omparative . . . in linguistics can be used in two senses, the one more specific and the other more general. [In the first,] . . . comparison entails the study of cognate forms and meanings within the discipline of historical linguistics. The second sense is more general, referring to the study of typological parallels, that is, of analogies between historically unrelated languages. While the establishing of cognates or borrowings is a matter of empirically proving a historical connection between the languages compared, the adducing of typological parallels need not be taken as proof for a given argument, but only as an intuitive reinforcement."[1]

But it is this "intuitive reinforcement" that has become so deeply problematic. Two previously undisputed (and central) players in the old comparativism are dispatched by postmodernism: object (the constructed transcendent or divine Self, God's Self [or gods' selves]) and subject (the constructing scholarly self). This exile has resulted, as David Tracy has written, in "the unreality of the modern subjects' self-understanding as grounded in itself."[2] The unreality of the divine object, once only a premise of anthropology and sociology, was surely also Durkheim's starting premise, and that of his countless intellectual heirs. It is now taken so much for granted in the study of religion as to go virtually unchallenged.

We will return to the latter below. The former charge, the unreality of the modern subject—or at least of its ability to be in any way objective—finds many permutations in our field, a number of which were anticipated by Jonathan Z. Smith in the volume *Imagining Religion: From Babylon to Jonestown*.[3] In the second chapter of that volume, "In Comparison a Magic Dwells," reprinted as our "Prologue," Smith argues that the act of comparison, which he remarks *"has been chiefly an affair of the recollection of similarity* [italics Smith's],"[4] is best revealed by the Frazerian typology of homeopathic magic. *"The chief explanation for the significance of comparison has been contiguity* [italics Smith's],"[5] the Frazerian description of the foundation for contagious magic.

While Smith is scarcely a postmodernist, grounded as he is in the history of Judaism and ancient Near Eastern civilizations, in anthropology, linguistics and, from college days on, deeply and persistently involved in the problematics of taxonomy, his exposition of the genre of comparison here is by all means an act of deconstruction. Furthermore, he shares the strong postmodern preference for difference over sameness, and its assumption that whereas the former is "real," the latter is "imagined" and exists only in the mind of the beholder. Since it often refuses to acknowledge itself simply as a useful scholarly fiction or language game, comparison is indicted by Smith for so often insisting that it can tell us how religious things "are"—suggesting or ascribing to such things an imagined common ancestry or matrix and "proving" (insinuating) that they "are" similar. In other words, comparative studies of religions are guilty of not strictly confining themselves to either of the two senses of comparison Nagy describes, but conflating them, working "backwards" from intuitive juxtapositions to imagined and unsubstantiated cognate ones. The mental act of comparison is historically revealed, according to Smith, as "the recollection of similarity . . . projected *as an objective connection* [italics mine] through some theory of influence, diffusion, borrowing, or the like, . . . a process of working from a psychological association to an historical one, . . . but this is not science but magic."[6]

In *Drudgery Divine*, drawing again from the vocabulary of biological taxonomy, Smith strongly values modes of comparison that are analogous over those that are over homologous. Analogous (or, in zoological terms, "homoplastic") relationships demonstrate some aspect of correspondence between things otherwise dissimilar: organs, or aspects of religious traditions that share the same specific function but emphatically not the same evolutionary origin. On the other hand, homologous ("homogenetic") relationships in zoology reveal a "real" correspondence in the structure of organs of different species that is due to a shared evolutionary origin: for example, the flippers of a seal and the arms of a human being. Homologous comparison in the study of religion, Smith has said repeatedly, is deeply to be mistrusted *because of the implicit, even if often occult, idea of a shared evolutionary origin.*

Now for the divine or consecrated "object" of comparative inquiry. Beyond the current allergy to comparison seems to dwell a deep suspicion of the assertion of similarity, as Smith makes clear. And when difference and *différance* compel so strongly, beyond the rejection of similarity or organizing pattern looms the specter of the now forsaken universal transcendent, the category of the "sacred." Like the slightest trace of arsenic in a punchbowl, any whiff of metaphysic, any attempt to re-couple the divorced religious signifier and its signified, any suggestion that each of the manifold forms of religious experience uniquely reveal a face of reality—"real" reality, not just the clichéd but ever popular "social construction of reality"—is met with alarm, or far more commonly, derision.

Consider the published self-description of the religion department at the University of North Carolina at Chapel Hill: "Today the History of Religions seriously questions the search for universals, and, especially, the tendency to find commonality at the expense of particularity. The field now generally assumes that universal patterns do not exist outside of concrete historical 'texts' (here a 'text' can mean a written document, an action, or an artifact)." The description then goes on to say that as a curious exception, the department *can* and is willing to support comparative work on mystical traditions, as though mysticism alone were able to liberate itself from historical context.

I recall an even more damning exchange a few years ago with one of my brightest former master's students, now pursuing doctoral work at a leading graduate program in New Testament at an Ivy League school. "I suppose that comparative religion is looked down upon in your department," I ventured. "Yeah," she agreed. "Well, I guess it's OK for undergraduate courses." I was too stunned to remind her that three years earlier she'd thrown herself without a whimper into my unabashedly comparative graduate course on the veneration of relics in ancient Greek hero cult, late Imperial Christianity, Shī'ite Islam, and Mahāyāna Buddhism. At the time, I had heard no complaints about the course being too remedial. Here, of course, is the facile equation of "comparative religion" with "generalization," the latter having been rejected in favor of area studies. That such a move might not have been completely felicitous—that there are attendant, and unacknowledged dangers therein, most importantly that of interpretive myopia—needs to be said.

In 1995, Benjamin Ray and I conceived of this volume as a forum for comparative religionists to consider the premises of postmodern thought as it has played itself out in our field. We encouraged panelists at two successive annual meetings of the American Academy of Religion to reflect on how they have salvaged comparative method from the wreckage of the great school of thought that produced *The History of Religions,* and how they employ comparison as a useful tool within their own special disciplines. Other comparative scholars later contributed additional essays on the problem.

Why and how is comparison still valuable? They argue that while comparative religion must come to terms with its past, it can be contextualized and refashioned so as to yield significant insight into particular aspects of religious ideas and practices, while still recognizing that comparison is the scholar's invention. Their work challenges certain of postmodernism's own generalizations; for example, the attempt of some postmodern scholars to reduce indigenous categories of experience to Western notions of "power" and "gender" has in fact often covered up and misrepresented a rich texture of cultural difference and individual perspective at the local level. The contributors to this volume argue that scholars can risk positing a comparative framework, not to reach closure in service of a particular theory, nor to achieve moral judgment or gain intellectual control over the "other," but to empower mutual dialogue and the quest for understanding.

The Gods Who Pour Sacrifice

My own comparative initiation was presided over by some three hundred fifth-century Attic Greek vases now in Athens, Rhodes, Berlin, London, Boston, and elsewhere, that caught my puzzled attention in 1985 and did not release me for seven years. These vases depicted Olympian gods, including Zeus, pouring libations at altars, burning incense, or even sacrificing animals. I spent those years trying to understand how those pots wanted to be read when they were originally, to borrow a term from Eastern Orthodox Christian iconography, "written."

After I had compiled my exhaustive catalogue and gingerly lifted, turned, scrutinized, sketched, and photographed scores of those feather-light, hollow vases created twenty-five hundred years ago, I was still no closer to knowing why Athena or Poseidon would offer libations. It occurred to me that the explanations of previous scholars who had looked no further than the ancient Greek religious imagination failed to account not only for the data, but also for the paradox it implied. Although I had been trained in classical religion and archaeology, my primary methodological grounding, and the one that interested me the most, was comparative—in the ideas of, among others, Wilfred Cantwell Smith, Huston Smith, John Carman, and Diana Eck. Therefore I thought I might shop elsewhere for some light on the subject, perhaps a historical connection or a phenomenological parallel.

When I did this, the curtain rose on a universe of ritualizing deities:

the Vedic gods who not only sacrifice Puruṣa to create the world, but even "sacrificed to sacrifice with sacrifice" (*Ṛg Veda* 10.90); Odin who hangs from the World-Tree as his gallows in the twelfth-century Icelandic *Hávamál* ("Hymn of the Lofty One"), having pierced himself with his own spear in the same manner that animals were hanged on tree limbs to Odin; Mayan gods who perform acts of ritual blood-letting on their own bodies, just like their adherents below; Buddhas who circumambulate the stupas of previous Buddhas; in first-century Christian tradition, a God who ordains the immolation of His own first-born son, beloved like Isaac or the daughter of Jephtha; God and His angels performing intercessory prayer for the Prophet in Sura 33 of the Qur'ān; in the Babylonian Talmud, a Lord who wears *tefillin* and *tallit*, studies Torah three hours each day, offers a heartfelt prayer that His mercy might overcome His justice—and bathes in a *mikveh* to purify himself after burying Moses: a *mikveh* not of water, but of fire.

The concept that I developed to unlock this problem, so surprisingly angst-ridden, particularly in scholarship on the monotheistic traditions, was that of "divine reflexivity." In a nutshell, I came to the conclusion that the standard question, "To whom do the gods sacrifice?" (or pray, or burn incense) is irrelevant in that, like so much recent scholarship in our field, it applies human categories to divine subjects. From the standpoint of the traditions themselves, the phenomenon is best understood as an expression of original divine essence and power. I thought that ancient Greek iconography cast the divine as the source of cult, rather than exclusively as its object. Thus cultic activity, just like cultic paraphernalia, might be thought of as divine attribute.

Was I right? Recalling the Northwestern native American who, when he was asked by the relative logician whether, if black spider and red deer always eat together, and black spider was eating yesterday, red deer was therefore *also* eating: "I don't know; I wasn't there." I didn't live in fifth-century Athens near the gates of the Kerameikos where those mighty red and black *kantharoi* and *hydriai* were being thrown and painted. And I don't know what those who threw and painted and bought and sold them, who dedicated them in temples and buried them with their dead in Attica and Beoetia and Agrigentum and Tarquinia thought they meant. To me, this idea of divine reflexivity—more than any other—seems most thoroughly to explain why the Greek gods pour libations at altars, particularly since on closer inspection one discovers that on the vases *only* Aphrodite burns incense, a key feature of her own cult—*only* Apollo, avatar of Delphic purity, washes his hands in the *perrirhanterion* or lustral basin—*only* Dionysos tears animals limb from limb in the Dionysiac act of *sparagmos*. Would such a theory have emerged had I not encountered the category of ritualizing god refracted in so many traditions? Absolutely not.

When I surfaced from my doctoral work, I got an ugly shock. Comparative religion, once a viable and even a respectable way to approach intractable problems like that of my libation-pouring gods, was held in abject disregard.

How did this come about and what does it mean? I want to consider three key philosophical moves made under the postmodern aegis, to remark on how these have been applied in our own discipline, and most of all to complain about how these premises are so seldom challenged or even discussed in light of their ongoing erosion of the respectability of comparative religion. It seems to me that these three in particular have had insidiously distorting scholarly consequences.

"Comparison Kills": The Historical Situation of Postmodernism

The first of these premises has to do with the intellectual act of comparison itself, which, as Lawrence Sullivan observes in this volume, seems to be a basic neurological function. Sullivan suggests that human experience itself is inherently comparative. However, a kind of murderous intentionality has been attached to comparative thinking. Critical language often charges extremity, destruction, or even obliteration of the matrix from which the compared object is "lifted."

What has happened is that the semiotic enterprise has collapsed. Thought structures such as "myth" or "grammar" by the power of which, as Thomas Docherty notes, a barrage of signs were "decoded" and discerned equivalences used to mediate or translate ostensible differences, have come under attack.[7] Adorno and Horkheimer, for example, declare, "Bourgeois society is ruled by equivalence. It makes the dissimilar comparable by reducing it to abstract qualities. . . . Abstraction, the toll of enlightenment, treats its objects as did fate, the notion of which it rejects: it liquidates them."[8]

The first postmodern premise, then, is that (ironically building on the taxonomic analogy) comparison kills before it even begins. I vividly remember the controlled outburst of a Reformation historian who was leading an AAR Teaching Workshop for junior religion faculty at which our assignment was to develop a new course. When I described a comparative course I hoped to introduce at Harvard Divinity School for master's students in divinity, mostly future Protestant ministers, on the variety of ways around the globe in which religious authority has been understood and transmitted, he began to fume. "But that's like my taking sixteen different birds and hacking out their livers and laying them out in a row!" he said. "All you end up with is sixteen dead birds!"

Never mind that I had not proposed anywhere near sixteen traditions in my syllabus. I've noticed that the simultaneous juxtaposition of any more than two religious traditions usually offends the newly drawn—and increasingly balkanized—lines of area study. Never mind that I could not imagine how deploying a common taxonomic category could "kill" its originating "birds," given that features of the birds themselves had suggested and generated the organizing idea. The category (religious authority) would obviously not only refract light differently in different religious and historical contexts, but also, as Jonathan Smith remarks in his "Epilogue," would itself also permute and be subject to "rectification" through the process of comparison. A month or so later, I pitifully related the story to my colleague Larry Sullivan and asked what he would have said in answer to this cruel charge. He shook his head. "How," he asked, "did he know that all of the organs were livers?"

It is, I believe, disingenuous to pretend that organizing or "overarching" categories do not exist in a wide range of forms of human knowing and thinking—in this case, the quasi-Platonic Idea of Liver, which although it was not perfectly represented by any one of the organs, nevertheless powerfully would dictate the criteria of *which* organs to select from among the corpses of the poor hypothetical birds. These are indeed "universal patterns . . . outside of concrete universal 'texts' "—not *divorced* from them in their particularity, but nevertheless *more* than them. Michael Polanyi's discussion of the classification of salt crystals proves enlightening here; his point still stands that *a meaningful taxonomic system can be formulated whose categories themselves cannot empirically be demonstrated.*[9]

It is profoundly misleading solely to assign the quality of "equivalence" or the act of abstraction to bourgeois (read dominant) society, to the critical eye that chooses, compares, and allegedly annihilates. If human religiousness did not function in equivalences, much missionary theology would have fallen on deaf ears, rather than in many cases relying so heavily on the translation of new concepts or divine figures into indigenous ones.

If only bourgeois religion scholars thought abstractly about phenomenological categories, a sixteenth-century theological dispute between Portuguese Catholic authorities and devout Sri Lankan Theravadan Buddhists over the authenticity of a relic of the Buddha could never have taken place. Brought to light recently by the Aśoka scholar and Buddhologist John Strong, historical accounts (most notably in the work of Diogo do Couto and Francisco de Souza) recall the capture and public destruction of the miracle-working Buddha's tooth by the viceroy of Goa, Don Constantinto de Bragança, during his invasion of Jaffna in northern Sri Lanka.[10] At the protest of the archbishop of Goa, who feared the reinstatement of idolatry, ransom attempts by the king of Pegu in Burma failed. The relic was publicly pulverized, burned in a brazier, and thrown into the river. The Sri Lankans responded that what had been destroyed was actually the tooth of an ape, a relic of Hanuman—a "folk" relic rather than the real Buddha's tooth. A number of others said the real tooth had been hidden till the end of time; some eventually claimed possession, such as Don Juan Dharmapala, the king of Kotte. Most interesting in the accounts are the testimonies of those who admitted that the true tooth had been captured, but since the remains of the Buddha were invulnerable, claimed that "just as it was about to be pulverized in the mortar, it miraculously slipped through the bottom of the vessel, and, passing through the earth itself, reemerged on a lotus blossom in its shrine in Kandy."[11] A real relic of the Enlightened One would have been unscathed by the fire, hammer, or water just as surely as would the hand of Mary Magdalene in the Loire Valley or the skull of St. Catherine at Mt. Sinai.

Now in this account we have something very interesting. Here, securely situated in global history, are representatives of two historically unrelated religious traditions, communicating with apparently picture-perfect mutual understanding in categories that span the supposedly unintelligible "concrete historical artifacts and beliefs" of their respective cultures. A relic is the venerated, miraculous physical remain of a holy person. Relics heal the sick and convert the heathen. Real relics cannot be destroyed; fake ones can. And so forth. Although the members of one group might be accused of having been Western bourgeoisie, those of the other surely could not. And not a professional comparative religionist in the lot; the discipline did not exist.

Postmodernism may fear "totalizing" for historical, not epistemological reasons. If there remains any doubt that postmodern thought, rooted as it is in the traumatic history of modern Europe, apocalyptically associates the discovery of paradigm or meaning with the pulverizing boot, one need only glance at the concluding paragraph of Jean-François Lyotard's essay, "What Is Postmodernism?" He writes,

> [I]t must be clear that it is our business not to supply reality but to invent allusions to the conceivable which cannot be presented. And it is not to be expected that this task will effect the last reconciliation between language-games (which, under the name of faculties, Kant knew to be separated by a chasm), and that only the transcendental illusion (that of Hegel) can hope to totalize them into a real unity. But Kant also knew that the price to pay for such an illusion is terror. The nineteenth and twentieth centuries have given us as much terror as we can take. We have paid a high enough price for the nostalgias of the whole and the one, for the reconciliation of the concept and the sensible, of the transparent and the communicable experience. Under the general demand for slackening and for appeasement, we can hear the mutterings of the desire for a return of terror, for the realization of the fantasy to seize reality. The answer is: Let us wage war on totality; let us be witnesses to the unpresentable, let us activate the differences and save the honor of the name.[12]

This passage reveals so much about the "situatedness" of postmodernism and its own goals and antigoals that it scarcely needs comment. The logic here is no logic at all; it is traumatized polemic. We can deeply sympathize with its inspiration, but we can also, just as surely, confront its irrational conclusions.

"Religion as Context"

The second postmodern premise I want to consider is the enshrinement of context as an absolute value virtually nullifying all others. This move begins as an attack on the person as independent "subject": "because individuals are both created and circumscribed by their location in the social matrix, the seeming autonomy of the individual is a bourgeois humanistic myth to conceal the social origins of personal experience and the social constitution of the self."[13] It ends, however, with a Cyclopean, monocular focus on social context that gives no quarter to any other constitutive element, in particular the religious construction of reality— *except as disguised social context.* That there can be no escape from this hermeneutical Möbius strip is eventually evident.

Consider, for example, this flyer for a symposium on Paradise Imagery in East Asian Art given on October 20–21, 1995, at Harvard:

Buddhist Art of East Asia has produced dazzling visionary tableaux of paradise. These imaginary configurations in turn have generated curious speculations about their meaning and function in medieval East Asian life and mentality. Rather than seeking answers purely in a set of over-arching and esoteric Buddhist doctrines and abstract teachings, the symposium attempts to place the medieval representations of paradise in local contexts and, consequently, turn matters of religion into more pressing circumstantial concerns of political and social interests.

Note the language here, and note the resonances with Adorno and Horkheimer: what is bad, irresponsible, delusionary is for the student of paradisical scenes to look for hermeneutical value in medieval Buddhist doctrine, characterized as "over-arching, esoteric, abstract." What is good is "placing the representations in local contexts." If we do this, we will be able to reveal "matters of religion" which, the conference flyer implies, are always superimposed from above and never of local interest, as "more pressing circumstantial concerns of political and social interests." Religion, like scholarship, comes from above as a universalizing conspiracy that inevitably distracts from what's "really" happening down here on the ground in a million places. It is inconceivable that an abstract or metaphysical question might itself be of pressing local concern.

Furthermore, when religious evidence is not allowed to present itself comparably or comparatively *except to denote difference*, we are left with only those "windowless monads"—each culture in its own little box: and an oversimplified box at that, as Wendy Doniger points out in this volume, one that often flattens out variations or contestations within the culture itself. This idea leaves us marooned in trying to reflect appropriately on nomadic cultures, such as those of the Central Asian steppes—on the tension between their integrity and their constant intercultural permeability through symbiotic interaction. As David White shows in his book, *Myths of the Dog-Man*, the most intense recombinations in the religious imagination occur and are creatively located between these peoples and the peripheries of "established" civilizations. Nomadic cultures can't be studied "contextually" in the same way that sedentary cultures can, because their context was and is continually shifting.

"Religion as Pretext"

This drastic overemphasis on context is, as we have seen, interlocked with the premise of pretext, the third idea I want to highlight. The pervasive, Foucauldian assumption is that what a religious tradition says it is about, that is, the mediation of the human relationship to the "really real," is not what it is actually about. What it is "actually" (allegedly) about is power—political relationships: who is included, and who is not, and how, and why. Catherine Bell warns, "[T]he deployment of ritualization, consciously or unconsciously, is the deployment of a particular construction of power relationships, a particular relationship of domination, consent, and resistance."[14] But is this all—or always—the story? In his recent book *Icon*, Moshe Barasch complains,

> Modern research on iconoclastic debates and conflicts in western history is indeed oriented mainly towards the "underlying" causes, the motives "behind" the slogans and doctrines that were explicitly claimed in the course of the debates. Many scholars see the great iconoclastic crises in European history essentially as power struggles, and therefore they look for the "true" causes or reasons, to use some of the terms frequently employed. We need not go into methodological discussions . . . in order to see the danger of approaching ideological attitudes—that is, what is explicitly said about icons—as if they were mere pretexts.[15]

"We do not, after all," literary critic Frank Lentricchia observes, "tell economists that economic systems are actually disguised examples of novels, poems, and plays. Yet this is exactly the form of absurdity that the professional study of literature has taken."[16] The same thing has occurred in the study of religion. We hear that the 1692 persecutions in Salem were "really" about seventeenth-century tensions rising from too little arable land or the paralysis of estate subdivision. Or adolescent delusional hysteria. Or ergot poisoning from bad wheat crops. Or anything but worldviews so powerful that they had far more influence on how people thought and acted than did the immediate, perceptible physical world.[17]

Again, this methodological condescension, which seeks to "overwrite" the claims about reality made by those who were or are themselves directly involved in the religious phenomena being considered, is in direct and irreconcilable conflict with the new emphasis on "context." Hence, in the case of Salem Village, the medical historian David Harley carefully insists on a distinction between "demonic possession" and "bewitchment" in the symptomology of the late seventeenth century, and forcefully demonstrates the accepted reality of both:

> Even in bodily disorders, it is often impossible to translate early modern case histories into modern terms. The patient's understanding interacted with the theory of the physician to produce a select list of signs worthy of note. How much more difficult, then, to translate the account of a demonic state into the terminology of disease or neurosis. Such a translation must remove the ideological and interactive elements of the original narrative.[18]

A disease, a neurosis, a "power struggle." If postmodern approaches to the Salem witchcraft episode privilege the socially driven "power" narrative over the narrative *about evil* informing seventeenth-century doctors, sufferers, and accusers, such approaches eviscerate history. They silence those directly involved as effectively as any colonializing overlay. "Historians of witchcraft often assume that their own explanatory theories are not culturally specific," remarks Harley; "[u]nlike the participants, they are engaged in discovering what 'really' happened. This is a condescending assumption that most anthropologists and historians of science or medicine try to avoid."[19] By this he means that they do not assume that their theories must be culturally specific in order to be valuable. One can extrapolate from Harley's point that when cultural worldview is—as it usually is—predicated on belief in otherworldly entities, then such belief cannot be dismissed out of hand as "unreal," or the theories have no explanatory value. "It is necessary to recognize the limits of such realism in order to listen carefully to the views of all the contesting participants."[20]

In the engaging post-panel discussion at the AAR in Philadelphia in 1995, a doctoral student in philosophy at Boston University rose to challenge William Paden's elegant concept of "multiple frameworks" when juxtaposing traditions. The student reminded the panelists and the audience that religious traditions actually make truth claims, and that those metaphysically descriptive claims often jarringly conflict with one another. The idea of simultaneously multiple frameworks, he argued, bracketed something which cannot be ignored: the seemingly obsolete and oh-so-unsophisticated issue of what is true.

Taking Kant's denial of any *direct* access to the noumenal realm to a new depth, postmodernism triumphantly refuses to discern what is real or true.[21] Yet what is at stake for the religious traditions that we study, no matter what their other agendas, and no matter how entrancing we scholars now find the fragmentary, the marginalized, the "transgressive," the grotesque, is nothing less. It is perhaps becoming increasingly more difficult to honor Jonathan Z. Smith's notion of "theory's obligation to be counter-intuitive," since many of us seem to have lost any connection with our own intuition when we think as scholars, and would hesitate to state its position. However, if we maintain a relentlessly closed mind toward the claims of religious traditions to describe what is real or true, how on earth can our descriptions of how they work, however "thick," be authentic? We end up then, as postmodernists insist we must, only talking about ourselves and our own prejudices, victims of a kind of narcissistic epigraphy that poses as methodological sophistication.

In fact, close inspection of allegedly deconstructive moves, especially textual historical ones, often reveals that what the scholar has so triumphantly flushed out as peripheral or subversive is actually in some way absolutely central to the tradition's ontology or self-construction. As an example, consider Robert Kiely's recently published piece, "The Saint's Underwear: A Postmodern Reflection on the Rule and Life of St. Benedict with Help from Gregory the Great and Hildegard of Bingen."[22] Kiely tackles Hildegard of Bingen's midrash on a passage from Benedict's Rule in which she "exposes her anxiety," according to Kiely, by insisting on the importance of monks wearing underwear to avoid sexual arousal. Kiely argues that "Hildegard's letter, however respectful and edifying her intentions may have been, points the way to a deconstructive reading of *The Rule*. . . . Hildegard takes a stitch from an obscure corner of the fabric and lets the whole unravel, if only a little. She does not engage in the kind of punning (with underwear, nakedness, and unraveling) that a Derridean disciple would revel in; nor does she attempt to leave *The Rule* in disarray. She does demonstrate, however, the way language can quite easily (some would say, inevitably) be made to deviate from the normative structure in which it is found. The Hildegardian 'decontruction' does not demolish the text, but, in selecting a marginal or 'hidden' entry point of ambiguity, sensitivity, or seeming triviality, it shows the whole to be less fixed and transparent than it may first have appeared." And finally, "in being so much more explicit about the dangers of naked flesh than Benedict, Hildegard opens a door to the postmodern scholarly fascination with sexuality (. . . especially if found in places where sexual activity is not supposed to take place or be mentioned). . . . Hildegard almost seemed to know that some day postmodern critics would be on the lookout for untraveled territory."[23]

I intend no disrespect toward the work of Professor Kiely, who is a distinguished literary scholar and a devout Catholic. However, the impossibility of an "absolute reader" does not absolve those of us who read, trapped in the present, from trying to discern how what *we* might consider deliciously marginal, hidden, or ambiguous, might in fact have to the author been just the opposite—might have knit up rather than unraveled the fabric of the tradition. It is not only just as likely, but even more likely, that Hildegard warns against a failure by monks to wear underwear because she believed, just as she writes, that such a lapse might lead ultimately to a critical failure in the living out of the monastic vocation, which involves absolute surrender of the earthly passions to God. Then was she instead the victim of a hegemonic ecclesiology, unable to appreciate reflexively the erotico-religious subtext of her own text? Perhaps. But whom have we negated with such a patronizing stance, and on what grounds? Deviance is in the eye of the beholder.

Nevertheless

The varieties of philosophical critiques grouped, however arbitrarily, under the term *postmodernism* have over the past several decades deployed important questions; these questions have been, I think, most acutely felt in the humanities and to some extent in the social sciences. They are not without their validity, nor are they useless in thinking about religion, as some of the essays in this volume reveal. I would maintain, however, that no matter where we want to locate the study of religion, at the level of method alone (not to mention anthropology or theology), it is particularly ill served by a thoroughgoing postmodernist stance. The match is a poor one.

There are myriad reasons for this, but I have tried here to illumine at least three of the most pressing. In the first place, European postmodernism originally emerges as a clearly reactive stance against the fascism and genocidal thinking of its generation. In lifting up the horrors of the Second World War, it often tends as well to reject any thought that occurs on a synthetic or "meta-" level as dangerous, and all "great stories" as potential weapons of the same destruction. By the same token, it wants to elevate the fragment, the margin, the "disconnect," the corporal above the metaphysical. But this is not a neutral token. As a historical product, postmodernism is potentially as fraught with ideological pitfalls as the bourgeois Western thought complexes from which it demands liberation. It is simply not true that abstraction or com-

[handwritten margin note: No total system, but attempts still lead to genuine understanding]

parison, as intellectual processes, lead inevitably to oppression. These processes, on the contrary, are often crucial to culturally nuanced comprehension.

Secondly, since most religious traditions do in fact construe and continually respond to some kind of "totalizing" worldview (that is their very goal!), the postmodern counterembrace of the "local" or "contextual" ("on-the-ground" study of religion) often boils down to nothing more than parochialism. To insinuate that even the remotest lives did not intersect with overarching ideas, cross-culturally shared categories of sanctity, or even numinous entities, must be inaccurate and is most surely unproductive.

Thirdly, we might challenge the rejection of the comparative study of religion on the grounds that it of necessity posits a shared notion of "the sacred," which postmodernism rejects as a socially constructed tool for hierarchical interests. No such assumption can be disproved, of course, but neither can it be proved. We must be very careful when we pretend to "unmask" religious entities as not what they purport to be, not "real." To discount as politically coded "pretexts" the theological, cultic, or philosophical motivations offered by participants themselves in religious phenomena, movements, or controversies, is arrogantly to disenfranchise those we purport to understand.

I used to believe that by trafficking in the study of religion we are playing a game that is purely intellectual, one that will leave us unaffected and free to go about our business. I know it now to be a bit more like juggling torches; either we will mishandle them, and they will burn and wither us, or else our faces will begin to glow. Even if we concede, with Bryan Turner, that "[t]erms, concepts and categories are inextricably meshed in social contexts and institutional arrangements; they can only be extricated from their social settings by great ingenuity and stealth,"[24] the fact remains that it is not a totalitarian—or even a silly— thing to try. Stealth it shall be, and sensitivity, and humility. But not surrender of the whole comparative enterprise just because it is hard to do it right.

Notes

1. Gregory Nagy, *Poetry as Performance: Homer and Beyond* (Cambridge, England: Cambridge University Press, 1996), p. 3.

As examples of each of the senses of the term "comparative," Nagy offers for the more specific sense a comparison of the meters of Song 44 of Sappho with those of Homeric hexameter: "[W]e are dealing with forms that are arguably cognate, that is, derivable from a common source." The more general application of comparison, and the one that interests us as controversial in this essay, is the one that, as Nagy writes, "comes into play if we compare, for example, the conventions of a performer's switching from second person to first person in Song 1 of Sappho with similar conventions in the female initiation songs of Athapascan language groups like the Apache and Navajo. Such a comparison is not a matter of proving something outright, since the ancient Greek and the contemporary Athapascan traditions are obviously unrelated to each other historically. What is achieved, rather, is simply the enhanced likelihood that parallel lines of interpretation might lead to a deeper understanding of the individual traditions being compared."

2. David Tracy, *On Naming the Present: Reflections on God, Hermeneutics, and the Church* (Maryknoll, NY: Orbis Books, 1994), p. 15.

3. Jonathan Z. Smith, *Imagining Religion: From Babylon to Jonestown* (Chicago: University of Chicago Press, 1982).

4. Ibid., p. 21; 25.

5. Ibid.

6. Ibid., p. 22; 26.

7. Thomas Docherty, "Postmodernism: An Introduction," in *Postmodernism: A Reader*, ed. Thomas Docherty (New York and Chichester, West Sussex: Columbia University Press, 1993), p. 9.

8. T. W. Adorno and M. Horkheimer, *Dialectic of Enlightenment*, trans. J. Cumming (London: Verso, 1986), p. 7.

9. See Michael Polanyi, *Personal Knowledge: Towards a Post-Critical Philosophy* (Chicago: University of Chicago Press, 1958), p. 47. Polanyi writes: "A classification is significant if it tells us a great deal about an object once this is identified as belonging to one of its classes. Such a system may be said to classify objects according to their distinctive nature. The distinctiveness of the 230 space groups [underlying three-dimensional atomic plans], like that of the 32 classes of crystal symmetry, rests purely on our appreciation of order; they embody in terms of specific symmetries the claim to universality which we necessarily attach to our personal conceptions of order. Yet this system was supremely vindicated, as was the geometrical theory of crystals in general, by its classificatory functions. It has controlled the collection, description and structural analysis of an immense number of crystalline specimens and has been richly corroborated by the physical and chemical characteristics which are found to distinguish these specimens. It has proved itself a natural classificatory principle. Here stands revealed a system of knowledge of immense value for the understanding of experience." I am indebted to Mark R. Kurtz of Harvard University for this connection.

10. John Strong, "Mortarized Molar or Canonized Canine? Some Reflections on an Episode in the Legendary History of the Buddha's Tooth Relic," unpublished paper, 1994.

11. Strong, "Buddha's Tooth Relic," summarizing the account in Francisco de Souza, *Oriente Conquistado* I:1:82.

12. Jean-François Lyotard, "Answering the Question: What Is Postmodernism?" in *Postmodernism: A Reader*, ed. Docherty, p. 46.

13. Robert Belknap, *Beyond the Great Story: History as Text and Discourse* (Cambridge, MA, and London: The Belknap Press of Harvard University Press, 1995), p. 6.

14. Catherine Bell, *Ritual Theory, Ritual Practice* (New York and Oxford: Oxford University Press, 1992), p. 206.

15. Moshe Barasch, *Icon: Studies in the History of an Idea* (New York: New York University Press, 1992), p. 4.

16. Frank Lentricchia, "Last Will and Testament of an Ex-Literary Critic," *Lingua Franca* 6 (September/October 1996): 64.

17. Some elements of the discussion in the two preceding paragraphs appeared in my article, "Stumbling Along Between the Immensities: Reflections on Teaching Religion," *Journal of the American Academy of Religion* 65 (winter 1997): 831–49.

18. David Harley, "Explaining Salem: Calvinist Psychology and the Diagnosis of Possession," *The American Historical Review* 101 (April 1996): 330.

19. Ibid. Note the similarity to the language of Barasch's independent complaint, above.

20. Ibid.

21. We might do well to meditate on physicist Alan Sokal's learned spoof, published in and at the expense of the journal *Social Text* (Alan D. Sokal, "Transgressing the Boundaries: Toward a Transformative Hermeneutics of Quantum Gravity," *Social Text* 14, nos. 1 and 2 [spring/summer 1996]: 217–52). In his opaquely written piece, bristling with footnotes, Sokal derides "the dogma imposed by the long post-Enlightenment hegemony over the Western intellectual outlook . . . that there exists an external world, whose properties are independent of any individual human being and indeed of humanity as a whole; that these properties are encoded in 'external' physical laws; and that human beings can obtain reliable . . . knowledge of these laws by hewing to the 'objective' procedures and epistemological structures prescribed by the (so-called) scientific method" (217).

In unmasking the sting, in "A Physicist's Experiment with Cultural Studies," *Lingua Franca* 6 (May/June 1996): 62, Sokal remarks that "[a]nyone who believes that the laws of physics are mere social conventions is invited to try transgressing those conventions from the windows of my apartment (I live on the twenty-first floor)." But what about the possibility that religion, which traffics in realities often no more visible that gravity, might be describing laws every bit as inexorable?

The point is that, aspiring social theorists all, we dismiss this possibility with as much cavalier superiority as learned trickster Sokal did gravity. "Perhaps it is time," as Pennsylvania State physicist Lee Smolin urges in response to the Sokal controversy, "to give up the notion that knowledge is 'constructed,' and replace it with the more generous conception that the products of culture are the results of a negotiation with a natural world of which we are a part" (Lee Smolin, letter, *Lingua Franca* 6 [July/August 1996]: 64). Replace the word *natural* in Smolin's remark with *supernatural* and we get an interesting, post-

Kantian working premise, one that might actually get us somewhere when we study world religions.

22. Robert Kiely, "The Saint's Underwear: A Postmodern Reflection on the Rule and Life of St. Benedict with Help from Gregory the Great and Hildegard of Bingen," in *Seeing into the Life of Things: Essays on Literature and Religious Experience*, ed. John L. Mahoney (New York: Fordham University Press, 1998), pp. 111–25.

23. Ibid., pp. 112–14, *passim*.

24. Bryan S. Turner, "Saint and Sheik," in *Weber and Islam: A Critical Study* (London: Routledge & Kegan Paul, 1978), p. 56.

METHODOLOGY, COMPARISONS, AND TRUTH

HUSTON SMITH

On its surface this essay may appear disingenuous if not hypocritical, for I begin by blasting methodology and then proceed with a straight face to describe my own. The discrepancy is more apparent than real, however. There is nothing wrong with methodologies *per se;* short of randomness, we all have our ways of going about things which amount to methodologies in the loosest sense of the word. What I am against is the attempt to extract methodologies that are *ad hoc*, embedded, and mostly subliminal, from their working contexts in the hope that getting straight about what we are up to and how we should proceed will improve our results; the project is sometimes called critical theory. To sharpen a chisel before using it makes good sense, but that model doesn't hold for knowing.

Against Method

Over twenty years ago Paul Feyerabend wrote a landmark book *Against Method*, but he was a philosopher of science, so (with a nod to him for the title of this section) I will develop my own arguments on the subject as they relate to religious studies.

Obviously, we can look at different aspects of religion—its history, its texts, its rituals, its truth claims, and the like. But after targeting which aspect of the subject we propose to study, to obsess over strategies for studying it is a waste of time and worse. For it's not just that it takes time away from *looking* at our subject as we back off and try to figure out *how* to look at it, as if a knowledge of optics could help art critics. More serious is the fact that any method we fix on will be edged by blinders that create tunnel vision. For methods are like the proverbial Zen finger pointing to the moon; they direct our gaze in a given direction. But how do we know that the moon is in the direction that our fingers point? If we need a methodology to determine that, we face an infinite regress, but let that pass. The point is: if our chosen methodology does not point in the right direction, it will divert us from where the pay dirt lies. One could offer pages of illustrations on how (a) the phenomenological method which van der Leeuw adapted from Kant, (b) Bultmann's Heideggerianly derived method for reading the New Testament, (c) Whiteheadianly vectored process theology, (d) deconstruction as fueled by Nietzsche, and (e) the critical-historical method that the Jesus Seminar employs are all, in their several ways, procrustean for *excluding* certain things we should be looking at—by my lights, the most important things. This isn't the place to argue that charge, so I limit myself to a single oblique question about the last in my list. Is the methodology of the Jesus Seminar capable of producing (as a sequel to Robert Funk's *Honest to Jesus*) a responsible book titled *Honest to Christ?* N. T. Wright's *Jesus and the Victory of God* allows for such a sequel, but that is because Wright works (with equal critical competence) outside the Seminar and relativizes its methods.

The subtitle of Walter Capps's recent admirable study, *Religious Studies: The Making of a Discipline,* is instructive here, for it shows that those of us who ply this trade have a dual loyalty. On the one hand we are beholden to our subject, religion, and at the same time (if we are orthodox), we are beholden to the way we study it: our discipline. That way is, in the bulk, an offshoot of the Enlightenment Project with its decidedly secular thrust. Accommodating to that thrust may have been necessary to get us back on campus after higher education went public and became secularized, but we need to be aware of the toll that the accommodation exacts. Using secular tools to interpret sacred materials is not an innocent enterprise. To cite only one indication, most of the giants who shaped the second-order traditions that structure our discipline accepted uncritically the Enlightenment's biological model of history, which links the history of culture to the life-cycle of individuals—the past was the childhood of the human race which has now (in the enlightened West) advanced to maturity. That assessment wipes out religion's key concepts, revelation and transcendence, with a stroke. Some of us may welcome that move; we may actually believe that transcendence and revelation are *passé* and that Max Weber's student and successor, Karl Mannheim, spoke the truth when he insisted that "there is no Beyond; the existing world is not a symbol for the eternal; immediate reality points to nothing beyond itself." So far fair enough. What is not fair either to our subject or to our students—or even by the university's professed commitment to objectivity—is to give our students the impression that our Enlightment-vectored courses show them what religion objectively is.[1] When we think of the way the university puts the finishing touches on the minds of students who go forth to rule America, and add to that the view of religion they derive from our Enlightenment-vectored courses, it is difficult to avoid the conclusion that we are partly responsible for the fact that, as Christopher Lasch pointed out in his final book, in public life today "religion is consistently treated as a source of intellectual and emotional insecurity, not as a challenge to complacency and pride."[2]

Returning to methodology *per se*, the fundamental point is that we always know more than we know how we know it, from which it follows that to channel our knowing through methods we are explicitly aware of restricts our field of vision. We would do well here to take our cue from the noetic experts of our age, the scientists. Abner Shimony, who was my colleague in the philosophy of science while I was at M.I.T., used to say (before Feyerabend said it) that the philosophy of science gives us a hind-end view of that enterprise. Scientists proper don't bother with it; they go streaking out ahead, discovering things right and left, and leave it to philosophers of science to try to figure out how they got there. Obviously scientists have devices for cornering their prey, but they are not fully aware of their strategies and feel no need to understand them before they apply them.

"Me either," I am tempted to exclaim, echoing one of our grandchildren, who meant to say "me too" before her grammatical grids had gelled. I don't recall having given a thought to how I have plied my trade until I was drawn into the discussions of this book. Having been corralled, however, I have to admit that I have found the project interesting. I feel self-conscious talking about myself, but in controversial waters examples help to ground things, so I enter the following brief methodological apologia.

My "Method"

As far back as I can remember I have wanted to know the truth; specifically, the truth about the ultimate nature of things, for how does one know in which direction to move unless one knows the lay of the land? William Sheldon tells us that continued observations in clinical practice reveal that the deepest craving in the human makeup is not for possessions, or sex, or power, but for "knowledge of the right direction—for orientation," and that calls for a map.

In my early, most formative years, the Bible was my map. In college and graduate school philosophy upstaged it for having (in the university's eyes) a wider purview, so I switched from religion (my undergraduate major) to the philosophy of religion. But then the strictures of modern philosophy obtruded—positivism, linguistic philosophy, analytic philosophy, and from the continental side, phenomenology and existentialism. Somewhat later I realized that those strictures derived from the deeper pervasive mindset of modernity, which has progressively lost sight of transcendence because science ("our sacral mode of knowing," Alex Comfort calls it) has no way of accessing it. Quantities science is good at but not qualities, the stuff of which values are made: better and worse, superior and inferior. Several years ago *The Chronicle of Higher Education* packed the consequence into a sentence. "If anything characterizes modernity," it noted, "it is the loss of the sense of transcendence—of a reality that encompasses and surpasses our quotidian affairs."[3]

When these realizations crystalized, I wanted out—out of modernity. So I cut back to the trunk of the tree, the traditional world from which modernity sprang, which I found to be more alive and interesting. Metaphysically more alive and interesting, I must quickly add, for I never fell for the romantic notion that the past as a whole was better than the present. Only its Big Picture—its ontology, its metaphysics, its worldview, religiously speaking, its revelations—is more commodious for being anchored in realities that far exceed the natural world. Naturally the hermeneutics of suspicion forced me to ask if those realities are only projections, but it didn't take much thought to see that most of the rhetoric about humanity's having come of age is shallow bluster. Modernity hasn't uncovered *any facts* that counter transcendence. It has simply turned away from it in the mistaken belief that the scientific worldview is more reliable, as if there could be such a thing as a scientific worldview when it becomes more evident every decade that science deals

science

with only part of the picture, not its whole. "Everything we know about nature," the physicist Henry Stapp writes, "is in accord with the idea that the fundamental process of Nature lies outside space-time."[4]

That's enough for my trajectory; how have I traveled it? Simply stated, by cornering the wisest representative of each of the major religions that I could find—preferably living so I could dialogue with them and receive their *darshan*, but where they had "dropped their bodies," as the Indians say, their writings have served. Then I apprenticed myself to them with all the focus and fervor I could muster. This has led me to say on occasion that I am self-taught in world religions, but all I mean by that is that my most important learning has taken place outside the academy. I know Asia's *ashrams*, monasteries, *khanaqahs*, and *zawiyahs* better than I know its universities. After my parents, the photographs of my principal teachers that line my office include a swami, a zen *roshi*, the Dalai Lama, a Sufi shaikh, a Trappist monk, and a Native American Road man. No professors, though I owe many of them a great deal and feel great affection for several.

Comparisons

It was the charge that religious comparisons are otiose that sparked this book, but it is difficult for me to take that charge seriously. Logically, everything is both like and unlike everything else; it is like everything else because it too exists, and it is unlike everything else or it would not be an individual in its own right. And since the crux of intelligence is the ability to draw distinctions, intelligence has no choice but to traffic in similarities and differences from the word go, and doing that requires comparing. So it cannot be comparing *per se* that is at issue; it has to be certain kinds of comparing, and in the case at hand it is comparing religions and cultures.

I am reminded of Robert Frost's last poetry reading in which he touched on the subject of hate. In the course of that aside he mentioned two things he hated. "I hate it when my books of poetry come to me in mailing jackets stamped 'educational materials,' " he said, "and I hate it when people say to me, 'Stop generalizing,' for that's all I have been doing my entire life." If I change "generalizing" to "comparing," I could say the same, and once more (because concrete cases help to settle the dust) I will turn the spotlight inward and try to ferret out how comparison has entered my work.

The first important time was in graduate school when I compared theology with philosophy and found it wanting. After I got my doctorate and stopped letting my teachers direct my thoughts, I reversed that judgment, and along with it my graduate school opinion that modernity has a better grasp of the Big Picture than our forebears had. Those were blanket comparisons. The first time I can remember comparing religions was when the Vedanta crashed over me and I found its concept of *nirguna Brahman*, "God beyond forms," more commanding than the personal God of Christianity I had been brought up on. Later I discovered that Christianity has its counterpart to *nirguna Brahman* in Eckhart's Godhead, but there is no point in itemizing the series of religious comparisons that followed that first one. I can skip directly to the conclusion of my personal story. Two of my books turned out to deal entirely with comparisons. *Forgotten Truth* presents what religions have in common; *Essays in World Religion* registers their differences. The second shows us what we can learn from others; the first finds at the heart of the world's religions a Truth which, because it is attested to by them all, we can wholeheartedly believe. That both books contain mistakes goes without saying, but I cannot understand how anyone could consider their projects to be misguided.

That has been my personal involvement with comparisons. Their place in religious studies centers in comparative religions, so again I turn to Walter Capps for what he says about that subdiscipline:

> So compelling has comparative religion become that it tends now to pervade religious studies in all of its aspects. It belongs to the context, the framework, of religious studies. It helps define the field's direction and compelling intellectual interests. Indeed, from this time forward, no aspect of religious studies can be thought through systematically—no aspect of religious studies can even be approached—without explicit acknowledgment of its cross-cultural dimensionalities. Already it is impossible to conduct scholarly research in religious studies except within an intellectual framework that treats cross-cultural sensitivities as being regulative.[5]

This strong endorsement of religious comparisons by the leading historian of our field doesn't make it any easier for me to take seriously those who dismiss the enterprise, but they must have something in mind, so what is it? As far as I can make out, they take two important half-truths and turn them into full truths.

First, it is indeed the case that thinking is embedded in cultural-linguistic contexts and is affected by them, but to argue that those contexts are so insulated from one another that it is impossible to understand what goes on in them except from the inside is going too far. (Complete understanding is a red herring here, for that is seldom achieved even by speakers of the same language when important differences are in dispute.) When Alasdair MacIntyre argues against "any overall rationality that can supply a sort of universal language among traditions, or any universal human practices that can elucidate understandings of the human good, and hence ground conceptions of virtue that can be shared and that are intelligible among and across traditions"[6]—when, as I say, MacIntyre so argues, I (whose life was once saved by Maasai warriors whose language and "practices" were as different from mine as the human species allows) have difficulty agreeing.

The second objection to cross-cultural comparisons comes mainly from the deconstructionists, who would have us believe that once one starts stepping across cultural boundaries there is no stopping short of oppressive totalism. The passage that Kimberley Patton quotes from Jean-François Lyotard in her contribution to this book is so instructive here that I shall reproduce and comment on it. "It must be clear," Lyotard writes

> that it is our business not to supply reality but to invent allusions to the conceivable which cannot be presented. And it is not to be expected that this task will effect the last reconciliation between language-games (which under the name of faculties, Kant knew to be separated by a chasm), and that only the transcendental illusion (that of Hegel) can hope to totalize them into a real unity. But Kant also knew that the price to pay for such an illusion is terror. The nineteenth and twentieth centuries have given us as much terror as we can take. We have paid a high enough price for the nostalgia of the whole and the one, for the reconciliation of the concept and sensible, for the transparent and the communicable experience. Under the general demand for slackening and for appeasement, we can hear the mutterings of the desire of a return of terror, for the realization of the fantasy to seize reality. The answer is: Let us wage war on totality; let us be witnesses to the unpresentable; let us activate the differences and save the honor of the name.[7]

What does this diatribe shake down to by way of sober claims? That, to generalize, wholes are bad because they produce terror, and, specifically, that they are responsible for the horrors of the last two centuries. Differences, by contrast, are good and should be activated; and in any case they are inevitable because language-games cannot be reconciled. That here too there is some truth is again not in question: wholes can be misused and have been, and differences do have their place. But the unnuanced, uncompromising dichotomy that Lyotard erects between wholes and parts is unconvincing, and nowhere in postmodernism do I find it argued straightforwardly and persuasively. To mention only a single problem with the thesis: predictably, Lyotard drags in Hegel for his whipping boy; but is the line from Hegel-the-lumper to Naziism any straighter than the line that runs to from Nietzsche-the-splitter to that *dénouement*?

Truth

The revolt against wholes—metaphysics, metanarratives, and pejoratively, totalism—has severely impacted the idea of Truth. In Foucault and much of postmodernism, truth comes close to being no more than a power play. Wilfred Cantwell Smith reports that though truth remains enshrined in Harvard's insignia, the word doesn't appear in the statement on the aims of undergraduate education that its faculty took two years to hammer out shortly before Smith retired.

Absolute Truth has to be grounded in absolute, all-inclusive Reality, for were it not, something beyond what it *is* tied to could relativize it; in fact, in the end the two come to the same thing, as the Sanskrit *sat* and the Arabic *haqq* attest. So what (allegedly) is wrong with Reality, and what is (actually) right about it? The arguments against it cannot be metaphysical, since metaphysics is what is under attack—human beings don't discern reality; the claim is that they project, invent, or construct it. This leaves deconstructionists with morality and epistemology as the directions to shoot from.

In both cases the objections seem to rely more on caricatures of the opposition than on solid reasoning. On the moral front, pressing the "terror" button relieves critics of the need to demonstrate that metanarratives necessarily marginalize. Why respect for the rights of others cannot be built into metanarratives as one of their moral corollaries is not explained.

As for epistemic objections, these too rely mostly on caricatures, the familiar ones here being that to think that reliable inclusive views are possible is tantamount to thinking that one can jump out of one's own skin; or (when the objection comes from historicism) like thinking that one can cross historical horizons in helicopters; or finally, like thinking that one can achieve a God's-eye view of things, as if omniscience were ever in the picture. The fitting metaphor is altogether different; it is the Himalayan range viewed from a distance. Its boulders, ravines, and glaciers don't show, but the contours of the range are reliably etched. That's all that responsible metaphysicians ever claim—that Reality's outlines are available to us respecting what human beings need to know about it; presumably other species approach those outlines from different angles. And responsible metaphysicians agree with Lyotard (and yes, as against Hegel if one wants to get into that), that "our business [is] to invent allusions to the conceivable which cannot be presented," and that we should be "witnesses to the unpresentable," for in their final, apophatic registers the wisdom traditions all recognize that finitude can only point to the Infinite, not deliver it.

One more epistematic bugbear needs to be laid to rest: the charge that belief in absolute Truth lands one in dogmatism. The truth is almost the opposite. Logically, it is fallibilism that is absolutism's corollary, for in the absence of a concept of the way things are, it is impossible to be mistaken about them.

If this tempers some of the objections to the big picture that the idea of Truth presupposes, I can round off my remarks by noting what such pictures contribute.

Religion, *religio*—presumably religious studies' primary reference point—has to do with being connected. Are deconstructionists, cultured despisers of metaphysics that they are, aware of how (to quote Lyotard one last time) their call to "wage war on totality [and] activate . . . differences" pulls against connectedness? If our century has given us all the terror we can take, it has also given us all the dismembering we need. Already at the opening of this century Yeats was warning that things were falling apart, that the center doesn't hold. Gertrude Stein followed him by noting that "in the twentieth century nothing is in agreement with anything else." Ezra Pound saw man as "hurling himself at indomitable chaos," and the most durable line from the play *Green Pastures* has been, "Everything that is tied down is coming loose." No wonder that when in her last interview Rebecca West was asked to name the dominant mood of our time, she replied, "A desperate search for a pattern." The search is desperate because it seems futile to look for a pattern when reality has become, in Roland Barthes's vivid image, kaleidoscopic. With every tick of the clock the pieces of experience come down in new array.[8]

Earlier and without using those names, I criticized communitarianism and holism for dead-ending meaning in cultural-linguistic wholes and their respective practices, but the position does connect us to something; it connects us to communities by recognizing that the meanings that inform our lives are solidly grounded in them. Its shadow side consists in limiting our meanings to the communities that generate them and questioning the possibility of trafficking between them. The providential feature of the human religious heritage is its consistent refusal to stop there—indeed, its refusal to let human connectedness stop anywhere short of Reality itself. That is the final explanation for religion's power.

One of the most arresting sentences I have come upon in the last two years relates to this. I regret now that I failed to make note of its author, but it reads as follows: "Liberals do not recognize the spiritual wholeness that can come from the sense of certainty." It has been one of the aims of this paper to argue that on ultimate questions, only metanarratives can provide that certainty, for only they elude the possibility of being relativized by things beyond themselves.

When the sense of certainty does explode within us, the image that comes to my mind is of our newly acquired, state-of-the-art air mattress. When, with a twist of my wrist, I screw its mouth into the electric pump that comes with it, it inflates with a sonic boom and such force that I have to release some air to make it comfortable to lie on.

That's *pneuma* for you.

Notes

1. Walter Capps opens his *Religious Studies: The Making of a Discipline* (Minneapolis, MN: Fortress Press, 1995) by saying that "little objective understanding of religion existed before inquirers learned how to make it intelligible" two hundred years ago. I don't know what to think about that statement. Are things intelligible, and to be understood, only from the outside?

2. Christopher Lasch, *The Revolt of the Elites* (New York: W. W. Norton, 1995), p. 242.

3. *The Chronicle of Higher Education*, 9 January 1978, p. 18.

4. From an unpublished public lecture delivered by Henry Stapp, professor of physics, University of California, Berkeley.

5. Walter Capps, *Religious Studies*, p. 340.

6. Alaisdair MacIntyre, in his *Whose Justice? Whose Rationality?* (Notre Dame, IN: University of Notre Dame Press, 1988), as paraphrased by Lisa Sowie Cahill in "Religion and Values in Public Life," supplement to *Harvard Divinity Bulletin* 26, no. 4 (1997): 8.

7. Jean-François Lyotard, "Answering the Question: What Is Postmodernism?" in *Postmodernism: A Reader*, ed. Thomas Docherty (New York and Chichester, West Sussex: Columbia University Press, 1993), p. 46.

8. Most of this paragraph repeats what I said in "The Religious Significance of Postmodernism: A Rejoinder," *Faith and Philosophy* 12 (July 1995): 409–22.

begin: tendency cosmic construction enter Eliade (handwritten)

ELEMENTS OF A NEW COMPARATIVISM

Smith-Rectification (handwritten)

WILLIAM E. PADEN

true (handwritten)

While comparativism in the study of religion for many has become as-sociated with the sins of the discipline—colonialism, essentialism, theo-logism, and anti-contextualism—it simply remains that there *is* no study of religion without cross-cultural categories, analysis, and perspective. Knowledge in any field advances by finding connections between the specific and the generic, and one cannot even carry out ethnographic or historical work without utilizing transcontextual concepts. Like it or not, we attend to the world not in terms of objects but in terms of categories. Wherever there is a theory, wherever there is a concept, there is a comparative program.

Though we cannot dispense with categories, we can fix them, change them, or make them better. I like to think that a certain reconstructed sense of comparativism is forming, and in this paper I will draw out some of its elements as succinctly as I can. After an introduction sketch-ing some new conceptual contexts of comparative work, the main sec-tion outlines five specific factors which form parts of an emerging pro-gram. These factors include attention to (1) the bilateral function of comparison, (2) the heuristic nature of the comparative process, (3) a conceptually expanded notion of the idea of patterns, (4) the controlled, delimitative function of comparison, and (5) the distinction of meaning-to-the-comparativist and meaning-to-the-insider. Brought together into a single picture, such features form a working framework for a broadly conceived comparative enterprise.

Contextualizing a New Comparativism

Exclusive attention to cultural specificity tends to overlook the salient fact that behind cultural variance we are all bio-human creatures who "do" universes.[1] Behind cultural formations, there are human actors, and here is one place where elements of comparability may be found. The act of forming a world or classifying its structures is not culture-specific, even though the content of a world is. In that sense, the plurality of cultural worlds does not bring the agenda of comparativism to an end, but enhances and recontextualizes it. There are diverse religious systems because humans are system builders and inhabitors, and socie-ties build and inhabit these systems as naturally as birds build nests. It is not just "cultures" but humans as a species that make inviolable boundaries and objects, interact and communicate in linguistic fields with agents believed to be endowed with prestige and power, reiterate sacred histories and defend traditions, follow the examples of ancestors and leaders, and absolutize or cosmicize symbols of authority and moral order. These, to take only a few examples, are broadly general, comparable activities, though their cultural contents vary and may in fact be what interest us most. Such worldmaking (to borrow Nelson Goodman's term[2]) points to generic human acts while also acknowledging unique social contents and contexts.

World-formation is an open-ended concept. It is as metaphysically neutral as the notions of system or environment. It includes not only the theoretical capital of categories like language, cognition, and social power, but also the specific categories used in religious studies, like myth, ritual, and postulated experiences of otherness, numinousness, and gods. There is no end to the content of world-experience. Moreover, the turn from the hermeneutical interests of theological schools to those of the secular academy is reflected in the shift from the revelational model of "the holy" (where the sacred manifests itself in a variety of kinds of objects) to the world-formation model, in which one looks for both difference and continuity in the way humans inhabit their universes.

Eliade's comparativism represents the old but has some resources for the new. Classical morphological analysis compared variations on structures—like cosmogonic myths—in order to amplify the meaning of the structure. The staticism and noncontextualism of this has since become fully apparent even if its function as a formative taxonomic staging in religious studies has not been fully appreciated, and this formalism may be juxtaposed with the model shortly to be described. At the same time, Eliade's thematic concern with world-construction adumbrates something more than just a slant toward timeless hierophanies. World-orientation in space and time is presented here as a human act that is comparable with the imaginal creativities, renderings, and systems of the "universes" of artists. It is this constructivist strand in Eliade which presents humans as builders who form their histories and environments through patterned acts and cognitive dispositions, for example, kinds of spatial orientation and memory retrieval, and who shape and fill these acts with cultural-historical style and content. This is not just theologism or ontologism. It is an example of a basis for looking at comparable human behaviors in a way that may link the work of comparative religion with the human and cognitive sciences.

Elements of a New Comparativism

The Bilateral Nature of Comparative Perspective

Comparativism misses its potential if it only collects parallels or only makes data illustrate an already conceived type. Rather, it should be a bilateral, two-way process that reveals both similarities and differences. The common factor in comparison is also a frame for showing differences relative to it. Only in relation to the point of comparability can difference emerge and become meaningful.

The area in which one looks for difference is driven by the selective interests of the interpreter. As Jonathan Z. Smith puts it, levels of difference are always constituted "with respect to" some particular factor that concerns the observer's theoretic interests.[3] The more such reflexive awareness and refinement one brings to the notions "common factor," "similarity," and "difference," and to the criteria for determining difference, the more systematically grounded comparativism becomes.[4]

For an example of how a comparative category works in relation to both the differential and common nature of world-formation, take the case of a pattern we may initially call "annual renewal rites," a recurring type of observance with endless cultural contents. Most religious cultures have major, periodic, collective times in which values deemed sacred are made explicit and intensified. This general pattern would constitute a common factor. But at the same time, the *content of these* observances is different in every case. Each religious system will have a different world, a different configuration of values that it is ritually re-affirming. Thus, the actual focus of the rites may variously have to do with the sacrality of hierarchic family relationships, or economic exchange alliances between villages, or the display of ideal military values, or exemplary meditative intensity, or the dependency of laity and monks on each other, or the prestige of the founder. In turn, any particular version of renewal can then be seen in differential relation to other versions, so that each adds a context to one's perception of the others and to the common theme.

The theme, "annual renewal time," represents a form of behavior, not a cultural content. A form, like a bowl, can have various potential shapes and fillings. Note how this reverses Eliadean terminology. For Eliade, the pattern or bowl is the content, the "transhistorical" content at that, to be extracted, and it has a meaning (e.g., the Cosmic Tree theme) that can be decipherable through sufficient variants. But in a bilateral comparativism where difference is important too, the content is equally understood as the historical, contextual configuration occupying the bowl.

Thus, the pattern of annual renewal allows focus on kinds of difference not otherwise discernible without the presence of the pattern. For example, it has the function of exposing and highlighting values that are particularly salient in the constitution of social worlds. The pattern does not obliterate cultural content, nor are its contents just replicas of "the same thing," à la the clones of a cookie-cutter mold. Where Eliadean comparativism states, "We compare or contrast two expressions of a symbol not in order to reduce them to a single pre-existent expression, but in order to discover the process whereby a structure is likely to assume enriched meanings,"[5] the post-Eliadean approach would point out that the new "meanings" reveal not only something about the theme (that a tree may be a center, an axis mundi, or a symbol of regeneration), but about the cultures and contexts themselves. Religions are not just variations on religious themes, but variations on different sociocultural environments, and different myths of origin not only show modalities of cosmogonic themes, but also reveal culture-specific social codings and the idiomatic textures of indigenous memory.

Just as the comparative pattern can bring into focus unforeseen differences, it can also bring into focus otherwise unrecognized connections. As Lévi-Strauss puts it, "[I]t is through the properties common to all thought that we can most easily begin to understand forms of thought which seem very strange to us."[6] Thus, rituals that might otherwise remain obscure, behavioral oddities, embedded exclusively in the horizons of their adherents, may be seen in a context of wider intelligibility that links their expressions with recognizable, familiar patterns.

The Heuristic Nature of Comparative Categories

"Points of comparison" are not static, essentialist entities, pinned down for all time. The initial choice of common factor—that is, the theme, concept, or pattern—once tested, usually needs refinement, differentiation, or reconstruction, as each element of the pattern is confronted by historical data, new questions, or possible misfits. So the parts of the formula "annual renewal rites" would all come under scrutiny and potentially give way to more complex understanding. Just identifying patterns, therefore, is not the end of the matter but the starting point for investigation. This open-ended method addresses what is perhaps the main criticism of comparativism, namely, that it overrides complexity and brings together incomparables.

So a major function of comparative categories is heuristic: to provide instruments of further discovery. This includes the possibility of their own further differentiation, subtypologization, and problematization through historical analysis. The comparative process is then a dynamic enterprise and not just a reiteration of fixed, Linnaean-style morphologies, and comparative patterns here are not timeless archetypes carrying ahistorical values or meanings which are simply replicated in historical material, but rather are exploratory and refineable.

Thus, one would need to face the complex questions surrounding the "pattern" of renewal rites. The festivals may have different purposes and functions in different cultures. Each culture may have a variety of genres of renewal rites. Rites change in time and are reworked to meet different situational needs. Some of their features may be internally important, some incidental. Different participants or social cohorts may find quite disparate significances in these occasions. The observances may be driven by the interests of royalties or peasantries, priesthoods or householders, men or women, warriors or merchants, established regimes or counterhegemonic groups—or all of these—and thus contain different political and economic messages. Moreover, every individual will have a different experience of the same festival. The initial pattern being compared will also have a different cluster of features depending on which culture's version of it we use as a prototype,[7] for example, Chinese New Year or Russian Easter. The very concept of renewal rites will have a genealogy in Western, academic discourse that will profit from decoding. And so forth.

Such factors give complexity and difficulty, but not impossibility, to the pragmatic, operationalist process of comparative work. Notice that for each shift in the analysis, for each new question or slant by which any pattern is pursued, the point of comparison shifts and is refocused too. So even where the scholar's interest turns to more refined focusings—for example, how is renewal related to male power?—the basic function of comparison remains at work through a succession of thematic foci and mappings.

Pattern analysis is not then the simple, univocal, and taxonomic pinning down or tagging of an already known phenomenon. The exemplifications of the topic and subpatterns continually modify and increase our understanding of the topic itself, including its limitations.

Enlarging the Concept of Pattern

The third element is the need to expand the notion of a comparative pattern. While our initial data compose that dimension of culture we label religious, the so-called common factor in comparison is not limited to religious themes, but should be understood as including any number of kinds of topical, conceptual, or classificatory categories, with different degrees of complexity geared to theoretic purpose.

Any concept creates a matrix for comparison. Thus the common, bridging factor in comparison could be a large metaconcept like authority, power, gender, or discourse, or it could be a function like class-empowerment, or a process like urbanization, or a complex combination of features like "the factor of secrecy in sacred space with reference to hieratic, male, political power in late nineteenth-century Korean annual renewal rites." The latter case of a multiform nexus of analysis shows how the comparative template easily becomes configured or loaded with a network of particular variables that guide the scholar's investigation. And this is the point: All such thematic material, and not just a list of kinds of religious objects through which the sacred is supposedly manifest, constitute "patterns in comparative religion," because the wider, academic task is not just to reiterate a morphology of overt, generic religious types like deity, sacrifice, or creation myths, but also to pursue a comparative study of religion. For this task, all language and concepts are at our disposal.

Comparison, then, builds its extended repertory by operating in all manner of conceptual matrices and at all levels of description and understanding, and this crisscrossing of religious subject matter with cumulative and newly generated reference points reshapes the evolution of religious studies itself. It needs to do this not only the better to engage the world's complexity and inexhaustible contents and to counteract our habitual propensity for conceptually monolithic packagings, but also to provide the stuff of theory and interpretation. Moreover, this broader concept of "referent" categories helps reestablish the connection that has been lacking between religious studies and the other human sciences, joining the interests of comparative religion and social history/theory which otherwise have been so disjunctive.

Controlled, Aspectual Focus

A new comparativism operates with an enhanced sense of conceptual self-control. Fitz John Porter Poole states this remarkably well: "Comparison does not deal with phenomena *in toto* or in the round, but only with an aspectual characteristic of them. Analytical control over the framework of comparison involves theoretically focused selection of significant aspects of the phenomena."[8] By defining the exact feature of the object being compared, the exact point of analogy or parity, the comparativist understands that the object at hand may be quite incomparable in *other* respects and for other purposes. Two objects can belong to the same reference class in one stipulated respect, but differ from other objects in that class in every other way and for every other purpose. The comparative pattern picks out one point of resemblance that has interpretive utility and leaves untouched all other meanings and contexts connected with that object that are not intrinsic to the limited theoretic function of the pattern. Muslim and Catholic pilgrimages may be comparable in some ways, but are not the "same thing." Because things are not identical does not mean they are not comparable according to some specific features.

This aspectualism challenges essentialistic categories in religious studies. Religion, ritual, and myth are not entities, but start-up words for looking into general, variegated areas of related phenomena. It is aspects of these conceptual building sites that we choose to look at, and the aspect chosen is already adumbrated by the lens of explanatory interests. Religious behavior draws on all varieties of human behavior and takes place in inexhaustible contexts of signification. The reason there are dozens of theories of religious behavior is that it has the same range of complexity as human behavior generally, and each theory addresses an aspect of the subject.

Distinction between Comparativist and Insider Domains of Meaning

Historians of religion, with their wide-angled lenses, are positioned to recognize and understand relationships that the insider does not. We are not comparativists simply to repeat what religions say and do, or to re-create their particular worlds, but more important, to find amidst those systems linkages with what we have learned from all of them and to form generalizations. These perspectives and significations are not necessarily totalizing, colonizing, juggernaut-like suppressions of real, local peoples' worlds, but can be understood as vocabularies that have their role and vision in the world and discourse of the interpreter rather than in that of the religious adherent.[9]

In William James's terms, the crab does not see its crustaceanness,[10] but the comparative anatomist does, along with the shared crustacean features of over thirty-five thousand other subspecies. One could extend this and observe that the zoologist sees the relationship of the crustacean class with other arthropod classes, studies the various subclasses with their respective ecological adaptations, and analyzes their developmental and genetic trajectories. For "crustacean," substitute any etic category from our field like "the paradigmatic function of myth," "sacred kingship," or even "religiousness" itself.

On the surface, James's biological reference appears to be dehumanizing. It could be taken as a subordination of the uniqueness of "the other" to the interests of cold, scientific classification. But James would be the last person to devalue the individual's experience. Rather, the example can be read as showing the relative place of insiders' and outsiders' perspectives,[11] and also showing the existence of continuities unobservable to the single species. The biological metaphor points not to dehumanization, recurrence of objectivism, or single-theory, scientistic totalization, but rather to liberation from the myopia of single-culture analysis and to an acknowledgment of the naturalness and structural variety of religious life on the planet. The crab's point of view, that of a single religious world, does not do this.

Concluding Points

Comparativism here is not just the study of different religions set side by side or considered serially, not just a classification of types of religious categories, and not just a hermeneutic which reconstructs or universalizes "the sacred" for an otherwise desacralized age. Rather, it is the basic, proper endeavor of religious studies as an academic field of inquiry—finding explanatory linkages and differentials among religious expressions, at either regional or cross-cultural levels, and seeking to discover otherwise unnoticed relationships among religious data.

A new model, rather than taking a lopsided interest in privileging the generic on the one hand (classical phenomenology), or the ethnographically specific on the other (anthropology), evenhandedly defends the bilateral prospects and character of the comparative process. A new comparative frame will neither ignore resemblances nor simplistically collapse them into superficial sameness; and it will neither ignore differences nor magnify them out of proportion to the human, cross-cultural commonalities of structure and function which run through them. In the end, the study of religion becomes an exercise in understanding what recurs, what is different, and why.

This approach unavoidably involves the factor of reflexivity: self-awareness of the role of the comparativist as enculturated, classifying, and purposive subject (which does not mean that patterns are fictions without substance); a cleaner sense of the process and practice of selectivity; an exploratory and multileveled rather than hegemonic sense of the pursuit of knowledge; the need for ongoing category critique; and the production of new or revisionary thematic collocations.

Finally, an expanded comparativism de-isolates the study of religion. The categories by which we typically scan religious worlds—for example, kinds of myth and kinds of ritual—turn out also to be templates for insight into human world-making generally, just as the categories of political authority and kinship bonding also become valuable tools for studying religious life. In this interdisciplinary way, comparative work pursues its fulfillment on a broader canvas and scale.

Notes

An earlier, embryonic version of this essay, which has here been thoroughly rewritten, was published in *Method and Theory in the Study of Religion* 8, no.

1 (1996): 5–14. The same issue contained responses by Marsha Hewitt, E. Thomas Lawson, and Donald Wiebe, and my reply to the respondents.

1. The anthropologist Donald E. Brown's *Human Universals* (Philadelphia: Temple University Press, 1991) is an important reopening of the issue of what is generically human, over against two generations of anthropological focus on cultural particularity. The notion of "worlds" is systematically related to comparativism in William E. Paden, *Religious Worlds: The Comparative Study of Religion*, 2d ed. (Boston: Beacon Press, 1994); and idem, "World," in *Guide to the Study of Religion*, ed. Russell T. McCutcheon and Willi Braun (London: Cassell, forthcoming). Not only traditional philosophical phenomenology and sociology of knowledge, but also more recent developments in cognitive psychology have utilized the concept of "world" construction as a fundamental human activity. Cf. Francisco J. Varela, Evan Thompson, and Eleanor Rosch, *The Embodied Mind: Cognitive Science and Human Experience* (Cambridge, MA: MIT Press, 1991).

2. Nelson Goodman, *Ways of Worldmaking* (Indianapolis: Hackett Publishing, 1978).

3. See Jonathan Z. Smith, *Drudgery Divine: On the Comparison of Early Christianities and the Religions of Late Antiquity* (Chicago: University of Chicago Press, 1990), p. 51.

4. Jonathan Z. Smith's compelling wake-up-call essays on the methodology of comparison focus particularly on the role of difference, and challenge the arbitrariness and inventiveness of comparison of cultural materials not contiguous in space and time. See "In Comparison a Magic Dwells," in *Imagining Religion: From Babylon to Jonestown* (Chicago: University of Chicago Press, 1982), reprinted as the prologue to this volume. In relation to Smith's terminology, I am proposing a model that allows for cross-cultural analogies with regard to human activities but that also can give "sufficient gravity to the historical encapsulation of culture" (26). The cross-cultural factor here is not an occult "psycho-mental unity of mankind" that encodes "universal" categories of thought, but the continuity of *actions* by which humans form communities, honor authorities and charismatic objects, defend territory (which comes in many genres), classify the universe, and so forth.

5. Mircea Eliade, "Methodological Remarks on the Study of Religious Symbolism," in *The History of Religions: Essays in Methodology*, ed. Mircea Eliade and Joseph M. Kitagawa (Chicago: University of Chicago Press, 1959), p. 97. Eliade's thematic work on space, time, myth, and ritual will assume renewed usefulness if it can be turned to generate differential knowledge about historical contexts, and not just instantiations of the common archetypal features of the theme itself.

6. Claude Lévi-Strauss, *The Savage Mind* (London: Weidenfeld and Nicolson, 1966), p. 10.

7. For a statement on the relevancy of prototype theory for the study of religion, see Benson Saler, *Conceptualizing Religion: Immanent Anthropologists, Transcendent Natives, and Unbounded Categories* (Leiden: E. J. Brill, 1993), especially chapter 6.

8. Fitz John Porter Poole, "Metaphors and Maps: Towards Comparison in

the Anthropology of Religion," *Journal of the American Academy of Religion* 54 (fall 1986): 414.

9. For a fuller response to the "colonization" problem, see William E. Paden, "A New Comparativism: Reply to Panelists," in *Method and Theory in the Study of Religion*, vol. 8-1 (1996), pp. 37–40.

10. James understood both the value and the limits of the scientific, classificatory mind. This particular example, however, illustrates the former, even though James appreciates the discrepancy of levels and ultimately acknowledges the value of the insider's self-described experiences, too: "Probably a crab would be filled with a sense of personal outrage if it could hear us class it without ado or apology as a crustacean, and thus dispose of it. 'I am no such thing,' it would say; 'I am MYSELF, MYSELF alone.' " *The Varieties of Religious Experience* (New York: Random House, 1902), p. 10.

11. Much as does the anthropologist's distinction of emic vs. etic language, the former representing the insider's culture-specific discourse, the latter representing the categories of the outsider. On the definition and relationship of etic and emic perspectives, I find particularly useful *Emics and Etics: The Insider/ Outsider Debate*, ed. Thomas N. Headland, Kenneth L. Pike and Marvin Harris, Frontiers of Anthropology, vol. 7 (Newbury Park, CA: Sage Publications, 1990).

THE MAGIC IN MINIATURE

Etymological Links in Comparative Religions

LAURIE L. PATTON

What binds
one shape to another
also sets them apart
—but what's lovelier
than the shape-shifting
transparence of *like* and *as,*
clear, undulant words?

— *Michael Doty, "Difference"*

Making More of the Uneasy Truce

The essays in this volume speak softly. In their defense of comparativism, they often mention a chastened, reformulated, and modified comparativism. While they establish a very clear break from the static, generic comparison of the previous generations, at the same time they hesitantly, tenuously, suggest links to that same comparativism. These links are formulated in modest terms, such as the ways in which comparative work has continued to be "suggestive" or of value as a "heuristic" device among other interpretive devices. Comparison can live and move and have its being in a postmodern world, but it must do so in a gentler, quieter way.

These more modest terms are a signature of what David Eckel calls here the "uneasy, hybrid character" in postmodern scholarship, whereby "modernist myths are broken, but they do not go away." Rather, "they coexist instead with the rediscovery of traditional patterns of life and thought that were considered long since out of date." In this essay I want to argue that this uneasy, hybrid character stems, in part, from an unwillingness to acknowledge openly some of the basic continuities of intellectual strategy which bind the two discourses together. There is at least one intellectual strategy which the modern and the postmodern study of religion share: the derivation of words as a way of making a normative argument. To put it another way, they both use etymology as a form of comparative ideology.

For the remainder of this article, I will examine two particular cases, those of Wilfred Cantwell Smith and Mark C. Taylor, in which etymology plays a critical theoretical role. In both cases, etymology's function is twofold: (1) to show, in the history of a single word, the ideas to which the study of religion must attend; and (2) to push scholars, by reference to the lesser known resonances of a single word, toward a more honest form of comparison that better incorporates those excluded from the discourse. In showing this similarity I will argue that, at the micrological level of word-derivation, there is little difference between the modern and the postmodern, despite the assertion of a radical "break" declared on both sides of the divide. In this way I am attempting to reverse the usual *modus operandi* by pointing out a similarity that ruptures and interrupts our assertions of radical break. A small study of the use of etymologies can ironically challenge the seamless web of "difference" that has come to dominate our comparative conscience.

Etymology and the Comparative Study of Religion

While space does not permit me to engage in a longer study of the relationship between etymology and the study of religion, some background might be useful here. As I have written elsewhere,[1] the study of the linkage between etymology and the gods has a long tradition in the history of religions. Max Müller, with his romantic notions about the origin of language and religion, is easily mocked. Yet it is time that the history of religions divorce itself from its all-too-facile patricidal perspective, and examine Müller's work from the perspective of intellectual history. Just as one might bestow a quiet, albeit disbelieving respect on the ideas of other intellectual ancestors, such as the conflict of Love and Strife in Empedocles or the spheres of Ptolemy, so too one might look at Müller's work as a kind of cosmogony, a new myth of creation in which the Hebrew was replaced by the Aryan in the misty dawn of time. The dangers of such a myth are more than well-known, but the remarkable similarities between it and other religious ideas about etymology, or word-derivations, might be outlined here.

Müller's approach is concerned with origins as they are revealed by names. Müller looks behind the "veil" of language to the actions and attitudes of the Indian rishis:

> I shall try and make my meaning clearer. You will see that a great point is gained in comparative mythology if we succeed in discovering the original meaning of the names of the gods. If we knew for example what Athena or Hera or Apollo meant in Greek, we should have something to start from, and be able to follow more securely the later development of these names.[2]

Andrew Lang, Müller's lifelong opponent on the question of primitive, makes the parallel between us and them more straightforwardly, emphasizing the fact that we are all scientists of mythology. Although linguists might term one "folk" and the other "scientific" etymology, both are born of the same spirit. Lang writes, "The explanations which men have given of their own sacred stories, the apologies for their own gods which they have been constrained to offer to themselves, were the earliest babbling of a science of mythology."[3] (The only difference, Lang implies, is that "they" babbled more than "we" do, a mistaken assumption at best.)

One of these so-called early apologetic strategies, according to Lang, was etymology, the science of finding the origins of a word. Lang should be given some credit for taking native commentaries into account when he rightly remarks that commentators on mythological traditions also write in harmony with the general tendency of their own studies. Yet he makes the mistake of assuming that they were also motivated by the same kinds of rational and moral needs as those of nineteenth-century scholars. While poets could but omit a blasphemous tale or sketch an apology in passing, it became the business of philosophers and of antiquarian writers deliberately to whitewash the gods of popular religions. Systematic explanations of the sacred stories, whether as preserved in poetry or told by priests, had to be provided.

For Lang, in the armory of religious apologetics, etymology has been the most serviceable weapon. He finds it easy to see that by the aid of etymology the most repulsive legend may be compelled to yield a pure or harmless sense, and may be explained as an innocent blunder, caused by mere verbal misunderstanding. Brahmins, Greeks, and Germans have found equal comfort in this hypothesis. Lang then goes on to discuss the same etymological strategy employed by Socrates on the name *Kronos* in the *Cratylus* of Plato, speaking of the procedure as a whole as "pious and consolatory," depending upon "individual tastes and preconceived theory." There is no consistency to such "cleaning up" if one believed Lang's nineteenth-century version of whitewashing. His criticism begs the question of whether or not the etymologists were up to something else entirely.

The nineteenth-century interpreters were the last to address the question of etymology in a thorough way. Their massive debunking has led to a feeling of contamination by association among later scholars, whereby even to discuss the issue of etymologies and the original meanings of words from a history of religions perspective becomes suspect. Ironically and yet quite significantly, the more recent turn to a hermeneutics of suspicion, of reading texts with a view to their ways of organizing knowledge, has provided an effective replacement for the more naïve approach of the nineteenth-century scholars. Yet for all of their seeming naïveté, our intellectual ancestors had one crucial insight: that etymology is a kind of intellectual strategy with its own investment, and can be examined in its own right as an effective tool for interpreting religion.

Modern Etymology: The Case of Smith's "Religion"

Let me turn to the first of my case studies. The entire argument of Wilfred Cantwell Smith's *The Meaning and End of Religion*[4] revolves around an etymology. In tracing the history of the word "religion," Smith makes the case that, in Roman times, the "archaic" meaning of the word *religio* was an awe that people felt in the presence of the dreadful power of the unknown. Cicero, writing in the midst of Greek influence, softened this usage somewhat by describing it as feeling, a quality of men's lives, and distinguishes "religious" from "superstitious" depending on the attitude with which people perform their observances. The early Church fathers used the term *religio* to designate the structural organization of the Church, and also the name of a relationship between god and human. In some of the debates between early Christians and pagans, *religio* becomes "a way of worshiping." For Augustine, *religio* is not a system of observances and beliefs nor an historical institution, but a vivid and personal confrontation with the splendor and love of God. For Aquinas, *religio* is man's prompting toward God. In the Reformation writers, the Latin term referred to something personal, inner, and transcendentally oriented—Zwingli and Calvin both thought of *religio* as a kind of piety and, Smith argues, used the term interchangeably. By the seventeenth century, "religion" becomes a system of ideas and beliefs, partly because of the influence of the Enlightenment understanding of religion as analogous to a kind of scientific system of beliefs. This schematic externalization reflected and served the clash of conflicting religious parties and the attempt to make sense of data coming in from other parts of the world.

Added to this was the Roman Catholic sense of practice and Schleiermacher's sense of feeling or disposition. Increasingly, it also meant the historical development of all this material over the sweep of the centuries. Building upon this, Hegel proposed "religion" as, in Smith's words, "*Begriff*, a self-subsisting transcendent idea that unfolds itself in dynamic expression."[5] And, as Smith goes on to put it, ever since, the hunt for the "essence" of "religion" has been on. The result of Smith's etymological explorations is the following: First, the English word "religion" has a sense of personal piety. Second, "religion" connotes a system of beliefs, practices, and values in relationship to a particular community, as well as an "ideal" system which the theologian tries to formulate. Finally, there is the term "religion" as a kind of generic summation, "religion in general." Given all the different definitions, no usage and no definition can be mature that is not self-conscious on this point.

W. C. Smith's own suggestion is that the word, and the concepts, should be dropped in all but the first sense of "personalness." This is on the grounds not merely that it would helpful to do so, but that it is misleading to retain them. The term "religion" is confusing, unnecessary, and distorting. The confusion arises because it is not clear whether religion is a form of practical piety or a system of beliefs. The distortion arises because most of the traditions that are objects of the study of religion do not themselves use the word, and the intellectual élites of each tradition would not know how to translate the term into their native or sacred language. Instead, Smith argues, the vitality of personal faith and the academic understanding of the history of tradition should be substituted for what has been called "the history of religion."[6]

The Etymology of Religion and Comparison

W. C. Smith discards the term "religion" in the service of clarity and of empathy. In performing a history of the term, he shows that what was singular about *religio*—the practice of piety and worship—cannot and did not remain singular over time. "Religion" has accumulated too many meanings which have strayed too far from the traditions of faith themselves. Thus, the work of Smith's etymology of religion is fourfold: (1) to strip the word down to its historical roots, if not "original meaning"; (2) to show the loss of the word's early force as a form of piety that expressed what was in human hearts; (3) to make possible, by clearing the rubble of accretions, new spaces for new words which *do* have the force of heart (e.g., "faith" and "tradition"); and (4) to engage in a program of comparative study that is more felicitous for the traditions being compared. Etymology, then, makes room for a new kind of comparison because it reveals the heart at the end of the derivation, the heart which is the only basis from which one can compare. Religion is at root personal piety, and new terms must be used to express this fact more accurately—new terms which will also be more in line with the traditions themselves.

But why should the history of the word be persuasive? It is, in the modernist sense, an act of recovery, of revealing the unifying principle behind the term. A word, an arbitrary collection of small signifiers, once meant something different. And it is the very nature of comparative thought to move the same element (in this case, a word) into different environments, and observe its interactions within that environment. This is the modernist etymology, the modernist history of a word.

But W. C. Smith's etymology is not just a story which reveals different usages at different times: his etymology has an "originary" flavor to it. It is not simply that the word "religion" once meant something different, just as the words "wheelbarrow" or "music" also meant something different. Rather, it is that the word "religion" has a seed of meaning to be recovered. The value of historical origin (in this day and age firmly eschewed in the halls of postmodernism) finds a safer home in the pages of W. C. Smith. In jettisoning the term "religion," Smith actually claims to recover its original meaning, in the sense of faith or piety. Thus, the etymology allows for a comparison on the basis of heart, wherein conversation can be established between people on the basis of the ethical commitment of the scholar toward the religious traditions she is studying. For Smith, this religious feeling has no residue, and no palimpsest.

It makes possible direct empathic conversation between representatives of a tradition without confusion, and it makes possible the scholarly study of the tradition without distortion.

Postmodern Etymology: The Case of Taylor's *Templum*

One might assume, then, that the postmodern study of religion might do away with etymologies precisely because of the concern they evoke with origins, essences, and the directness of speech. Yet postmodernists use them perhaps even more than modernists do. However, they use them playfully, in order to set up a set of possibilities and questions that are introduced, but never answered, by looking at the history of a word. Mark C. Taylor, in his postmodern theology *Nots*,[7] also uses etymological procedure, but does so as a way of criticizing Jacques Derrida's study of negative theology. Yet, as we shall see below, even in its more postmodern forms, this etymology also has very important, and deeply similar implications, for comparative thinking.

Let us begin with the text that Taylor is reading: Derrida's "How to Avoid Speaking: Denials."[8] In his analysis of both Greek and Christian apophatic movements, Derrida writes of de-negation—the process of creating a negative discourse that ultimately asserts a positive value. While space does not allow for a full exposition of the immense complexity in Derrida's essay,[9] in sum, Derrida traces and analyzes the images of negative theology, from Plato's *khora* (χώρα) to Eckhart's sieve to Heidegger's *Riss* (*Riß*). Derrida's view of the *khora* begins his exposition of de-negation. In Plato's *Timaeus,* the *khora* appears as the place or non-place into which the Demiurge introduces images of the paradigms that are essential to the process of creation. As such, the *khora* must have been there beyond becoming, and since it is beyond being; it is neither being nor non-being. The *khora* involves a negativity that escapes both the positive and the negative theological register. Derrida goes on to assert that the Christian *logos* incorporates the *via negativa* and shows it to be implicitly affirmative. In Christian theology, God is beyond being, but is not discontinuous with it. When carried to completion (and completion is possible for theology), the negative becomes positive. This is true in Augustine, pseudo-Dionysius, Bernard of Clairvaux, and Meister Eckhardt. And the process of de-negation also finds its traces in the philosophical writings of Heidegger, particularly in his essay "The Origin of the Work of Art." In all of these writers, the place of negative speech acts as a kind of boundary to the dramatic possibility of ultimate being; its "place" is therefore a kind of threshold, like the outer sanctuary of a temple. As Derrida writers,

> This is to speak in order to command not to speak, to say what god is not, that he is a non-god. How may one hear the copula of being that articulates this singular speech and this order to be silent? Where does it have its place? Where does it take place? It is the place, the place of this writing, and more precisely, a threshold . . . the place is only a place of passage, and more precisely, a threshold. But a threshold, this time, to give access to what is no longer a place. A subordination, a relativization of the place, and an extraordinary consequence; the place is Being. What finds itself reduced to the condition of a threshold is Being itself, being as a place. Solely a threshold but a sacred place, the outer sanctuary of the temple.[10]

It is at this very discussion of the temple that Taylor begins his critical reading of Derrida. And Taylor begins with etymological proceedings, playing with Heidigger, Eckhart, and the idea of the temple. While Derrida argues that philosophy and Christian negative theology extend and expand the domination of Greek ontology, Taylor responds that domination requires repression and that the repressed never goes away but always returns to disrupt, interrupt, and dislocate. What is repressed, argues Taylor, is the break: "The origin of the work of art . . . is a certain *Riss*—tear, fissure, gap, flaw, crack. Perhaps this *Riss*, which rends the text of negative theology, points toward a different space and time." Taylor wants to argue here that this *Riss* is a part of the temple, but not in the usual, organized sense of a sanctuary that we associate with the word. Hence his etymology:

> "Temple," after all, derives from the Latin *templum*, which, like *tempus* (time) comes from the Greek *temnos*. While temno means "cut" *temnos* designates that which is "cut off." Accordingly, *templum* is a section, a part cut off. What, then, is the time and place of the severed part . . . *la part madudite*. Perhaps the time/place of the *templum* is the time/place of a threshold that cannot be crossed or erased: something like an invisible sieve . . . a filter that allows the eye to see.[11]

What exactly is achieved by this etymology of Taylor's? Let us go back and retrace the steps that Taylor takes. We should be aware, at this point, that we are now at a playful six steps removed from the actual texts at hand. I am writing about Taylor, who is writing about Derrida, who is writing about Heidegger, who is writing about Eckhart, who is basing his negative theology on traces of the Greek ontology. It is precisely etymology that brings Taylor back through the many layers with which he (and we) are working: etymology brings him to the Greek root of the word *templum* and its historical resonances.

The most important resonance is Taylor's questioning of the location of the temple; he suggests that it may not be a threshold which "belongs" to the temple, but it may be a part cut off, *la part madudite*. Derrida has written that, in negative theology, such a temple acts as the threshold of the seeing eye, that which all things must pass through. "The eye thus passes the threshold [read: *templum*] of being toward nonbeing in order to see what does not present itself."[12] Taylor takes up this suggestion and criticizes it by elaborating upon it etymologically, showing how the temple in negative theology is not just a threshold belonging to two spaces, but also "a part cut off," that which does not belong. Thus it is not the eye which acts as a filter or sieve, as Derrida would have it, but the amputated part which acts as a kind of filter, or sieve *for* the eye. As Taylor writes, "perhaps the time/place of the *templum* is the time/place of a threshold that cannot be crossed or erased: something like an invisible sieve, a filter that allows the eye to see."[13] Taylor's etymology of *temple,* then, as a part cut off, gives us its resonance as an uncrossable threshold, which is the sacred space between Being and non-being.

Yet the other resonance of the temple is that which tears, a fissure or a gap. It is the gap which rends the text of negative theology: the difference between Being and non-being is found in the outer sanctuary of the temple. The temple becomes, for Taylor, a figure for Heidegger's "ontological difference," that which is the boundary between that which can be said about god, and that which cannot be said about god—the threshold which will eventually lead us back to an assertion of god through not-speaking. So, for Taylor, the etymology of *temple* implies that there is no center, but only a perpetual crossing back and forth between the assertion of being and that of non-being.

The Etymology of *Templum* and Comparison

This etymology of the temple as part cut off, or uncrossable threshold, has very important implications for comparison. For the temple as threshold of ontological being is rooted in the Christian and Greek traditions, that ground upon which the philosopher Heidegger builds. But Taylor points out that there is still a part cut off, an essential part of negative theology which is not included: in his essay Derrida also decided not to speak of the apophatic movements in the Jewish and

Islamic traditions. As Derrida writes, "To leave this immense place [of the Jewish and Islamic traditions] empty, and above all that which cannot connect such a name of god with the name of the place, to remain thus on the threshold, was this not the most consistent possible apophasis?"[14] Taylor argues that, no matter how consistently apophatic his silence about the Muslim and the Jew is, Derrida is not building a temple of the threshold, but a temple in the sense of the part cut off. For Taylor, Derrida cuts off—retains—a huge gap and fissure in his treatment of traditions of negative theology by remaining silent about the Muslim and the Jew.

Taylor shows that, in his choice not to speak about the Muslim and the Jew, Derrida does not cross the threshold into comparison, comparison which would be the most riskily autobiographical, that of the Muslim and the Jew. "For lack of capacity, competence, of self-authorization, I have never been able to speak of what my birth, as one says, should have made closest to me: the Jew, the Arab."[15] Instead he analyzes what is more distant from him—the Greek, and the Christian, and the German philosophy.

And thus, Taylor's etymology of the word *temple* and his emphasis upon the uncrossable, cut-off threshold forces the issue of comparison in a new way: even in its denial of the possibility of translation, the postmodern chooses some texts as worthy of the always doomed attempt to "cross," to "translate," and others as beyond the pale of the threshold itself. Taylor shows that, because of Derrida's unwillingness to be direct, the Jew and the Arab are beyond this pale of his study of negative theology. To put it directly in terms of the comparative study of religion, by his simple word-derivation, Taylor implies that Derrida has refused to cross a threshold into the Jewish and Muslim traditions, and thus has refused an important comparative move. And it is this comparative move which would most fulfill the postmodern agenda of incorporating some of the "alterity which haunts the Western theologico-philosophical tradition."[16] Taylor's critique of Derrida implies that the comparative move is one of the most significant ones to make—the only one which will allow the Greek and Christian to move aside from their dominant intellectual space and allow the Muslim and the Jewish traditions in.

In concluding this section, it is perhaps only necessary to point out that Taylor's etymology of "temple" as "threshold which cannot be crossed," "that which is cut off," affords him a new reading of Derrida, and thus, perhaps, of the postmodern project. Taylor shows that the temple is a kind of place into which Derrida cannot cross, but it is the very place to which he might go if he were to admit those Jewish and Muslim traditions of which he cannot speak. The historical resonances of the word "temple" allow Taylor to make this critique, and to suggest that Derrida himself could broaden his comparative horizons in order to incorporate his own traditions as an Algerian Jew into his work. In his critique of Derrida, Taylor shows that comparison would entail being brave enough to be autobiographical.

Conclusions

Let me begin my conclusions by delineating the differences between the two etymologies: It is clear that Taylor's etymology does not achieve a clarifying history, as it does in the work of W. C. Smith. Instead it achieves a set of resonances, a set of possible meanings which are to be explored but never fully realized and finalized. The etymology of the word "religion" allows Smith to reestablish a directness and empathy in the scholarly study of religion and in inter-religious dialogue. The etymology of the word "temple" allows Taylor to show that Derrida, in leaving out the Jewish and Islamic traditions, cuts himself off from his own postmodern project of decentering the Greek and the Christian logocentric perspectives. W. C. Smith uses straightforward, declarative sentences; Mark Taylor uses playful questions and negations of negations to make his points.

Yet both Taylor and Smith are fundamentally concerned (as Lang was, and Müller was before him) with how the path of a word through history can expose a flaw in thinking and correct it. Both give weight to this micrological study of a word, so that when the term is reintroduced, it can have new meaning. The newly deployed word can itself become efficacious, even magical, much as the miniature functions in ritual.

I would describe the process in the following way. As Susan Stewart writes of the process of miniaturization, "[T]he reduction in the physical dimension of an object depicted can, in fact, increase the dimension of significance. . . . The miniature always tends toward exaggeration—it is a selection of detail that magnifies detail in the same movement by which it reduces detail."[17] Analogously, we can see etymology as a kind of "miniaturization" of a word. The history of particular, "charged" words in which both Smith and Taylor engage is a kind of selection of detail that magnifies meaning. In this magnification of detail, the word's efficacy is thereby increased—a kind of magic of scholarly ritual.[18]

Thus, "religion," correctly etymologized, can be a term designating piety that other faith traditions can understand and can translate; "temple," playfully etymologized, can remind the postmodern student of religion that she, too, has left something out. And this corrective etymology involves a new understanding of comparison that underscores an ethical connection between traditions. W. C. Smith implies that the term "religion," in its confusion of meanings, also creates distance between those who study and those who are studied, whereas religion understood as piety (and supplemented by the terms "faith" and "tradition") would create more connection between them. Mark Taylor implies that the term "temple," used as a crossable threshold, enables Derrida to ignore the problem of Muslim and Jewish traditions; whereas "temple," used as a lens for that which has been cut off from Derrida's study, would allow Jewish and Muslim traditions directly to confront the dominance of Christian and Greek. Even in their difference, then, both Smith's and Taylor's intellectual moves insist on comparison, and what is more, they insist on forms of comparison which liberate thinkers about religion.

I return, then, to the similarities that interrupt the seamless web of difference between the modern and the postmodern study of religion. Both have traced words through history, and in doing so, have discovered new possibilities of meaning. But why does it matter that both approaches use etymology? *Because both approaches use it toward the same end.* Both have used this word-tracing, this re-membering of words, to show the ethical value of comparative thought in its abilities to re-member the Other. Comparison reinforces ethical relations between scholars and their objects of study. In our case studies of their use of the same etymological tools, we have seen that modernist and postmodernist agree on at least this—that the comparative move and the ethical move can be one and the same. Perhaps this fundamental agreement should become an openly acknowledged and crucial link between the two approaches. In this sense the essays in this volume need not be so softly spoken. Perhaps the similarity between the modern and the postmodern can become not simply an uneasy truce, but can become, to use the words of the poet Michael Doty, a lovely and shape-shifting transparence.

Notes

1. Laurie L. Patton, *Myth as Argument: The Brhaddevata as Canonical Commentary* (Berlin: DeGruyter Mouton, 1996), pp. 138–42; see the larger discussion in the chapter in the same volume, "Language and Cosmology II."

2. Max Müller, *Contributions to the Science of Mythology*, 2 vols. (London: Longmans, Green, 1987), 1: 410–11.

3. Andrew Lang, *Myth, Ritual, and Religion*, 2 vols. (London: Longmans, Green, 1899), 1:14.

4. Wilfred Cantwell Smith, *The Meaning and End of Religion* (1961; reprint, Minneapolis: Fortress Press, 1991). The crucial etymological discussion is on pp. 20–50.

5. Ibid., p. 47.

6. Ibid., p. 50.

7. Mark C. Taylor, *Nots* (Chicago: University of Chicago Press, 1993).

8. Jacques Derrida, "How to Avoid Speaking: Denials," in *Languages of the Unsayable: The Play of Negativity in Literature and Literary Theory*, ed. Sanford Budick and Wolfgang Iser (New York: Columbia University Press, 1989), pp. 3–70.

9. Here I am fully and ironically aware of the quixotic nature of trying to write a clear exposition of Derrida—an endeavor which is perhaps fundamentally opposed to the playful and coy nature of his own (and Taylor's) writing.

10. Derrida, "Denials," p. 52.

11. Taylor, *Nots*, p. 50.

12. Derrida, "Denials," pp. 52–53.

13. Taylor, *Nots*, p. 50.

14. Derrida, "Denials," p. 50.

15. Ibid., p. 66.

16. Taylor, *Nots*, p. 54.

17. Susan Stewart, *Nonsense: Aspects of Intertextuality in Folklore and Literature* (Baltimore: Johns Hopkins University Press, 1980), pp. 100–101. See also idem, *On Longing: Narratives of the Miniature, the Gigantic, the Souvenir, the Collection* (Baltimore: Johns Hopkins University Press, 1984). This is treated by Jonathan Z. Smith in "Trading Places," in *Ancient Magic and Ritual Power*, ed. Marvin Meyer and Paul Mirecki, Religions in the Graeco-Roman World, vol. 129, ed. R. van den Broek, H. J. W. Drijvers, and H. S. Versnel (Leiden, New York, Köln: E. J. Brill, 1995), pp. 13–27.

18. For a discussion of the uncomfortable use of the term *magic* in Indological writing, see Laurie L. Patton, "Making the Canon Commonplace: The *Rgvidhana* as Commentarial Practice," *Journal of Religion* (January 1997): 1–19. For a discussion of miniaturization and metonomy in Vedic ritual, see idem, in the forthcoming "*Viviyogavijñāna*: The Uses of Poetry in Vedic Ritual," *Journal of Hinduism*, special issue on Hinduism and the Arts, ed. Bruce M. Sullivan.

THE NET OF INDRA: COMPARISON AND THE CONTRIBUTION OF PERCEPTION

A Conversation with Lawrence E. Sullivan

This is the edited transcript of a discussion between Kimberley C. Patton, co-editor of this volume, and Lawrence E. Sullivan, Director of the Center for the Study of World Religions at Harvard University. The original interview was recorded on 29 October 1997.

Comparison and Cultural Fashions

KCP: Larry, I want to ask you first of all about your own formation as a scholar. What was your training as a comparative religionist? Of course you had training in your own particular field of study in Central African and South American indigenous traditions, but could you identify some of the working methods and assumptions about the possibility of cross-cultural or synchronic comparison you encountered? Secondly, have those premises been challenged or evolved in your mind since then? Maybe we could start with the personal history first.

LES: I began doctoral studies at the University of Chicago as an Africanist. There were nice seminars with participants who formed a good company of intellectual peers, and there was good intellectual stimulus from faculty, but there were no other people working in Francophone Central Africa. There was a historian of Africa, Ralph Austin. He and Victor Turner were really the only Africanists. Turner left after my first year and a half there to go to Virginia. That was before Jean Comaroff and John Comaroff came. Stimulating intellectual conversation was, by necessity, comparative, for no one worked in my area of specialization. With regard to specialization and comparison in graduate school, the old African proverb seems to hold: "He who thinks Mother's cooking is best hasn't traveled." I traveled a lot to visit other intellectual kitchens. At the very least I had to compare in order to transpose what I was learning from those who taught Hinduism, like Ralph Nicholas and Bernard Cohen, or Buddhism, such as Joseph Kitagawa and Frank Reynolds. I tried to take their methods and the questions they generated from their materials and see what analogous applications I could make in my area of concern.

From the beginning of my training, then, I was making efforts to compare. It was built into the setting of my intellectual formation. Both of my advisers in anthropology, Victor Turner and Marshall Sahlins, had conducted extended periods of fieldwork and knew how to write a thick description, a case study emphasizing language and context. But both of them, as well as other anthropologists with whom I studied, were also interested in the comparative study of certain kinds of issues. Ritual and liminality, let's say, for Turner, including utopian communal movements and other questions concerning the comprehension and operation of symbols, especially symbolic actions and social dramas. Marshall Sahlins was comparing structures of history, as he came to call them. Nancy Munn was comparing cosmologies of space; Valerio Valeri, systems of sacrifice. Michael Silverstein was conducting fascinating research in linguistic reflexive structures and Paul Friedrich continued his work in comparative poetics and mythology. I studied with them. I worked especially closely with Mircea Eliade during my years at Chicago.

KCP: Were these scholars sympathetic to your efforts to think comparatively about the African material, or did you find it more of an individual intellectual effort you felt compelled to pursue?

LES: Grad school was an experience of solo flight in many respects; "sympathy" is not the word that looms large in memory. That may be intrinsic to the effort, but in my case I lived and worked in Pilsen neighborhood elsewhere on the South Side. In the beginning of graduate school you looked for methods to help you face your questions. There was a great debate among students about whether comparison was a viable method at all. I think that for a long time I was persuaded that comparison of any sort was something passé, and that the answers lay

deeply embedded in a close-grained analysis of social organizations—
the social, economic, and material bases of the context of the Lega people in the Kivu Province of Zaire on which I was focusing in particular.

KCP: At that time, why was comparison passé?

LES: The main voices in declaring comparative methods in the study
of religion bankrupt were cultural anthropologists whom I admired and
still admire, but who really were not trained in comparative religion.
They knew of the study of religion only as an obsolete predecessor to
the current trends in their discipline. They saw comparative religion as
part of the primeval period. While their own discipline had changed
since then, they thought that comparative religion had remained unal-
tered since Sir James George Frazer or Edward B. Tylor. We students of
religion read anthropology, but anthropologists had not generally kept
up with work in the comparative study of religion. Ironically, these anthropologists were unaware of the comparisons that inevitably filled
their own work: the comparisons that mapped the differences between
"home" and "abroad." For the most part, they were field anthropologists whose lives swung dialectically between times of fieldwork, especially early on in their careers, and times of research and teaching in the
university. Without really noticing it, they fell into what Jonathan Smith
calls ethnographic comparisons in an attempt to render their exotic field
experiences familiar to themselves and their student-readers. Some provocative voices like those of Fred Eggan, following E. E. Evans-Pritchard
before him (studying Shilluk, Nuer, and drawing on Godfrey Lienhardt's
work on the Dinka), and Wyatt MacGaffey cautiously talked about the
possibility of something Eggan called "controlled comparison." I found
that attractive for a while. Eggan's notion was to study a small number
of cases—four or five, say—that were historically and culturally cognate. These cases had reasons for being comparable because they had
grown out of the same nexus. The relations and permutations would be
historically related, part of a single complex set that could be mapped
in geographic space and historical time.

Then I realized that the intellectual grounds for justifying Eggan's
kind of historical comparison couldn't possibly be exhaustively historical. Inevitably such comparisons had to base themselves as well on the
nature of the symbol, on the perceptive capacities of the retrieving historian, and on the hermeneutical constitution of the cultural scientist
who was not a part of that historical horizon. I should point out that
Jonathan Smith was my teacher also during this time. I found Jonathan

Smith's views exciting and encouraging as well as cautionary; he challenged us to undertake new and more self-critical kinds of comparisons. So I began to feel, on the one hand, that a close examination of justifiable historical comparisons necessarily opened up much wider possibilities for comparison at several levels. On the other hand, I viewed the attempt to narrow or eliminate broad comparison as a suspicious proposal to place our contemporary cultural experience—which is always fragmented, open-ended, polygenetic, and multileveled—into a vacuum in order to analyze it, like the early study of ballistics. The desire for simplicity and control was overcoming our willingness to disclose meaning and pattern in the complexities that inevitably constitute culture.

The Deep Structure of Comparison:
Brain-Mind Pattern Formation

LES: The kinds of comparisons I encountered in graduate school were generally of a historical sort in the widest sense of history. Later through Mircea Eliade in phenomenology, Victor Turner in cultural anthropology, and the work of Claude Lévi-Strauss in linguistics and structural anthropology, I was exposed to a range of comparative hypotheses or let's say alternative platforms for mounting comparisons. As grad students, we were asked to come to grips with the shortcomings of these comparative methods—their failings, in some sense. We studied the risks of doing comparison in any of these ways. And yet there was no general consensus, such as one might encounter now, that comparison ought to be abandoned altogether—that our understanding may be completely defeated by our cultural experiences, which are inevitably and widely comparative. Comparison was to be undertaken warily, with a high degree of critical self-awareness. In fact, keeping in mind the proverb about home cooking, wariness and self-criticism were good reasons to study religion comparatively; comparison uncovered one's methodological mistakes and exposed one's cultural biases in ways not easily arrived at in any other fashion.

One of the helpful things about structuralism, and the cause of some of the excitement that Lévi-Strauss generated all through the seventies, was that he took linguistic models—and later other models such as musical and mathematical ones—and demonstrated how these models might be suggestive for cultural studies as well (for example, studies of myth, masks, and village space). The symbolic codes in diverse models were mutually enlightening for one or both of two reasons. Either they were all expressions of *the same mind* (and therefore music, math, and myth are all genetically related symptoms of the same operations of the same mind)—Kantianism without a subject. Thus the co-arising of all symbolic codes of whatever kind is the reason for their inherent comparability. Or the relationship between diverse codes exists because the study of linguistics or genetics, say, provides metaphors that excite and empower the mind. These metaphors both illustrate and over-determine certain mental operations—a science of the concrete that applies itself analogously to the treatment of diverse cultural and material realities.[1]

KCP: And do you agree with him?

LES: I find the theory very stimulating: that from the close examination of the tropes of language as one domain of cultural expression one might generate so many ideas of how to compare mythologies. I wish not to reject that project entirely, but to criticize the central concepts of "science," "concreteness," and "binary opposition" so that we can broaden the base from which we draw inspiration, moving beyond just language in a written text. How about language in performance settings, language as it's lived or practiced in oral performance? This is not meant to strike down the value of the written text, which obviously occupies a special place in Biblical cultures. However, after all, the bulk of our linguistic experience occurs outside of written language. Once you step beyond writing, language opens up to cultural sounds in general, music and other culturally valued sounds.[2] How about building our theories on the fuller range of visible and audible expressions? Could we use those as a baseline for inspiring comparative methods in the study of religion? I have been asking recently whether we can learn from studies of the nature and structure of sound itself or sight—not simply in physics but, inevitably, when these are viewed as sensory experiences examined by the neurosciences?

After all, a lot of the terms of comparison found stimulating in the 1970s and, indeed, ever since De Saussure and Franz Bopp, were generated from the world of linguistics and also, increasingly, from that of genetics, as these comparative sciences borrowed notions of codes of communication and signals from one another. These discourses about codes, switches, transmitters, and receptors, for instance, are centrally important in neurobiology as well, it is worth noting. This common analytic vocabulary in itself should signal the promise of exploring the neurosciences more profoundly.

KCP: When, in reflecting on comparative studies, you direct our attention to neurophysiology, are you urging a focus on the operation of *the mind of the one who is comparing*—recombining fields of perceptible data? Or are you speaking about a more biological version of what Lévi-Strauss was talking about—a deep structure of the mind that is shared by those whose religious activities are being compared?

LES: The real excitement lies in retaining an openness to both. In fact, I would say that this is the lesson that hermeneutics can bring to neurophysiology. Observing the brain and mind implies that there are brains at work at both ends of the observing microscope: mindfulness is the general condition infused through the entire investigation at all levels. This is why neurophysiology calls for attention from those in the humanities. We have important considerations to offer. In turn, the study of the *brain* might offer to us new, substantive perspectives on how the *mind's* expressions work, because minds are both enabled and constrained by this physiology. There is always some close link between what we see in culture and what the brain allows us to see—the patterns that are represented to us—largely because of the way the brain processes and arranges these representations in vision, in memory, in association with emotion, and so on. The brain receives stimuli and perceives them in a patterned way. Let's call that the basis of the innate or nativist point of view. I'm not using the term *nativist* in regard to culture here, as Ralph Linton did when he studied nativist movements, for example, but *nativist* in the sciences of brain study. The nativist view privileges the innate capacity to order and refine messages received from the fallible senses. The nativist view of mind and brain descends from Descartes through physiologists like Ewald Hering in the first part of the twentieth century. Psychology, in this view, is largely conditioned by neural activity which is innate.

On the other side from nativism, you have empiricists or culturalists who would want to stress the role of the cultural world in shaping the patterns that form the basis of understanding. Championing the view that all knowledge is based on the senses were empiricists like John Locke, Bishop Berkeley, and David Hume, whose points of view descend to us through physical psychologists like Hermann von Helmholtz. From these thinkers comes the realization that the meaning of sense stimuli remains inherently undetermined and ambiguous. The culturally conditioned perceiver actively participates, through conscious and unconscious inference, in perceptions of patterns and their meaning.

In either view, the brain's operations can provide incredibly stirring metaphors for how the relationships among mind, brain, body, behavior, and culture can be understood. Thus I would find it exciting to be open to both directions, that the study of the brain would let us know something about the physical apparatus that perceives—its constraints and its potentialities. But it's also my belief that the study of the brain might shake loose for us or deploy into our own field of the study of religion, new metaphors, forms of organizing that have not come forward from linguistics or genetics. Let us keep in mind that the human brain is the most complex organ that exists in the universe, as far as we know. Learning more about how it is organized and functions can prove very suggestive about the order and function of other realities in which it is deeply involved.

As an example, there is now functional MRI (magnetic resonance imagery) that lets us see what parts of the brain are "lighting up" as it performs different functions. Physiologists had realized long ago that there were certain trigger points in the brain that were more responsible for vision, for hearing, for smell, for certain kinds of memory, and so on. But now what we are seeing with these non-invasive technologies is that the brain lights up in surprising ways. Although the idea that there are specialized modules is born out by the MRI, in response to stimuli, the brain lights up holistically. Certainly the occasion for the brain activity might be a certain sound or image, which triggers activity in a specific modular area, but in processing that input the brain links it to memories and emotions. In response to triggers in specific modules, the entire brain is glowing all together. The result is a holistic effort on the part of the brain, but not one that is undifferentiated or unpatterned.

KCP: If I understand you correctly, you might be extending the possibility of this patterning and this concurrent holistic functioning to the possibility of such patterns in the brain (or mind) existing inherently, that is, preexisting the incoming stimulus.

LES: It's a question being explored now, one that I am learning about from colleagues who study the brain.[3] For example, thirty years ago two Harvard researchers, David Hubel and Torsten Wiesel, discovered that individual brain cells responded respectively to very specific visual stimuli, short horizontal lines, or lines that were long and vertical, or lines that were at specific diagonal angles somewhere in between. Moreover, particular neurons fired only when their preferred stimulus appeared in a specific location in the field of vision: at or near the center, for instance, or off to one side or another. The specific cells responding to these various stimuli detect very specific features such as motions of various speeds and directions. The neurons fire in patterns sparked by stimuli. Building on that work, very recently scientists have discovered that sometimes single neurons also respond only to extremely complex stimuli. Some neurons fire, for example, only when presented with one human face, but they will not fire when presented with many other faces. So there do seem to be patterns inherent and innate to the brain's biology, in response to your question. However, studies of brain plasticity and development, such as those published by J. R. Cronly-Dillon, show that the brain's innate coding systems can also be modified by experience.

So we find ourselves suddenly talking about billions of brain cells with incredibly specialized functions that respond not only to a single-stroke stimulus but also to complex patterns. *Now where do we say the pattern is located at this point?* We could talk about the pattern "out there" in the culturally conditioned world, but the truth remains that the single neuron as well as clusters of neurons are innately built (or have evolved) to respond to patterns of tone, color, distance, motion, or an aggregation of features. The best course is still the more challenging course of seeing pattern in both directions at the same time—holding open questions and hypotheses that force us to compare expressions in the innate biology with those in the mental and cultural realms. This is, after all, what the brain seems to be doing. In addition, such comparison and openness pluck us from the deadly jaws of oversimplicity.

KCP: Might it then be possible that the complex brain is hardwired, as it were, to receive religious data—ritual data, or even perceptions of the metaphysical or supernatural sort? I'm just wondering if that is what one might legitimately infer.

LES: I'm not sure if that's the way it's going to work! Ever since Ernst Weber and Gustav Fechner postulated in the nineteenth century that sensations in all realms of the senses obeyed the same constant laws of measurement, others like S. S. Stevens and now Donald Laming of Cambridge University have hoped to develop something of a physics of the mind, replete with mathematical laws of surprising elegance and efficacy. Like the cosmological questions that arise in astrophysics, the physical and neurobiological studies of mental phenomena, such as judgments about sensations and ideas like math or myth, approach metaphysics. Though these studies are fascinating, I don't think of hardwired structures as the most fruitful way to locate religion in the brain.

Let's just step toward the possibility of a link in another way and see how close we get. Returning to how innate comparison is to human perception and understanding, recent research indicates that some brain cells will fire only after a complex process of comparison has been executed—a comparison of traits and features. This is very clear in the binocularity of vision, for example. Most of the individual cells in the visual cortex fire in response to signals coming from both eyes. The left and right eye, however, see differently. Many elements of those two different retinal images cross over in the brain to yield, in the end, only a single perception of one visual world. Disparities in crossed and uncrossed visual images are sorted out in the brain. Stereodepth perception is one result of that sorting, when the different receptive fields in the two eyes stimulate corresponding points on the two retinas and fuse to form one vision. When they instead stimulate noncorresponding points, one eye's image is suppressed, in whole or in part, to yield one picture. Every person's visual field is therefore full of suppressed images or "ghosts" of which the viewer is totally unaware, but which compose the full experience of vision.

What is most provocative is that the cues which trigger the fusion or suppression of images are not completely mechanistic. Instead, these fusions and suppressions are often the outcome of *interpretations* based on the cultural meaning of experience. Such interpretations can override the built-in physiological system that processes depth impressions. This is significant for those of us in religious studies: the role of *meaning* in the integration of diverse visual stimuli into a representation of reality— and in the processing of brain activity more generally—is looming ever larger in neurobiological research.

I would not look for religion in the brain's operations primarily at the level of a "gene for religion" or at the level of a hardwired neural pattern for specific religious experiences. Rather, given the meaning-making character of religion, the role that meaning plays in brain function opens the broadest avenue for consideration of religion in the light of the brain sciences and vice versa.[4] The human being characterized by this brain is also the religious being, religious imagination being a distinctive mark of the human species. Here exists a promising prospect that the study of religion and the study of the brain will prove mutually illuminating. In the process, what we learn about comparisons executed within physiological and mental operations may well offer stimulating suggestions for comparisons on other levels of cultural understanding.

KCP: This suggests at the least an interpretive interactivity between the perceiving and processing brain and the cultural environment. I want to ask you a bit about the natural environment, about the problem of whether, after all, we really can see the tree in itself, or whether the "real" tree even matters in religious construction.

LES: In the short term, I'm probably a culturalist. I think it's hard for a human being to see a tree and have some meaningful notion of it without that perception being rooted in that person's cultural history, language, poetics, scientific knowledge, emotional associations, and so on. A given tree, insofar as it really appears distinctive, probably is helped to appear distinctive by its place in these cultural systems and personal histories of associations.

That said, there is still a question in the longer run—and here I'm talking about the longer evolutionary run—of the role of the outside world in shaping the brain. Brain evolutionists speak more than casually about the history of evolution being contained in the brain. They expect to see footprints of evolutionary development reflected in the processual structures of the human brain and its operations. Even anatomically speaking, we can see that the body's heavy elements like calcium appear to be, from all we know now, the outcome of astronomical events in the development in the universe, like the explosions of supernovae, so that human physiology itself, and the chemistry and processes of the brain all bear the stamp of the "outside world." Neurobiologists don't identify the brain with the head; rather, they more accurately speak of the body as the brain, with all its axons and nerve endings that extend from the neurons in our heads to the nerves in our bodies. We not only "have a brain" but we also "are one."

Once you're rolling outward from the cranial brain cells to the extensions where contact and sensation occur, you encounter the wider world whose stimuli have always provoked the brain into operation and development. The brain and the outer world are intimately related parts of a whole system that has generated itself through time. Religious perceptions of nature and scientific ideas about the brain's development are both human reflections on this system. Our new understandings of its development, as refracted through the evolution of the brain and the natural environment, may succeed in drawing the world of science and the world of mystical experience into new relationship.

KCP: Might one not then leave oneself open to the postmodern charge of reification, or even of essentialism? Are you implying that a material feature of humanity—the brain—is a foundational starting point from which we can or even must consider religious experience?

LES: Speaking only in terms of material evolution may indeed leave one open to that charge. However, even the least spark of self-awareness brings home the realization that in that very act we are *speaking* and *thinking*. I am suggesting that a particular mode of *thinking* about the material universe, and the brain within it, may offer a new starting point. The materiality of the world, upon reflection, soon undergoes a strange inversion. For example, the materialist philosopher in France, Mikel du Frenne, who had been imprisoned with Paul Ricoeur during the war, remained an evolutionary materialist. However, he realized that the span of evolution—and the complex web of material preconditions—are so infinitely beyond the historical compass scribed by our human species, and certainly beyond the history recoverable by communal memory, that the term "infinite" comes into play with full force. Now an authentic infinity rooted in physical matter and not only in metaphysical fantasy. While staying material, du Frenne felt compelled to restore notions of infinity and apriorism as well as a whole series of concepts that had been associated to essentialist philosophies and metaphysics. It's as though the two parallel lines of brute material existence and unfettered metaphysical imagination are bound, by their very nature, to encounter one another when each is explored to its utmost reaches.

Taking such a tack toward questions of biology and the evolution of the brain opens new ways of reflecting on these perennial philosophical issues. The infinite number of variables in brain circuitry as well as in brain development over evolutionary time which result in our thought, speech, and sensation summon us to grapple with the notion of infinity as a precondition of our own meaningful expressions. Religious and philosophical arguments about such cosmological themes as random chance, fate, determinism, freedom, providence, and design are revisited in attempts to come to grips with our place in the world, and the human brain's place and role in the universe.

Adverting again to the issue of comparison, biological models recast the nagging questions that surround comparison, such as those concerning purpose or design or pattern. Discovering patterns in evolution or uncovering patterns in the residues of evolutionary development re-poses the troublesome questions about intention and design and re-frames them within apparently self-organized natural systems. Can we locate the mind in which patterns of this kind were intended?

KCP: Or the question of whether the pattern is internally created or whether it is in fact already "out there," to be perceived and responded to. This parallels in many ways the Enlightenment-fueled debate about the existence of the transcendent—about where this sense of divinity or power originates! The sociology of religion posits, as Hubert and Mauss put it, that "religious things are social things," that we create them. Whereas traditional theology responds, no—*we respond to them*, to a reality that is greater than and apart from us. The academic study of religion has increasingly sided with the former.

LES: The debate that has taken place in religious studies over the past century concerning the representation of reality can be of value to our scientific colleagues who are steeped in imaginative and symbolic for-mulations about the world. In some ways they are still playing out or, in some specialties, just entering the conflict between the nature/nurture viewpoints or innate structure versus social construction of reality—debates we ourselves have long contended with because religion was one of the first realities deconstructed in the Enlightenment. Often today, critical studies in the history and philosophy of science are taken as anti-science by scientists. When Locke and Descartes were the main players, it was easier to see the theological relevance of the debate. It's harder to elicit the theological relevance of brain sciences and the neuroscientific relevance of religious life today because of the parting of the ways of science from the humanities, including religion.

But, as you are suggesting, these questions and thoughts from diverse sciences today converge just one step away from a theological language that has been the subject of religious studies. Conversely, those in the-ological and religio-historical studies easily could step over the line into scientific and material essentialism, on the one side, or perhaps step over the line into the rhetorical persuasions of political speech, on the other side. We are made aware through the critical studies of deconstruction and postmodernism that we are standing on the head of a pin. It is no step at all to vastly different kinds of talk, posited on vastly different premises about the nature of the world and the nature of the mind and the relationship between the two.

I appreciate your pointing us back toward the notion of patterns and the process of comparison that seems to disclose or generate them. Where are patterns located? Are they located in the mind? If so, what kind of "mind" is that? The universe itself? Is there an instigating intentional subject who can act as an agent, generating patterns that affect the world; or is the universe itself the sum total of all correlated, self-referring permutations, a kind of interdependence of co-arising expressions, none of which has any final determining efficacy? These were questions pursued by the late historian of religions Ioan Couliano. Although many of his ideas were almost provocatively sprinkled throughout his writings both playful and serious and not grounded in ways totally persuasive for all readers, he wanted to focus attention on these kinds of questions in, among other works, *The Tree of Gnosis*. He was suggesting that the individual human mind is part of some larger universal mind. Surely there are not a lot of historians of religions building comparisons based on that kind of paradigm.

Still, it is hard to know whether one is ever finding a pattern in such diverse realities as light or stone, or in the long sweep of human history, or the short sweep of a myth told during a night around the fire. Is the pattern not in the eye of the beholder—as Jonathan Smith would have us remember, in the scholar-magician? On the other hand, are there not also concrete patterns in the history of culture or religion that are analogous to the patterns in our perceptions? After all, what accounts for the irrepressible sense we have of an outward reality available to our senses almost without effort? The magnetism and intimacy between the world and our perceptions may be almost magical, in Smith's sense. If so, that attraction of mind for order in the universe may, for all practical purposes, be a manifestation or at least a mirror of the creative forces that constitute it. This seems to be Kukai's Shingon Buddhist view when he describes the ten worlds that are also ten ways of perceiving and experiencing *dharmakaya*; or, in a different Buddhist exercise that also posits a magical intimacy between viewer and world, in the Ten Ox-Herding Pictures. Each one of the ten pictures frames views of all the others, but never of itself.

KCP: Postmodernists have chosen the former of the two alternatives: "Pattern must only exist in the eye of the beholder." At the end of his essay, "In Comparison a Magic Dwells," Smith, too, argues that all forms of comparison are epistemologically invalid. They might work as "magic," as working fiction, or even as heuristic tools. But they emphatically do not work, he says, as accurate descriptions of outside re-

ligious realities. For Smith, comparison is possible, but only if it is acknowledged as located in, and contrived by, the comparing mind.

LES: Maybe at its simplest and most powerful, comparison is magical
in this sense: comparison that consciously disavows persuasion and argument, and that presents itself as arbitrary rather than grounded in any
justifiable reason, nonetheless can function efficaciously. Doesn't irony
function in just this way, as a trope: an unlikely and sometimes startling
juxtaposition of two terms which discloses yet a third meaning previously unseen? In language use, comparison flourishes physiologically
and also semantically, as Roman Jacobsen and the Prague school of
generative phonetics demonstrated, noting that we process all manner
of comparisons between sounds each time we understand a sentence or
even a word. When I speak, you not only compare the sounds I am
making to one another, in order to distinguish them, but you compare
them also to ones I am not making, all those possible, implicit sounds
which remain suffocated below the expressed articulations that carry
meaning. Here are the noted bundles of binary oppositions that inspired
structuralist comparisons with their magic.

In spoken communication, just as in the case of binocular vision, we
are constantly processing these comparisons. Notably, these comparisons of features do not take place in the foreground of our conscious
awareness. Though we may not even recognize these comparisons when
they are demonstrated, nevertheless these ongoing comparisons are
clearly efficacious in the sense that they galvanize our thought, convey
our communications, mobilize our common action, and so on. They
make things happen in the "real" world. The comparisons constructed
in the study of religions offer the distinctive promise of pulling into the
foreground of consciousness many of the comparisons that are suppressed or implicit in the exercise of conscious expression. This is so not
only because religions often focus on experiences gleaned in altered
states of consciousness (dreams, ecstasies, possessions, trance) but also
because a comparative history of culture allows the interpreter to draw
together expressions that the idiosyncrasies of different cultural histories
kept separate. For arbitrary reasons of the constraints of history, many
of the expressions of the religious imagination have never been set beside
one another before. Only recently is simultaneous examination and evaluation possible through new creative comparisons.

Category Formation

KCP: Part of what you are suggesting is that the study of religion can at least draw from and be inspired by neurobiology, cognitive psychology—as Lévi-Strauss suggested, comparative linguistics—or as J. Z. Smith sometimes intimates, from comparative anatomy. What I want to ask you about now is the problem of category formation. Whereas in those other disciplines we just mentioned one can think about a category and can examine cases that might not necessarily be contiguous but that seem also to demonstrate the patterns that one hopes to investigate, the case has been made that the very category that organizes the comparison necessarily originates from a subjective, an imperialist, a bourgeois, or a Western academic context. At Harvard when you informally presented at a faculty-student colloquium your *Encyclopedia of Religion* article on "supreme beings," there was considerable controversy.

LES: I think it is probably unavoidable in our work as religion scholars that we conjure some category or other which catalyzes around it a cluster of ideas or images or expressions. For better or worse the *summum genus* term "religion" itself evokes a galaxy of other terms, concepts, practices, and histories. Our discipline labors to recharge the meaning of words that have a strongly different sense in everyday use: myth, cult, ritual, symbol. I am not sure that people today want so much to talk about the "correctness" or "incorrectness" of a category as they do about whether it has value for the intended purposes. Much depends on how a category can be explained and what kind of plausibility structure supports that particular value the category serves. "Supreme being" is not a notion that is attractive in circles of religion research today. This strikes me as a great irony. Whether the lack of interest is due to intrinsic reasons, linked to the otiose and spent character of the deity in question, or whether it is due to a momentary fad, is not clear. William James complained that the category of "possession" had fallen out of favor because of the tendency of scientists to be tyrannized by fashion. He predicted, however, that given its long history, the idea of possession "would surely have its innings again." Except for a few people like Andrew Lang, Wilhelm Schmidt, and Raffaele Pettazzoni, there has been little comparative study of supreme beings. On the one hand, theologically grounded studies, especially those rooted in the Abrahamic monotheisms, have been unwilling to compare their God to others. On the other hand, social scientists and historians have been drawn away from the task on account of methodological impediments. My view has been that the method should adjust itself to the task and not the other way around. Though the "supreme beings" article is lengthy, it serves as a sketchy table of contents for future research.

KCP: Do you feel that the construction of a comparative category could of necessity be oppressive? One thinks of Adorno and Horkheimer's characterization of abstraction as a form of killing by distortion because of the radical destruction of the context surrounding that which is abstracted.

LES: Metaphors can be powerful, just as can be the manipulation of images and their understandings through comparison. Those powers have different effects. Surely unjust effects have issued from comparison. Just look at the stultifying effects of the totalizing metaphors that have come from such universalizing, blanket comparisons as "All abstract comparisons are a form of killing"! On the other hand, I don't think there is anything intrinsically noxious about comparison as an operation. Of course there can be comparisons that are invidious, even odious. Human beings can be harmful in their language and thoughts, but I don't myself feel that there is something "bad" about systematic thought, or comparison, or particular kinds of metaphor, such as holistic or organic metaphor. In *Reenchanted Science: Holism in German Culture from Wilhelm II to Hitler*, Anne Harrington recently traced the history of the suspect metaphors in science, particularly images of holism deployed in Nazi medical research. Due to the manipulation of the ideas and language of holism in German medicine under the Nazis, many have been frightened of holistic, organic, and totalizing imagery in analysis. Harrington offers an extremely careful analysis of the history of images of holism in German culture throughout the period, and is able to condemn certain inclinations more roundly than heretofore, while at the same time allow for a more critical, which is to say more open, evaluation of the positive possibilities of images of wholeness.

KCP: It is interesting that you mention the intellectual impact of the Third Reich. If one looks carefully at, for example, the writings of the postmodern French philosopher Jean-François Lyotard, one finds exactly what you've implied, namely that the *fear* and suspicion of the "metanarrative" or totalizing concept really has its origin in a philosophical reaction to fascism.

LES: That legacy was one of overwhelming destruction and evil, and

I would say that historical reality would compel us to walk very carefully. But even in walking carefully, we nevertheless can review wholesale condemnations of comparison, holistic metaphor, or the study of myth, fantasy, and so on. To condemn them out of hand, without first examining how they are phrased and to what ends they are deployed, is the kind of negation that Lyotard elsewhere warns against.

In *The Postmodern Condition*, Lyotard insightfully hypothesizes that knowledge, which had always been viewed as tied to the interior life of knowers, was increasingly becoming an exteriorized productive force in its own right, a commodity in the form of quantities of "information." Knowledge would circulate like monetary currency. Lyotard predicted a future in which nations would struggle over information as they had previously fought over territory. But this information would be emptied of the cognitive content and credibility associated with metanarratives of the past industrial age. Those historical metanarratives he categorized by their distinct teleologies: positivist evolutionary science headed toward a goal of human progress through empirical observation; Marxian political economy aimed at liberation through class struggle; and the hermeneutical strategies descending from German Idealism led to human self-construction. In Lyotard's view, those metanarratives are no longer believable, but they are instrumentalizable discourses used, like performative speech acts, to produce desired effects. A multiplicity of such language games exist, each one following its own rules. In *The Differend*, Lyotard proposes an agonistic way to speak meaningfully and to lodge moral contestations. He needs to do this, even to explain the nature and basis of his own writing and analysis. The credible unit of communication for him is not the metanarrative, of course, but the small phrase which draws names into meaningful relation with one another. Phrases are joined creatively into an interdependent network of names whose weight is evaluated less on grounds of verifiability than on usefulness, suggestiveness, and productivity. I believe that Lyotard provides additional and quite startlingly different grounds for comparison, especially the construction of comparative morphologies such as I explained in *Icanchu's Drum* and exemplified recently in an article on the Duomo of Firenze.[5] I view morphology of this sort as consonant with Lyotard's view of phrases. Morphologies, as I envision them, are the opposite of master metanarratives; they work within the fragmentary state of our knowledge and, indeed, of our historical and cultural existence. I believe that Jonathan Smith's invitation to work comparatively with what he calls (following Needham) polythetic taxons, in which each classificatory taxon is something of a bricolage of elements rather than a single determining feature, is also compatible with the situation Lyotard describes.

In *The Differend* Lyotard also sets in a new light an important realization already expressed by Gottlob Frege and elaborated by Paul Ricoeur in his *Interpretation Theory*—every phrase always evokes *the world* in which it appears, the world of interdependent relations in which it makes sense. In keeping with his earlier injunctions, Lyotard wants to emphasize that no phrase or phrase-world should negate or obliterate others. But what is also opened up here is the cosmological dimension, or I would even say the cosmological nature, of all knowledge. James Fernandez has ably argued this view in his studies of metaphor, especially puzzling metaphors. Puzzling metaphors prompt the listener to carry meaning from one term of the metaphor to the other, from one set of referents to another. The puzzled mind is provoked to turn toward ever wider, more inclusive sets of reference in search of some common term—a direction of thought which leads to construction of the widest possible set of references, which is the world itself. All knowledge, in this view, is not only comparative, moving from known to unknown, but is cosmological, pushing toward relationships among the widest set of references, names, or distinct phrases that can be known. To my mind, Lyotard's analyses of the contemporary incredibility of metanarratives in no way denies the world-conjuring power of any phrase. In order to use phrases well and understand them in their world-contexts, then, those world-auras must be taken into account. Moreover, if no world or discourse should obliterate others, as Lyotard commands, we are compelled to hold the various worlds and discourses together in our thoughts, which is a powerful exercise of comparison.

Lyotard's views about the performative nature of knowledge lead us to another issue important to comparison in religious studies. Comparison holds matters up to view, displays them in a striking manner and in a new arrangement, in order to disclose relationships and significances that may have been less evident or absent. Good comparisons can be moving on many levels of appreciation, aesthetic and social as well as intellectual. When knowledge is judged by its effectiveness, comparison can also be viewed as a theorizing knowledge in the root sense of the word *theorein*, to view, look at, or spectate. There is something of the theater here, just as demonstration in the operating theater was part of the persuasive performance of comparative anatomy in the developing knowledge of physiological systems. A comparativist holds up to view a set of relations in an arrangement that she or he has composed, not unlike the mixture of tonal relations set together and displayed in an original jazz composition or the flowers arranged in *ikebana*. Though items in the arrangement may be subject to factual scrutiny as "correct" or not, I agree with Lyotard that the response to the overall phraseology of comparison should not occur finally on that level of verification and legitimation of fact but rather on the level of the effect it has on understanding and relations. Seeing comparison in this way, as a suggestive arrangement of diverse and distinct parts rather than as a single meta-narrative whose parts bear one-to-one correspondences to a single cultural history, avoids the common misconception that comparisons among cultures should rise or fall in light of quotations imputed to native informants within a single given culture: "The so-and-so's have no word for 'religion' "; or "The so-and-so's don't use the term 'sacred.' " An effective comparison need not be—should not be—a mirror image of life on the ground, for comparison operates in between things; it cannot be disallowed simply because a given cultural actor does not see himself as he wishes to be seen. At its best, effective comparisons add value to culture and do not simply replicate existing expressions. As in any performance, the value is determined also by the relationship of the performer to the audience.

Astrophysics: The Making of True Myth?

KCP: I can understand the argument for efficacy as a criterion for determining whether a category is helpful, or whether a comparison has value. But doesn't that throw us back into a kind of hermetically sealed, reflexive or even self-referential environment of reference? Doesn't that prevent, for want of a better term, the study of religion (in addition to its poetic or imaginative or noetic function) from becoming a kind of science of the humanities?

You've spoken in the past about astrophysics as a good way of understanding how a "real mythology" still works today. While it has become highly problematic in the history of religions to attempt to discuss the "real world" of the sacred or religious reality, you've observed that astrophysicists, like myth-makers, don't qualify their ideas by speaking about the universe in terms of symbolic structures or as bundles of metaphors. For them, it is unabashedly the "real world"!

LES: Well, if we all agree that our homologies and terms of comparison are nothing but conventions used among the *cognoscenti*, and that the terms bear no reference to the world of religious life as lived, then there is little hope that we are talking about something real and moving, either to ourselves or to the larger public.

I was intrigued by your remembering the allusion I made to astrophysics during the AAR seminar. We held a session here at the Harvard Center, and invited several gifted astrophysicists to discuss an issue of their choosing: "The Age and Fate of the Universe." Present were Alan Guth from MIT, Michael Turner of the Fermi Lab at the University of Chicago, Robert Kirschner from Boston University, and John Huchra of the Harvard and Smithsonian Observatories. They were full of metaphors about primal stew, the universe as a set of resonating strings, dark matter and anti-matter, and so on. At one point several quickly agreed that clear indicators pointed to the existence of other universes, perhaps even an infinite number of universes, though by definition nothing could be known about them. In any case, certain arrows or vectors of energy pointed toward more universes than the known one. These scientists were fantastically imaginative, spinning out a mythology of the origins and destiny of the universe. Though their mythology was rich in symbol and image, it was ironic that they did *not* want their ideas to be described as symbolic or in any way metaphorical.

KCP: They saw no separation between the designating language and what was designated.

LES: No. They emphasized that they were talking about the "real thing." They were irritated with several people (I think I was one of them) who suggested as a friendly notion that theirs was a rich symbolic discourse that might stimulate creativity in other cultural realms. In their view, there was nothing symbolic at all—this was the real goods. Few in our discipline, on the other hand, wish to speak essentially anymore. One thinks as well of the issue of literalism, and of the insubstantiality of language, the arbitrariness of the sign, the indeterminate relationship between word and the signified to which it points.

KCP: Now uncoupled by the semiotic project of deconstructionism.

LES: I would not give full credit to deconstruction alone. Trust in the primacy of experience and in the unmediated relationship between an expression and its referent was broken long before. In linguistics, de Saussure had already announced the arbitrariness of the sign in 1916. Max Weber and Sigmund Freud pointed to disenchantments and alienations that set distance between the valued world and the place that human culture had constructed in it. For those of us in religious studies, a most significant break occurs with the iconoclastic impulse of Protestant reform whose questioning of "real presence" in signs is felt from the early sacramental debates to the demythologization of Bultmann's critical methods. The concomitant lack of trust in the immediacy of the senses stretches from Descartes and Bishop Berkeley to Mark Taylor.

This is one reason I would like to turn as a historian of religions to performance as a basis for cultural analysis and comparison rather than solely to linguistics. Performance studies is a promising area because performance is ephemeral; it takes place only while a particular spectacle is going on. The spectacle is co-involved with existence itself. There are ontological implications: the play *is* the thing; the performance is only while it lasts. Whereas it is hard to talk about the script *being* the play, just turning to oral performance, for example, resituates many key problems of representation. With performance theory we are closer to the *ex opere operato* efficacy of sacrament, as has been realized by the linguistic anthropologist Charles Briggs and the ritualist Richard Gardner in Japan. Performance is a setting quite different from the literalness of well-formed sentences that ground linguistic analysis. A performance exists only in its signs and the quality of knowledge of those who perform them, whereas a well-formed sentence may be written in a context different from the one in which it is uttered, and showcases the arbitrary link between sign and meaning. There is room for a rapprochement of these different approaches, for the notion of well-formedness is predicated on the competently performed intuitions of a native speaker who utters a sentence in real cultural time. The performance offers clues and gives us pause to think about what we have labeled arbitrariness. In the context of effective performance, the unity of signifier and signified appears less arbitrary and is even indissoluble. Lyotard is suggesting that we reframe cultural analysis in terms of the names linked in a phrase. He and thinkers from other disciplines suggest new grounds for generating comparisons.

KCP: To bracket the approach of deconstruction . . .

LES: Or to supplement in some way, or set up encounters between that view and other knowledgeable people who are wrestling with very similar issues, and who because of the texture of neurosciences and the imagery they work with, are able to raise different questions than the ones raised by linguistics or by those who treat religious ritual primarily as "text," and text worthy of deconstruction at that. Performance is held in existence through the very signifying gestures that one seeks to analyze. The questions concerning perception and sensation are set within a context of reflexivity which contests with arbitrarinesses associated with the sign. What is the proper interpretive response toward that reflexive quality of the performed gesture?

KCP: As in Greek tragedy, where the tragic chorus sometimes collectively asks as it dances, "Why should I dance?" Or in the performative reflexivity found in ancient narratives like *Gilgamesh* or *The Odyssey*, wherein the performance and future memorializing of the epic are referred to within the epic itself: the stele set up by Gilgamesh, the songs of the Trojan War sung to the disguised Odysseus by the bards Phemios and Demodokos.

The Drive toward "Centeredness"

LES: That's the very notion. Let's think some more, if we could, about issues of system and pattern. In regard to Hugo Winckler and Alfred Jeremias and some of the Pan-Babylonianists, Jonathan Smith takes them to task. At the same time, he expresses an appreciation for the rich heritage of comparative systematics they bequeath to the field of history of religions. Smith's reading of the Pan-Babylonianists, in my view, is that their complex notions of system and pattern were driven by some species of reflexivity internal to them. Where they failed was in their oversimplification of history. Elsewhere in his lecturing and writing Jonathan Smith has pointed out correlations between the Pan-Babylonianists' mindset, their notions of *Weltanschauung*, and their political *Sitz im Leben*, all of which worked together to stunt their notions of history. I do not take Jonathan's criticisms of Pan-Babylonianists or, indeed of all existing comparative methods, as a defeat of all attempts at systematic comparisons, nor do I think he intends that. I read Smith's work as an invitation to integrate a comparative systematics of patterned cultural expressions with complex notions of history. In that light, although he has been strongly critical of paradigms of centeredness (for instance, in his opening essays of *To Take Place*), I do not think that Smith's critiques apply *tale quale* to the proposals of Anthony Aveni, for example, who studies Mesoamerican astronomy and cosmology, nor to David Carrasco, who examines Mesoamerican urbanism and empire, nor to Gary Urton, who investigates Andean astronomic and land-use systems. Without relying on shaky theories of diffusion or textual dating that so weakened the Pan-Babylonianists in Smith's view, Aveni, Carrasco, Urton, and others (such as Johanna Broda and Reiner Tom Zuidema) are delineating worldviews with strikingly similar dynamics: centered on temples and sacred precincts, mirroring in the earth's liturgical calendar the movements perceived in the heavens, threading repeatedly the course from chaos to creative order, unifying distant tributary units into an overarching identity of empire, and so on. The theorists of Mesoamerica and the Andes are rooted in cultural circumstances very different from those of the Pan-Babylonianists (and from those of one another) and bring different epistemological assumptions to their analyses.

Paul Wheatley conducted a large comparative study of city archaeology in the twelve most ancient urban centers around the world. In the earliest archaeological substratum of these urban settlements Wheatley finds ceremonial centers with many specific features in common. Reading the landscape and architecture, Wheatley postulates principles of a cosmo-magical mindset that repeatedly accompanies urban ceremonialism. Wheatley deals with vastly different areas than those treated by the Pan-Babylonianists. He forwards no theory of historical diffusion of the sort that rendered the Pan-Babylonianists incredible. Wheatley does hypothesize about the nature of religious experience at ceremonial centers and about the concomitant religious nature of the center. He engages dirt archaeology, stripping back layers of finds to the earliest horizons of certain city centers to show ceremonial sites to which people have pilgrimaged before there was dense settlement. Someone like Wheatley and the evidence he marshals are very moving and important for historians of religions. I don't see his work being a big part of the debate in religious studies, but it almost certainly should be: he came over to look at religious studies in order to understand his comparative archaeological project. If we are to joust over heuristic concepts like "centeredness" in systematic comparisons, Wheatley (or Zuidema, Carrasco, or Aveni) would prove less of a straw man than Winckler or Jeremias. I'm not dismissing the importance of a reasoned critique of the Pan-Babylonian school. But there is more to centers than was convincingly dismantled by Jonathan's critique of Winckler and Jeremias.

In *Icanchu's Drum* I showed how a notion of center was crucial to cultural systematics in non-urban societies of South America. Concepts of "center" were key to hydraulic systems, color schemes, tonal scales, anatomical functions, psychic life, and artistic expression. It would be an error to view the notion of "center" primarily in terms of politics of empire. It is wrapped up with a quality of perception that includes a critical, reflexive perception of the perceiver as well as of the perceiver's world.

In each case, one has to work within the constraints of the given physical topology of perception in a locale to say, "This is the way we can center ourselves *here*." The deeper issue you wish to open, which Aveni chooses not to enter, but which Wheatley does broach, is *Why do people want to be centered anyway?*

And this very notion of centeredness, and what constitutes the *perception* of being at the center, is not only a question in religious studies; it is a problem in the brain sciences also, for example. You can talk about it at so many levels—what is the center of attention in the retina, and how is it determined? The role of centeredness in maintaining constancy of focus—how do you keep someone at the center of your attention as they walk away from you? The perceiver carries on all manner of adjustments and differential calculations in reference to a center, calculations which some researchers feel can be mapped logarithmically with strict laws and formulas. It is clear that "centeredness" is part of intellection—part of the intelligent operation of stimuli reception. The centered nature of the central nervous system itself raises questions even on the physiological plane—the role of such central and unique structures as the amygdala and hippocampus and the processes that engage them in cognition, for example. Or the notion of centeredness required to understand the normal synesthesia that succeeds in giving us the sense of being one person though we receive data from many relatively separate sensory modules and channels.

Conclusion: The "Net of Indra," Interconnectedness, and Perceptual Influence on the Object of Perception

KCP: I want to ask you one more thing. You have wondered aloud on a number of occasions whether human experience is inherently comparative. In 1995, at the AAR panel on comparison in Philadelphia out of which this volume grew, you said, "To borrow a metaphor, all things known are linked pneumatically like the net of Indra." Would you elaborate?

LES: I think in that context I was alluding to works by Ioan Couliano, such as *Eros and Magic in the Renaissance* and *Out of This World*, which examined relativity and physics, on the one hand, and contemplated mystical expressions and poetry, on the other. Couliano was very taken by the notion that the outer physical universe, as it is known, is continuous with the inner universe of mind, the two sets of interdependencies being joined at key points, something like the mystical net of Indra. Conjunctions in the net could be pulled upon when desired: made susceptible to rhetoric, magic, or scientific manipulation. Disclosure of any conjunction was no less a function of desire (to know, to relate, to attract and be attracted by reality) than of the existence of some objective chain of being. The links between different aspects of reality possess, in addition to their physical quality, a pneumatic one that animates desire for union (through knowledge and otherwise).

KCP: Does that concept attract you at all? Do you find it useful?

LES: Well, I find its possible ubiquitousness attractive—that the world with its constituent elements is always also the world as perceived, reality as desired. All the various things we know are also an expression of human desire—the desire to be intimate with the world, to unite with reality through knowledge of it. Our link to the known world is therefore spiritual, pneumatic; moreover, this means that all the realities we know are related to one another through the same pneumatic links of knowledge, fascination, attraction. This frees us to take perceptions, desires, interpretations, and meanings seriously, as constitutive of our universe. In this frame we can place the ideas of cosmologists like George Smoot at Berkeley. In describing the COBE Project that located *Cosmic Background Radiation to Explore* the forms it took in the first fraction of a nanosecond after the birth of the universe, Smoot got himself into trouble for talking about the mind of God. But in some way he meant it . . . to point to "that than which nothing greater can be conceived," to borrow a phrase from Anselmian ontology, and demonstrate that all existence is interconnected. In Smoot's case he has a picture of it! He can see the whole universe, or least its cold, fifteen-billion-year-old shadow cast by the light of the Big Bang. The universe he envisions through his instruments is interconnected, as the term "universe" suggests. If, in any measure, mind or pneumatic links are seen to affect any significant portion of the universe—through sciences like genetics, biology, aeronautics, and nuclear science or through environmental change, visual art, or music—we can picture patterns of shifting relations when, provoked by our desire to know the physical universe, our senses tug on the net of interconnections through our experiential and experimental attachments to it.

KCP: And isn't this precisely what string theory is proposing? It is sustained, at least thus far, as the only workable theory that can comprise and potentially explain all empirically known observed, physical phenomena, and those that can only be speculated about as well.

LES: I gather that, in particle physics, superstring theory promises to offer a fully unified theory both of all known particles and of all known forces: for example, of gravity as well as the variety of electromagnetic forces. Each elementary particle is treated as having extension in one dimension only, like a string with no mass. Though massless, each particle-string is one Planck in length, which is just long enough to register the effects of gravity. Depending on the kind of particle, each string vibrates distinctively and interacts with other strings vibrating in resonance with their respective particles. String theories solve anomalies but also pose new questions about matters not yet observed, such as multiple dimensions and new particles of "shadow matter." As historians of religions we may be familiar with precedents of such speculations.

When I was in Florence [at the Villa i Tatti in 1996–97], I spent some time working with Giordano Bruno's *De Vinculis in Genere*, where he speculates about all existence as an interactive chain of being. And in *Enchanting Powers* I have traced the idea of the universe as a system of overtones, from Ficino and Kukai to Kepler and Schönberg, all tones being related to one another through mathematical proportions. If you can chart your way through the entire system, however, you can affect those relations with deliberate forethought through magic or science. Through your stirring entry into this pneumatic net, chiming in, so to speak, with your own desire, you too can affect the system of tones, the ripple of effects. This intriguing notion extends from modern particle physics and quantum theory to psychological sciences, musical theory, mass media, and modern advertising.

It is a ubiquitous enough notion to ask, *Does this work?* Is there something here worth understanding in the study of religion? Bruno and Ficino offered explanations suited to their own times in their own way. Obviously, their analyses would not satisfy us today. Only a short time ago, other totalizing theories were forwarded, descending from German Idealism or Feuerbachian or Marxian natural history—Marcel Mauss's notion of a "total social fact," for instance, which made such a mark on Franz Boas. These proposals strike us as dated now. The question of systemic interrelations among empirical entities and between observer and observed continue to press on us. I think of the studies of natural self-organizing systems and emergent structures like galaxies and the immune system. The Paris-based physician and philosopher Henri Atlan and the Belgian physical chemist Ilya Prigogine propose that we view our universe and its subparts as self-organizing systems, moving from chaos to order. They raise the philosophical question of where to locate the source of non-random design.

Where shall we "put" the notion of an organizing mind or principles of order? Such comparative studies of self-organizing systems raise questions about freedom or determinism precisely because the human observer affects outcomes. Comparison seems inherent in the working out of self-emergent systems, whether they be mental and ideal, as math appears to be at times, or reflexive, as are the notions of self, or empirically observable, as the material universe seems largely to be. Lawrence Krauss once explained why the emergent structures of the physical universe disclose themselves through comparison of different levels of structure. It is because there exists a deep bond between the macrophysical structures of the universe as a whole—the interactions on the largest scale imaginable—and those microphysical structures on the scale of the fundamental particles that compose all matter. The difference between the two kinds of structures is only a matter of time, for we believe that 15 billion years ago, when the entire universe may have been no larger than a single point of infinite density, the macro- and micro-structures were merged—that the structures of largest scale unfolded on the infinitesimal scale of fundamental particles. Holding the macro- and micro-views side by side in comparative perspective is the distinctive labor of the human mind, the comparative process of reflection that redimensions time and space and recasts them in memory and imagination.

KCP: Perhaps there is resonance here with one of the more trenchant contributions of postmodern thought, extrapolating as it does from Kantian trajectories, namely, that the perceiver is necessarily very much a part of and affects that which is perceived; there is no truly "objective" stance about "things." So we are actually participating in the history of religions by studying them.

LES: Right. Following this logic, then, *inner dispositions and understandings will affect the perceived universe,* with the emphasis falling on "universe," rather than on "perceived." No matter how we settle what is inner perception and what is outer reality, we must admit that the two can have a direct bearing—a substantive effect—on one another. We can see this, for example, in the consequences of human thinking on the global physical environment where a self-organizing system like the atmosphere can be deleteriously affected by human scientific intellection, technological ingenuity, and accompanying habits of practice such as burning fossil fuels.[6] Through our knowledge of the universe and our ability to apply that knowledge technologically over the past two centuries, humans have become a cosmic force on a scale similar to the asteroid that eclipsed the life of the dinosaurs. We are altering the life of our planet and witnessing the consequent mass extinctions of species on a global scale. Our inner consciousness, ideas, and perhaps even our religious character affect the larger natural and social environment, having been a part of them all along. It is a mistake to think of inner consciousness and our world as entirely separate. Deciding in what measure and mode they are engaged with one another and are comparable can be stimulating and disclose new distinctions helpful in our studies.

Notions of comparison can be drawn from aspects of the material universe such as the brain, where there is a promising possible convergence of the study of material structure, formation through time, and reflexive understanding of these processes of structure and development. Given what the comparative study of religious history can bring regarding human intention, imagination, and orientation, it can look forward to joining the effort.

Notes

1. Lawrence E. Sullivan, "Lévi-Strauss, Mythologic, and South American Religions," in *Anthropology and the Study of Religion*, ed. Robert L. Moore and Frank E. Reynolds (Chicago: Center for the Scientific Study of Religion, 1984), pp. 147–76.

2. Lawrence E. Sullivan, ed., *Enchanting Powers: Music in the Religions of the World*, Religions of the World (Cambridge: Harvard University Center for the Study of World Religions, 1997).

3. Lawrence E. Sullivan, with Daniel L. Schacter, Joseph T. Coyle, Gerald T. Fischbach, and Mere-Marsel Mesulam, eds., *Memory Distortion: How Minds, Brains, and Societies Reconstruct the Past* (Cambridge: Harvard University Press, 1995).

4. Lawrence E. Sullivan, "Looking at Vision: Reflections on the Role of Re-

ligious Vision in the Project of Visual Truth," in *The Papers of the Henry Luce III Fellows in Theology*, vol. 3 (Atlanta: Scholars Press, 1998).

5. Lawrence E. Sullivan, "The Recombinant Nature of Ritual Space," *Vivens Homo: Revista Teologica Fiorentina* 8 (December 1997): 237–54.

6. Lawrence E. Sullivan, "Toward a Geology of Religions," edited text of presentation delivered at the United Nations General Assembly Headquarters, New York, to open the conference *Religion and Ecology: Discovering the Common Ground*, 21 October 1998.

EPILOGUE

THE "END" OF COMPARISON

Redescription and Rectification

JONATHAN Z. SMITH

"In Comparison a Magic Dwells" was delivered as a lecture some twenty years ago. Now, shorn of its tactical setting, it is open to comparisons both to its subsequent reevaluations in my own work, on a trajectory from the initial typologies of "*Adde Parvum Parvo Magnus Acervus Erit*" to the constructive proposals of *Drudgery Divine*,[1] and to its reconsiderations and reconstructions in the works of others, beginning with the most suggestive article on comparison of the past two decades, F. J. P. Poole's "Metaphors and Maps,"[2] and continuing through the writings of several scholars in this volume.

"In Comparison" took its starting point from the relationship of comparison to memory, as developed first by Aristotle,[3] extended in mnemotechnics, in associationist epistemologies and psychologies, and reconfigured, critically, with respect to magical thought by Tylor and Frazer. In this history, Aristotle's category of the different or other (the *heterōn*) has largely dropped out; similarity and contiguity remained. However, with the possible exception of Jakobson's extension to a general account of cognition, under the rubrics of metaphor and metonymy,[4] similarity and contiguity have proved incapable of generating interesting theory. The perception of similarity has been construed as the chief purpose of comparison; contiguity, expressed as historical "influence" or filiation, has provided the explanation. In a deliberate adoption of Frazer's caustic language for magic, "In Comparison" argued,

> In the vast majority of instances in the history of comparison, this subjective experience [of the recollection of similarity] is projected as an objective connection through some theory of influence, diffusion, borrowing, or the like. It is a process of working from a psychological association to an historical one; it is to assert that similarity and contiguity have causal effect. But this, to revert to the language of Victorian anthropology, is not science but magic.[5]

Such a view, giving precedence to similarity and contiguity at the expense of difference, is deeply embedded in Western discourse, especially since the amalgamation of biblical and Greco-Roman anthropologies in Christian cultural thought. This was a totalistic system that prevented surprise whenever similarities or differences were encountered in the peoples mapped upon it. The genealogies that underlay the system, as well as the biblical anthropogonic narration, guaranteed the essential unity of humankind. All were children of Adam and Eve, even though their lineages must be traced through Noah's three sons. Differences were, therefore, accidental. Somatic and economic differences were the results of climate and ecology. Cultural variegations were caused by a particular group's forgetfulness of primordial knowledge, and by mixtures brought about by processes of contact, conquest, migration, and diffusion. Even when the biblical framework was repressed and the myth of primordial knowledge rejected, essential unity was continued through the postulation of some post-Kantian universality of cognitive capacities (in older language, the "psychic unity" of humankind) still linked to historicistic, genealogical explanations.[6] Such an explanation could even be adapted to a more atomistic view of cultures, where similar mentalities in similar natural or social environments produced "independent inventions" of parallel phenomena.[7]

Genealogical comparisons have been successful and provocative of thought in a few cases: in comparative anatomy, in historical linguistics, as well as in more recent developments in folkoristics and areas of archeology. Each of these cases fulfills three preconditions: first, the comparative enterprise is related to strong theoretical interests; second, the data for comparisons form an unusually thick dossier in which microdistinctions prevail; and third, as a consequence of the first two preconditions, the genealogical comparison has been able to provide rules of difference.[8] At present, none of these preconditions are fulfilled in the usual comparisons of religious phenomena, but there is nothing, in principle, to prevent their successful deployment.

In light of subsequent work, the turning point in the article, displaced by its typological concerns, was the replacement of the language of discovery with that of invention. As elaborated in later writings, there is nothing "given" or "natural" in those elements selected for comparison. Similarities and differences, understood as aspects and relations, rather than as "things," are the result of mental operations undertaken by scholars in the interest of their intellectual goals. Comparison selects and marks certain features within difference as being of possible intellectual significance by employing the trope of their being similar in some stipulated sense.[9] It is this relationship between invention and difference which grounds the conclusion of "In Comparison" as expressed in its penultimate paragraph: "Comparison requires the postulations of difference as the grounds of its being interesting . . . and a methodical manipulation of difference, a playing across the 'gap' in the service of some useful end."[10]

The "end" of comparison cannot be the act of comparison itself. I would distinguish four moments in the comparative enterprise: description, comparison, redescription, and rectification.[11] Description is a double process which comprises the historical or anthropological dimensions of the work: First, the requirement that we locate a given example within the rich texture of its social, historical, and cultural environments that invest it with its local significance. The second task of description is that of reception-history, a careful account of how *our* second-order scholarly tradition has intersected with the exemplum. That is to say, we need to describe how the datum has become accepted as significant for the purpose of argument. Only when such a double contextualization is completed does one move on to the description of a second example undertaken in the same double fashion. With at least two exempla in view, we are prepared to undertake their comparison both in terms of aspects and relations held to be significant, and with respect to some category, question, theory, or model of interest to us. The aim of such a comparison is the redescription of the exempla (each in light of the other) and a rectification of the academic categories in relation to which they have been imagined.

Notes

1. J. Z. Smith, "*Adde Parvum Parvo Magnus Acervus Erit,*" *History of Religions* 11(1971): 67–90; idem, *Map Is Not Territory* (Leiden: E. J. Brill, 1978), pp. 240–64; idem, *Drudgery Divine: On the Comparison of Early Christianities and the Religions of Late Antiquity* (London: School of African and Oriental

Studies, University of London, 1990; Chicago: University of Chicago Press, 1990).

2. F. J. P. Poole, "Metaphors and Maps: Towards Comparison in the Anthropology of Religion," *Journal of the American Academy of Religion* 54 (1986): 411–57.

3. Aristotle, *De memoria et reminiscentia*, 451b. 19–20, which employs the terms, "[starting] from something similar, or different/opposite, or neighboring." It is the category of the different that marks an advance; Plato had already identified similarity's and contiguity's roles in memory in the *Phaedo*, 73D–74A. See further the translation and useful commentary in *Aristotle On Memory*, by J. Sorabji (London: Gerald Duckworth, 1972), pp. 42–46, 54, 96–97.

4. R. Jakobson, "Two Aspects of Language and Two Types of Aphasic Disturbances," in *Fundamentals of Language*, by R. Jakobson and M. Halle (The Hague: Mouton, 1956), pp. 53–82, and often reprinted.

5. J. Z. Smith, "In Comparison a Magic Dwells," in *Imagining Religion: From Babylon to Jonestown* (Chicago: University of Chicago Press, 1982), p. 22; 26.

6. Note that even in the case of Eliade and Lévi-Strauss, incorrectly understood in the article as being ahistorical, diffusion theories play a central role in their interpretations of myths and rituals. That is to say, both scholars work with an essentially spatial rather than a temporal construction of the historical.

I am quite sensitive to the justified criticism that my treatment of structuralism in the article was more than "exceedingly brusque." Rightly chided by Hans Penner's review (*History of Religions* 23 [1984]: 266–68), I spent the next three years reworking the materials, which resulted in the sustained meditation on and dialogue with structuralist theory in *To Take Place* (Chicago: University of Chicago Press, 1987). For the purposes of this volume it suffices to state my deep indebtedness to structuralism's focus on relations of *difference* for enlarging my understanding of that term with respect to the comparative enterprise.

7. I shall not here repeat previous discussions on the issue of homology versus analogy, which is the locus where these issues have been most thoroughly debated in both biological and cultural comparisons; see Smith, *Drudgery Divine*, pp. 47–48, n. 15. I should note the technical terminology of homogenetic (homologous) and homoplastic (analogous) similarities, originally coined by E. R. Lankester, "On the Use of the Term Homology in Modern Zoology and the Distinction between Homogenetic and Homoplastic Agreements," *The Annals and Magazine of Natural History* 6 (1870): 34–43, and reexamined in a recent symposium, M. J. Sanderson and L. Hufford, eds., *Homoplasy: The Recurrence of Similarity in Evolution* (San Diego: Academic Press, 1996).

8. Archeology has been less successful than the other named fields in fulfilling this third precondition. For example, the meticulous classification of pottery types was linked to strong historicist theories of "artifactual cultures," invasions, migrations, and diffusions, but rules governing difference only become possible when relations of identity, such as pottery type = particular culture/ change of type = change of culture, are challenged. See, among others, the general critique of C. Renfrew, *Archaeology and Language* (New York: Cambridge University Press, 1988), pp. 3, 18, 23–24, 86–94, *et passim*. For an in-

fluential example which meets all three preconditions, see the work of J. J. F. Deetz, *The Dynamics of Stylistic Change in Arikara Ceramics* (Urbana: University of Illinois Press, 1965); Deetz and E. Dethlefsen, "The Doppler Effect and Archeology: A Consideration of the Spatial Effects of Seriation," *Southwestern Journal of Anthropology* 21 (1965): 196–206; and Deetz's summary, *In Small Things Forgotten* (Garden City, NY: Anchor Press/Doubleday, 1977).

9. In this paragraph I have drawn on Smith, *Drudgery Divine*, pp. 50–53. In those pages I insisted on the priority of analogous to homologous modes of comparison in order to reinforce the notion that "comparison does not necessarily tell us how things 'are' (the far-from-latent presupposition that lies behind the notion of the 'genealogical' with its quest for 'real' historical connections)" (p. 52). For the purposes of this epilogue, I have relaxed that insistence and provided (above) three preconditions which might properly ground comparisons in the service of an homologous theory.

10. Compare the reformulation of this sentence in Smith, *To Take Place*, pp. 13–14.

11. Compare Burton Mack's insightful elaboration of these four "moments" in my work in Mack, "On Redescribing Christian Origins," *Method and Theory in the Study of Religion* 8 (1996): 247–69, esp. 256–59.

CONTRIBUTORS

Wendy Doniger is Mircea Eliade Distinguished Service Professor of History of Religions in the Divinity School at the University of Chicago. Recent publications include *The Implied Spider: Politics and Theology in Myth* (Columbia University Press, 1998) and *Splitting the Difference: Gender and Myth in Ancient Greece and India* (University of Chicago Press, 1999). Forthcoming are *The Bedtrick: Telling the Difference*, and a novel, *Horses for Lovers, Dogs for Husbands*.

Diana L. Eck is Professor of Comparative Religion and Indian Studies at Harvard University. She has published in the fields of Hinduism (*Banaras, City of Light* [Princeton University Press, 1982]; *Darsan, Seeing the Divine Image in India* [Anima Books, 1985]), theological reflection (*Encountering God: A Spiritual Journey from Bozeman to Banaras* [Beacon Press, 1998]), and American studies (*On Common Ground: World Religions in America*).

Malcolm David Eckel is Associate Professor of Religious Studies at Boston University, where his courses on the religion and philosophy of South and East Asia have been recognized by a university-wide award for excellence in teaching. His books and articles include *Jnanagarbha's Commentary on the Distinction between the Two Truths* (State University of New York Press, 1984), *To See the Buddha: A Philosopher's Quest for the Meaning of Emptiness* (Princeton University Press, 1994), and "Is There a Buddhist Philosophy of Nature?" in *Buddhism and Ecology*, ed. Mary Evelyn Tucker and Duncan Ryuken Williams (Harvard University Press, 1997).

Jonathan R. Herman is Assistant Professor of Philosophy and Religious Studies, Georgia State University. His field is Chinese religion. He is the author of *I and Tao: Martin Buber's Encounter with Chuang Tzu* (State University of New York Press, 1996) and several essays on comparative religion.

Barbara A. Holdrege is Associate Professor of the Comparative History of Religions at the University of California at Santa Barbara. Her research has focused on historical and textual studies of Hindu and Jewish traditions, as well as cross-cultural analyses of categories such as scripture, myth, and ritual. She is the author of *Veda and Torah: Transcending the Textuality of Scripture* (State University of New York Press, 1996); an edited collection, *Ritual and Power, Journal of Ritual Studies* 4, no. 2 (1990); and numerous articles on representations of scripture in the brahmanical tradition and the rabbinic and kabbalistic traditions. She is currently completing *The Mythic Dimension of Religious Life* (Routledge) and a book on Hindu discourses of the body.

William E. Paden is Professor and Chair in the Department of Religion at the University of Vermont. His publications include *Religious Worlds: The Comparative Study of Religion*, 2d ed. (Beacon Press, 1994), and *Interpreting the Sacred: Ways of Viewing Religion* (Beacon Press, 1992).

Kimberley C. Patton is Assistant Professor in the Comparative and Historical Study of Religion at Harvard Divinity School. Her research and teaching are in ancient Greek religion, archaeology, and iconography as well as in the fields of phenomenology and the history of religions. She is co-editor of the present volume and author of the forthcoming book *The Religion of the Gods: Ritual, Paradox, and Divine Reflexivity* (Oxford University Press, 2000).

Laurie L. Patton is Associate Professor in the Department of Religion at Emory University. Her interests are in Vedic interpretation, comparative mythology, and theory in the study of religion. In 1994 she published an edited volume, *Authority, Anxiety, and Canon: Essays in Vedic Interpretation* (State University of New York Press, 1994). Her authored work, *Myth as Argument: The Brhaddevata as Canonical Commentary*, was published by DeGruyter Press in Berlin in 1996 as the forty-first volume in the series *Religionsgeschichtliche Versuche und Vorarbeiten*. Another volume, co-edited with Wendy Doniger, *Myth and Method*, appeared from the University Press of Virginia (1996). She is currently completing a second book on the use of poetry in Vedic ritual, and an edited volume on women and textual authority in Hindu India.

Benjamin Caleb Ray is Daniels Family NEH Distinguished Teaching Professor, Department of Religious Studies, University of Virginia. He is co-editor of the present volume and author of *African Religions: Symbol, Ritual, and Community* (Prentice-Hall, 1976) and *Myth, Ritual, and Kingship in Buganda* (Oxford University Press, 1991). He has written a variety of articles on African religions and on the myth and ritual of the ancient world and hunting-gathering societies. As adjunct curator of African art at Bayly Museum, he has created several exhibitions of African art at the University of Virginia and on the World-Wide Web.

Huston Smith is Thomas J. Watson Professor of Religion and Distinguished Adjunct Professor of Philosophy, *Emeritus*, Syracuse University, and sometime Visiting Professor of Religious Studies, University of California, Berkeley. He is a philosopher and historian of religions who works cross-culturally. His books include *The World's Religions* (HarperSanFrancisco, 1991), *Forgotten Truth*

(Harper & Row, 1976), *Beyond the Post-Modern Mind* (Crossroad, 1992), *Essays on World Religion* (Paragon House, 1992), and, edited with Reuben Snake, *One Nation under God: The Triumph of the Native American Church* (Clear Light Publishers, 1996).

Jonathan Z. Smith is Robert O. Anderson Distinguished Service Professor of the Humanities at the University of Chicago. He specializes in the history of the study of religion. He is the author of *Imagining Religion: From Babylon to Jonestown* (University of Chicago Press, 1982). He served as general editor of *The Harper-Collins Dictionary of Religion* (1995); his most recent book is *Drudgery Divine: On the Comparison of Early Christianities and the Religions of Late Antiquity* (University of Chicago Press, 1990). He is currently completing a manuscript, *Close Encounters of Diverse Kinds: Elements in the History of the Western Imagination of Difference.*

Lawrence E. Sullivan is Professor of the History of Religions at Harvard Divinity School and the Director of the Harvard University Center for the Study of World Religions. He is a scholar of Francophone Central Africa and of the native traditions of South America, with particular research interests in ethno-history, cosmology, myth, and ritual. He is the author of *Icanchu's Drum: An Orientation to Meaning in South American Religions* (Macmillan, 1988). Under Mircea Eliade, he was Associate Editor of *The Encyclopedia of Religion* (16 volumes, 1987). He has also edited *Healing and Restoring: Health and Medicine in the World's Religious Traditions* (Macmillan, 1989), and, with Daniel L. Schachter, co-edited *Memory Distortion: How Minds, Brains, and Societies Reconstruct the Past* (Harvard University Press, 1995). Most recently he edited *Enchanting Powers: Music in the World's Religions* (Harvard University Center for the Study of World Religions, 1997).

Winnifred Fallers Sullivan is Assistant Professor of Religion at Washington and Lee University. She teaches and writes about American religion and about the comparative study of religion and law. She is the author of *Paying the Words Extra: Religious Discourse in the Supreme Court of the United States* (Harvard University Center for the Study of World Religions, 1994).

David Gordon White is Associate Professor of Religion at the University of California at Santa Barbara. He is the author of *Myths of the Dog-Man* (University of Chicago Press, 1991) and *The Alchemical Body: Siddha Traditions in Medieval India* (University of Chicago Press, 1996). He is also the editor of *Tantra in Practice.*